Postmodernism and Race

Postmodernism and Race

Edited by
Eric Mark Kramer

PRAEGER

Westport, Connecticut
London

Library of Congress Cataloging-in-Publication Data

Postmodernism and race / edited by Eric Mark Kramer.
     p. cm.
  Includes bibliographical references and index.
  ISBN 0–275–95367–X (alk. paper)
  1. Race awareness. 2. Ethnic attitudes. 3. Postmodernism—Social
aspects. I. Kramer, Eric Mark.
HT1521.P625 1997
305.8—dc20   96–26281

British Library Cataloguing in Publication Data is available.

Library of Congress Catalog Card Number: 96–26281
ISBN: 0–275–95367–X

First published in 1997

Praeger Publishers, 88 Post Road West, Westport, CT 06881
An imprint of Greenwood Publishing Group, Inc.

Printed in the United States of America

The paper used in this book complies with the
Permanent Paper Standard issued by the National
Information Standards Organization (Z39.48–1984).

10 9 8 7 6 5 4 3 2 1

To my three *hidamari*

Contents

1

The Spiders of Truth

Eric Mark Kramer

Working out the logic of ethnic and racial conflict may be aided by a time-honored discursive form, the parable. Let us imagine an American high school biology teacher named Mr. K. Shortly after the popular festival known as Halloween (when children in costumes go door-to-door to get candy), Mr. K's advanced biology class is doing the part of the curriculum that focuses on poisonous arachnids. Mr. K keeps a small menagerie of creatures in his garage for instructional purposes, including a couple of black widows and brown recluses. Over the years, he has found that allowing the students to see the real thing is a very good way to teach them how to identify and avoid certain kinds of spiders, and it makes the material much more relevant and fun for them.

One bright morning Mr. K is rummaging around for a means to transport his creatures to school. As he steps out into his garage he notices a shoe-sized sturdy cardboard box that his wife recently discarded. It had been used as a container for a large quantity of Halloween candy bars. It has the logo of a popular candy bar prominently displayed on its top and sides. He takes the box, creates separate compartments for each creature, and creates cellophane ''windows'' in the box through which to view the stars of the show. He carefully loads his pets into their temporary home and is off to school.

Mr. K walks into his morning class and sits the box on the table at the front of the room. He explains to the class that these are real, living, and potentially very dangerous specimens. He tells the class that he wants two people at a time to come to the front to have a look. At that moment the principal appears at the classroom door and asks Mr. K to step outside. The principal informs Mr. K that he has an important phone call. Mr. K sticks his head back into the classroom and tells the students that he will be right back and, of course, not to bother the spiders.

Excited conversation breaks out around the room. A moment later, Joe, a football player who has been down in the whirlpool nursing a bruised thigh from the last game, comes late to the class. At first no one notices Joe. Bob, one of Joe's buddies, is sitting in the front row talking with a girl. Joe, being happy-go-lucky and a bit of a cut-up, sees the candy bar box and immediately starts to reach into it while winking at Bob. Bob yells, the girl gasps, and Bob tackles Joe just in the nick of time, saving him from a nasty bite. Joe is very upset with Bob. Just then Mr. K reenters the room yelling, and is very relieved to discover that Bob not only saved Joe, but his job and probably a lawsuit against the school.

Now, is Bob's violent act morally justified? Insofar as Bob truly believed that Joe was about to stick his hand into a box full of poisonous creatures, it seems that his actions are justifiable. In fact, to knowingly watch someone make such a mistake without taking action to stop him or her would be very immoral. It was more than just pleasant etiquette on Bob's part. It was his *duty* to tackle Joe. By Bob's action, Joe was saved from a nasty bite, and maybe even his life was saved.

Now, up the ante from mere mortal suffering and death to eternal damnation. If a religious person (''A'') *truly, really*, absolutely, and positively believes that someone (''B'') is making a mistake that will cost him his eternal soul, and if person ''A'' does nothing to alter ''B's'' behavior, then ''A,'' in his indifference, has perpetrated a terrible sin, one that could even cost him his soul too. Thus, violence, far beyond tackling, can be justified. The stakes are absolute (nothing less than the essence of the self—the soul). Under such conditions (definitions), the actions which are taken are beyond the pale, ''out of principle.'' As such, no act can be too harsh, too violent. And once ''A'' starts killing (converting) people from group ''B'' (identifiable by a different cosmological set of parameters for the, of the, self), it is highly unlikely that people in group ''B'' will appreciate the ''help.'' If people in group ''B'' really and truly do *not* believe as group ''A'' people do, then the situation is bound for endless conflict. Hence, the many ethnic clashes around the world in Pakistan/India, the Middle East, the former Yugoslavia, Rwanda, Ireland, and so on.

''Race,'' which is often a part of ethnic identity, is a semiotic marker, and is usually accorded moral (absolute) significance, *because* it signals the other. Minimally, the other ethnic group is seen as ''other.'' More intensely, the other group may be an eternal enemy. Principle breeds intolerance. However, even totalitarian systems, where everything exists by definition (like mathematics), exhibit great variety among themselves and also internal provisionalism (Merleau-Ponty, 1973; Kuhn, 1962). Over time, religious (qua divine) and natural laws change. Thus, appreciating the world synairetically may avoid privileging one reality over all others. Integral awareness allows one to see the others in the one.

Synairesis is not transcendental, in the Platonic, other-worldly sense. Synairesis is not ultimate perspective or judgment, but rather, it is the process of appresentiating integral differentiation. One might say that the synairetic awaring of comparative civilizations is an awaring of comparative validities, and the realization that one has no way to rank-order them in terms of referential or epistemic force without capriciously assigning privilege to one set of criteria over all others. To choose one set of criteria (or world) over others presupposes a metacriterial authority, *ad infinitum*. Like Ludwig Wittgenstein (1971), Jean Gebser (1985) argued that the most that can be said of a world-structure, as such, is that it is, or is not, vital (surviving by its own criteria). Each world, by definition, manifests different rules and criteria. The deconstructive tactic of reversing the duality of margin and center, for instance, presumes a modern power hierarchy that is not universal. Championing the ''marginal voice'' is basically Western Enlightenment liberal pluralism. Very few cultures value equality. Most are very ethnocentric.

RELATIVE "KNOWLEDGE"? JAZZ AND AMPHIBIAN LOGIC

The mistake of arrogance made by Freud, Heidegger, and many others has been to presume that their conceptualizations of world-consciousness are absolutely generalizable (definitive). Given the struggles evident between various worlds, perhaps the most generalizable claim to be made is that most people make claims that they presume to be universally true.[1] The study of comparative civilizations has revealed fundamental differences in styles of awaring. The unique qualities of each modality are seen through other modalities.

For instance, very often when people travel abroad into a very different world, they come to see and learn more about their home culture (themselves) than the new one. The first realization may be that one's home culture is not the only one. But most systems, especially the more explicitly structured ones with well-defined feedback loops (written laws and transgressions), attempt to outtrope relativity, which would severely challenge their exclusive claim to validity (their onto-political might) by deploying the most formidable (even absolute) barriers to choice imaginable, such as threats of eternal torture or oblivion. Such barriers dissolve in the aperspectival world.

Nor is the experience of difference limited to binary opposition. Each different experience enables a different, ''new'' verition (not ''revelation'' because nothing is speculatively presumed to be hidden, but instead something is made) about one's home culture (and the other), with implicate change in the fluxing clouds we call ''the'' self and ''the'' other. However, unchecked perspectivism is not only a closed system (mind), but, as such, it inflates to totality via blind ignorance and arrogance. Totalitarians believe themselves to be exclusively and absolutely ''right.'' The utterly blind prejudice favoring the taken-for-granted home culture is often articulated by the sense that the other, ''strange'' culture is somehow less ''natural,'' less ''real,'' or ''valid.'' Such a sensibility is expressed as ethnocentrism, xenophobia, nationalism, and other dangerous responses to difference, experienced as competition and threat. At the same time, this process has the tendency to deflate the internal arrogance of ignorance which characterizes closed systems (minds) by opening the potential for other, including unsystematic, validities. Modern mental-rational nation-states, which legally define the citizen/noncitizen, generate legal definitions as a veneer of perspectivism added to ancient tribal tendencies. Tribalism is rationalized, not abandoned or surpassed.

Protean Play

Proteus is the name of an ancient Greek water divinity. Proteus had the power to change its shape at will, to transform. After embracing the revolutionary realization that the world-game is not predetermined ("fixed"), that it is conventional, protean vitality is enabled. Aperspectivity is essentially protean. A good example of fluid "boundary conditions" is jazz, which presumes the structure of instruments, music, and coordination, while playing off of these stabilities (Gilroy, 1993; West, 1993; also see Chapter 2). Jazz is integral music. Difference need not be antagonistic. While fascists (like the Bolsheviks and Nazis) typically ban "discordant" music, without it their order would not be recognizable or "necessary." To be a "champion," one needs an opponent, even if one has to be invented. A jazz ensemble has no opponents.

One of the first college basketball games ever played between a white and a black team highlights the problem of determining a systematic norm. Early in the game, the black players brought the ball down the court. A black player dribbled behind his back, between his legs, and spun around. This was perceived by the white players, who never did this during games, as antagonistic taunting—not playing "right." A fight broke out which ended the game. Although technically no rules had been broken, improvisation of that kind was not tolerated. The attitude of the white players was perspectival, diacritical.

If appreciated aperspectivally, improvisation is pleasing because it is unpredictable (even to the players/musicians/communicators). It opens to creativity. It can be seen as an invitation to create and improvise. This may help explain the excitement that usually receives a new technology like the automobile and the Internet. The fervent and explosive interest in the Internet, which is not systematically structured, comes from its aperspectival diffusion. The Internet has no hierarchical or pyramidal structure. It (not counting servers) does not (yet) pay "dividends," which divide profits and investors from producers and consumers. Nor is it a closed modern system dedicated to feedback, or "cyberspace," as William Gibson conceived of it in his 1984 science fiction novel *Neuromancer.* Instead, it is a shared autonomy (equality of expressed difference). It is a manifestation of aperspectivity, where no *one* owns or controls it, traditional identity cues are superfluous, clock time integrates with other forms of time, and the sense of "being somewhere" "together" in the same (but also different) room, as John Perry Barlow (1995) puts it, is both real and not real.

The Internet manifests integrum. The Internet changes by the second, and more importantly, many who constitute it understand this and celebrate its mutability, its amphibian logic.

Being comfortable with uncertainty and difference is a sign of aperspectival awaring. Such comfort often depends upon the dissolution of conventional identity. Anonymity is liberating. This modality is very different from Hegelian systematic destiny (even when it presumes it). As one famous film actor/director (Orson Welles) said about creativity, if he knew what he was doing, then he would not be creating something new. Instead, he would be too systematic, formulaic, repetitive, predictable. Artistic life is a constant experimenting without the benefit of prophecy—prediction. Sometimes experiments "fail"; that is why they must be made.

Potent(ial) is the nondistinct, indeterminate origin of empowerment. If something is not readily predictable, then, and only then, is it significant. Where/when prediction is successful, one has located redundancy, powerlessness, a sense of nihilism (surveillance of the future). Why try, it makes no difference? The game is rigged. Tautology allows no play.

Despite the best efforts of some who would know us better than we know ourselves, life is open. It is a continual experiment. It is not always positive or happy. That is why it is still worth living. But the ever-present origin of aperspectivity, like a blank slate, makes it possible (is a necessary condition for) for various arrangements to emerge. This is why any expressive process that is vital, like science, cannot be predicted. Scientists cannot tell us when, where, how, by whom, or what breakthroughs will be. Because it is a surprise, discovery (not tautological definition) is exciting. When the creative activity that is science is strictly controlled, as in the former Soviet Union, there is little invention or discovery. The same used to be true of the restrictive authoritarian system of knowledge in Japan. Science, as Husserl (1962) argued, is part of life too.

"Breakthroughs" (like taking a "break" or having a "breakdown") violate the system (paradigm), crossing the liminal boundary between nothing and something, absence and presence. As Linus Pauling (the only American to win two Nobel Prizes, in 1954 and 1962) used to say, "I work in the dark."

DANCING ZOMBIES

Potency is dynamism. Whether human civilizations began as accidents or not, their maintenance is not accidental. Human behavior is a constant striving against entropy; creativity includes making predictions which we then "outrun," and laws that we break. The hump in the bell curve moves. We try harder.

Dead materialism is not evinced by all worlds. It is the modern consciousness, with its dedication to a materialistic, metaphysical faith, that exhibits a paternal power-drive which conceives a world as essentially dead stuff that can be endlessly dissected and reconstituted into any use-form desired. Animals, and less-than-human slaves, suffer from this attitude. The idea that matter is "ripe" for indiscriminate manipulation betrays a particularly modern patriarchal attitude.

"Matter," "*mutter*," "mother" all share a common Sanskrit root *mat*, which became Greek *mater* and *meter* (both meaning "great mother" as in Demeter). Unlike matter, however, humans continually *make* plans and predictions (project complex future horizons), read them, and then decide whether or not they will attempt to make them happen or deny them viability (abandon them). Today, species do not survive solely because they are adaptable or the "fittest." They survive if humans *want them to*. The systatic process is one of a continual integrating function of *human* existence. For instance, on the basis of all past experience we predict that future population growth will be disastrous. We don't want a disaster so we take action to falsify our own prediction. Dead matter cannot do this. In the modern world, matter is truly disinterested.

Humans are not merely in motion but in action. We can therefore "outrun" predictions by variance. We can change the rules, abandon the system precisely because we are not exclusively systematic creatures. So it always was, even as leaders went to hear the Oracle at Delphi. They did so because they believed that they could use the information in order to make plans, not because planning was irrelevant in the face of inevitability. If determinism had been the faith of the classical Greeks, telling the future would have been an utterly senseless activity. It would not have existed. The attempt to predict is a proactive form of agency. *Because of agency*, people want to hear predictions (oracles have a rationale) and *adjust* accordingly. The irony is that the cultures that are most obsessed with seeing the future are also most active in making it fit their vision.

By contrast, deterministic fatalists postulate a dead world that is lethargic and unadventurous, totally systematized, and consequently, predictable; so much so that prediction is irrelevant. It is no accident that the German word *Tot*, as in "totalitarian," means "dead." Prophetic (visionary) cultures move and make. This is why Soren Kierkegaard (1941) called Hegel's grand systematics a splendid and solid edifice unfit for human habitation, a tomb of pure logic. According to Hegelianism, there are "reasons" why things happen, not emotions. It does not matter what you *want*. Often visionary, prophetic ideologues (who personify hypertrophic emotionalism, reveling in pageantry and political theater) exploit the same rhetorical tactic as operational definers. They evoke "destiny" as a way to inoculate their desires from criticism. Adolf Hitler decreed that the Third Reich would last a millennium, not because he wanted it to happen (besides, he identified himself with the Reich) but because the Aryan race was "naturally" superior to all others, and the laws of nature are said to be utterly unbreakable. Likewise, the Communist revolution is inevitable because the reason of history (not human consciousness) unfolds with "iron necessity" (Marx, 1967: 8). History will change minds, not the other way around. Unfortunately, the followers of Napoleon, Hitler, Stalin, Mao, and many modern "organizational men" have not caught the drift of Kierkegaard's insight into the prison-house of systems thinking.

Unlike molecules, humans have minds to change. They can anticipate and interpret what the method is "trying to get at." That is why researchers of humans must sometimes exercise their ingenuity to trick their subjects by using placebos, confederate respondents, redundant questions, and other deceptive techniques such as the fake shocks utilized in the famous experiments about obedience conducted by Stanley Milgram (1974). Humans are temporal creatures (where time happens). Death is timeless. Civilizations that lose vitality are "lost." Vital, open processes continually integrate predictions into plans; the past into the future. Predictions are always made in the past, while "history" is yet to be enacted in the future, and histories written after that. And this integrating process is continually "now," which is never "the same."

As Jean-Paul Sartre (1960) said, humans are condemned to freedom. We cannot avoid the responsibility of our actions *or failures to act*; our jazz. We make our music and endure it. Many "historic figures" have noted that the absence of behavior can be more important than its presence (Niebuhr, 1976). History is the story of changing architectures, fashions, paradigms, languages, boundaries, philosophies, cosmologies, worlds. But it is a story with no meta-narrative, no transcending rhyme or reason. Communicating is an effort, an expressed potent(ial). A steady-state, self-correcting system yields no history. Humans *make* history and vice versa, which means that (unless one posits a superordinate, divine plan or inescapable natural system) humanity is a process of self-production without a goal. Consequently, it is not a simple, two-valued dialectic, nor is there a final synthesis. The aperspectival science of genetic engineering demonstrates that even human "nature" is subject to human evaluation. Human nature is no longer perceived as a determinate and unalterable coherence (a perspective), and neither is "material" nature, as quantum physics has demonstrated.

SIGHT-BASED MODERN TRIBALISM

Despite the manifest unfolding of aperspectivity in the sciences, the arts, and "letters," currently the dominant structure that characterizes "the West" is the mental-rational perspectival manifold. Modernity is synonymous with perspectivism. Racism is essentially perspectival. No matter what colors are involved, racism posits an intolerantly exclusive identity. Its origin can be found in tribal boundary conditions which almost always lead to violent confrontation.

According to perspectivism, only matter, as extension in space, is real. Therefore, only statements about extension can be valid. In the modern world, only things which can be seen (material surfaces) and measured "count" (are valid). By definition, empiricists cannot do historical research, or make predictions or discoveries, because such actions are more than simply reactions to "real-time" stimuli. Furthermore, such actions involve the invisible. Materialism does not recognize magical identity and mythical imagination/emotion as "real." As Marshall McLuhan (1967) noted, the modern preaches that one should believe none of what one hears and only half of what one sees. "Typographic man" is visually oriented, which expresses an obsession with lineality (but is not restricted to that form alone but to space generally) in opposition to Jacques Derrida's concept of phonocentrism (Kramer, 1988, 1993b; Derrida, 1974).

Unlike Derrida, who argues that modernity is marked by phonocentrism (the "Voice of Being"), I argue that modernity (at least since the advent of Athena's concept of kn*owl*edge and the well-aimed lance) is obsessed with visual presence (visiocentrism) and absolute truth ("constants"). The modern Athenian orientation is evident in such processes as surveil-lance and ba-lance. Already in 1913, in the book *Ideen I*, Edmund Husserl described as "naive" the thesis of the existence of the lifeworld as being exclusively restricted to concrete extension. In the 1930s and 1940s, Gebser more specifically traced the modern lifeworld to the emergent dominance of a spatializing attitude and its consequent perspectivism.[2] Building on these ideas about the ideological force (ontopolitical inertia) of the "natural attitude," the current author calls the modern (neo-Aristotelian) emphasis on a material/spatial metaphysic and its correlated visual epistemology "visiocentrism."

Visiocentrism is an epistemological prejudice that stresses spatial orientation and sight (the category known as "empirical" observation). Physical surfaces, such as phenotype, are all that "matter." By describing this metaphysical prejudice, one can understand not only the tremendous power that faith in physical observation entails, but also the birth of phenotypical identity. The idea of "surface" (which is an ideational category) phenomena is a manifestation of the natural attitude of the perspectival consciousness structure. The modern is preoccupied with correlating surface color with behaviors. What difference does it make?

In the modern world seeing is believing. Empirical observation (though premised upon the direct *personal* perception of a free, nondogmatic subject—romantic individualism) is the only valid path to reality qua truth. Being "straight" is being "true," "honest." But seeing is also perspectival. It does not admit the validity of the not seen, such as meaning, context, and history. That which is "outside" of the cone of vision does not "count." Thus, observation is distorting. As any sleight-of-hand artist knows, the more exclusively we trust our eyes, the more we are tricked. We confuse perception with stimulation, and both with knowledge.

In the hypertrophic modern world of screens and images, what people look like is more important than their quality of thinking. The televised political theater of today is evidence enough. Instead, the label "genius" is increasingly applied to the slick management of image, the "shadow part of politics," and a "knack," as Socrates called it in Plato's *Gorgias*, which has become centralized and professionalized. According to visiocentrism, the "internal process" of thinking is defined as nonexistent. Hence, the absurd antagonism between the brain and the mind. Information (no matter in what quantities) is not the same as knowledge. The potential for a third sophistic, a new darkness caused by the snow blindness of the screen, is not impossible (Kramer, 1993a).

In the modern world, inequity is rationalized via naturalization expressed as Spencerian eugenics and "market forces." The autonomous systematics of "free" markets are preached to others by those who control them. Such market forces thrive on sexual and military/vigilante imagery. However, as Cornel West (1993) has noted, it is disingenuous to chant the mantra that market mechanisms can do no wrong in the face of chronic underemployment and slavery, which, according to The Anti-Slavery Society for the Protection of Human Rights in London, is a still a thriving institution. Over 200 million people worldwide are suffering under various forms of servitude including debt bondage, serfdom qua "contract labor," sham adoptions, concubinage, and chattel slavery (50 million of whom are children).[3] Many in servitude are identified by their phenotype, which is a convenient way to avoid mixing and mingling with the master class, and/or escaping and "blending in."

Stark empiricism leads to nihilism because meaning is not a thing. Discourse is seen as discord. Debate about action is preempted (deemed irrelevant) because values are not things and agency is reduced to stimulus/response. Logically, nothing should move. So long as those who are movers and shakers can opiate everyone else with this ideology, resistance is defused by the hegemony of "objective" determinism. We bind ourselves with chains of causation and systematic surveillance and behavior modification ("corrections" or "re-habit"). Amnesia is encouraged. There should be no history, for that would undermine the apodictic force and eternal inertia of the system. Contingency must be exterminated, transcended. If the system gives itself as eternal, then we forget that we make it and, therefore, can change it. This amnesia is the essence of disenfranchisement, disempowerment. Empowerment presumes the potential to make a difference, to discourse and play.

The greatest threat to community is deterministic (redundant, automated) nihilism. This is the death of hope, the closure of the future. This is the horrendous message of conservative social "science" (like Herrnstein and Murray's *The Bell Curve*) that tells minorities that they have been scientifically determined to be doomed to failure. So much for family, or any other kind of values. At the moment of its apodictic triumph, human science reduces (explains) its subject matter out of existence.

However, unlike Newton's idea of the conservation of energy requiring an "outside" force (such as "the market") to make us move, there is phenomenologically evinced "internal forces" that manifest proaction. Proaction is not conservative or reactionary (to "external" stimuli), but creative. Internally motivated movement is usually goal-establishing, with an idea to produce a difference in the not yet present future. Action and reaction are differentiated by the presence or absence of consciousness. So long as we allow ourselves to be defined as piles of reactionary atoms, we surrender to existentialism, self-loathing, and despair. Systematized complexes of causal chains do not escape dead empiricism. In fact, in its attempt to conceptualize the genuine reciprocity of communications, systematization inadvertently overrationalizes by introducing "feedback" as a solipsistic control mechanism. Again the model is the zero sum conservation of energy. Creativity dissolves this barrier to change.

Systasis integrates time with static system. This involves liberation from systematics. System exhibits dynamism only according to internal criteria. Flow charts do not flow. They exempt themselves from their own logic. But as soon as dynamism becomes reflexive and disrupts criteria, the system is breached ("fails"). Life is creative, revolutionary. Systasis recognizes the momentary validity of systems in time. Systasis is morphological, meaning interested in transformation as much as reactionary efforts toward equilibrium, control, conservation. Systasis is not metamorphical, because the Platonic/Cartesian concept of a two-world system of transcendental rules, and rescendent things that follow the rules, is seen as pure metaphysical speculation. Systasis is a recognition of relativity and dynamism. Systasis does not deny, or deconstruct the validity of perspectival system, but temporalizes it. The dualistic perspective is no longer seen to be totalitarian (eternally and exclusively valid).

Dynamism continually reintegrates systematic structures while affirming their validity as only momentary. Each sentence is a new invention. Even the rules change. Communication is play. Claude Levi-Strauss's (1978) and Noam Chomsky's (1968) genetically grounded prison of universal grammar is swallowed by Kronos.

SYSTEMATIC RACISM

For many, race is a system which precludes the potential for change. However, the "system" of race is continually changing. But, it is not necessarily moving toward a goal in teleological fashion. In other words, race relations are not necessarily "progressing" or "getting better." However, we can be proactive rather than reactive. We can establish a goal and work toward it. Contingent though it is, we can set valued direction.

Relationships between things are not fixed material things. And since the meaning of "things" is dependent on their mutual vitality, things themselves are mutable. Despite every systematizing effort, time, as change (including human agency), is not "arrested." It is not a criminal, but instead it is the essence of potential. Time is the necessary condition for inessential contingency. Empiricism argues for a steady-state universe. Empirical systematics take many forms such as the modern nation-state with its self-maintenance via internal surveillance (feedback or "cybernetics"). Under such conditions, "progress" becomes a permanent condition guided by functional rules and laws.

The synairetic awaring of the continually integrating process of the integrum enables one to appreciate the fact that writing about race relations changes race relations so that what one was referentially describing is no longer the case. Take H. B. Stowe's *Uncle Tom's Cabin* as an example. The description invalidates itself via time. The universe is not a steady state. Humans are creative agents, not merely unconscious responders to stimuli. Humans create stimuli. One could observe the entire prehistory of humanity and not be able to infer from it space flight. Quite the contrary, after observing human behavior from say 40,000 B.C. to 1000 A.D., it would be more rational (presuming a linear steady-state universe) to predict that humanity would never fly because in fact it *never* had flown. But, aperspectivity, which acknowledges indeterminacy and discontinuity, presumes the unpredictability of mutational change, discovery, invention (genuine creativity, free association, and free dissociation).

Aperspectival systasis does not accept only the perspectival mode of given-ness to be the whole story. Nevertheless, the abandonment of race by biologists does not affect the everyday interactions of most people. Racism is real. The claim that the "dilemma of race" (in America at least) can be resolved by learning history, or by generating a "prophetic vision" or plan that will generate leaders, and soon, begs the question of which history (that of Malcolm X or Thomas Sowell) and which unifying vision/identity? Both solutions presume criteria that are not stipulated and categories that are presumed but ill-defined. For instance, West (1993) wants to avoid essential statements in favor of a "prophetic framework" from which to launch ethical evaluations of black behavior! His (1993: 43, 44) attempt to avoid categorical claims collapses almost immediately when he discusses black style, specificity, "mature" black identity, "dominant modes of expression," humanity, and ethics, thus:

[typically, wrongly] . . . blackness is understood to be either the perennial possibility of white supremacist abuse or the distinct styles and dominant modes of expression found in black cultures and communities. These styles and modes are diverse—yet they do stand apart from those of other groups. . . . Mature black identity results from an acknowledgement of the specific black responses to white supremacist abuses and a moral assessment of these responses such that the humanity of black people does not rest on deifying or demonizing others.

Identity is dependent upon difference. Insofar as we minimize difference, we must be prepared to surrender our identities, to supersede the focus of the perspectival modern world, the individual self. Writers on race are fundamentally modernists. They must presume the category "race" in order to begin. And as they attempt to distance themselves from the charge of being racist, they are caught in the contradiction of denying the validity of the concept they are discussing. It is similar to the quagmire of being an atheist. Being an atheist is a logical impossibility because one cannot demonstrate the nonexistence of something.

A good example is Tony Brown (1995), who likes to say that he has no interest in people who go around calling themselves "white" or "black." But he does this after expending great energy talking about how "blacks" own no hotels, how many "blacks" there are and how much "they" collectively earn annually, how "blacks" could finance programs in their "own communities," and how no instrument designed to measure "white" cultural literacy can accurately assess a "black" youth's abilities, and so on.

Another confusion that permeates the vast race literature is the call for an abandonment of selfish individualism (hedonism) in favor of personal responsibility and a moral reasoning based on the Protestant ethic. This has been preached by King, West, Farrakhan, X, Brown, and others. Of course, responsibility presumes the modern self as autonomous from institutional and orthodox determinisms. This ethical call away from selfishness toward individualism is senseless. What is required is a clarification of dimensionality, and identity.

So we are faced with several kinds of spaces, times, histories, and selves. Magical and mythical dimensions must not be ignored because they are not extinct, but actively constitute what the surface color means, which (despite rationalizing objectivation) is presumed by mental-rational organization. Racism is more than simply acknowledging phenotypical differences. Nor is it adequately appreciated by reducing it to "mental illness." Racism involves magic and mythic attitudes that identify phenotypical characteristics with all sorts of emotional "associations," numeric correlations, and magical attributions. Association is in quotes because to associate presumes a separation. But the magic dimension of race perceives no separation between color and qualities. For instance, Blacks *are* lazy. Whites *are* cruel and unjust. When I see a black man I see a lazy man. This is magic identity. There is no thinking involved, no "about." Perspectival thinking involves strategy, rationalization of, and correlation with.

Race is a reaction; a communication. Race is an interpretation and therefore an expression. "Race" is not a physical thing but a cultural artifact, an interpretation. It is ideational in that everyone, regardless of color, has "race." Physical differences alone do not constitute "race." Physical difference is not a sufficient condition for racial identity. Physical difference may not even be a necessary condition as in the case of Jewish identity. However, for those who do not reflect upon their own prejudices, race is an aspect of passive synthesis, and is therefore believed to be "physical," "real," "natural," and as such a legitimator of all sorts of contingent comparisons and "correlations." In other words, the innate conditions of color and facial features are always already meaningful; self-evident.

Physical features are meaningful and are real. Like it or not, the color of Michael Jackson's skin "matters" to many people. For those suffering from what Husserl (1962) called the "naive natural attitude," (from the illness of metaphysical prejudice), the word "matter" indicates or means reality. Jackson's skin tone really means something about his politics, his economics, his character, even, and especially, his identity. Because as Husserl (1962) demonstrated, experience is always experience of meaning, physical features are experienced as an expression that is quite unintentional and as such, prereflectively blind. Ironically, our preoccupation with what we see (our visiocentrism) exposes a profound blindness (Kramer, 1993a). However, simply because one's color or type of hair is not intentional it does not follow that the myriad of interpretations and associations attached to it are "natural" or inescapable.

From the perspective of a phenomenologist, "naturalism" is a metaphysical proposition and as such is considered speculative. Nevertheless, the ideological (meaning unreflecting naive attitude) danger of naturalism is that it inoculates its propositions from reflection. What is "natural" is "self-evident." What is natural is Reality, and what use is it to argue with reality? While color and other physical features are visiocentrically powerful (even "natural"), interpretations of them are not—they are cultural (Kramer, 1992). But interpretations, though relatively mutable, inconsistent, and contingent, are no less real. In fact, the metaphysical doctrine of empiricism itself is an interpretation. Therefore, race is real; just as real as physical features. But importantly, for the unreflective person, they (meaning the physical and the ideological) are identical; race is a *physical thing* and therefore a legitimate, meaning "objective," point of reference for evaluating the quality of a person. In the cultural world, which is the human world, race is real. Regardless of one's metaphysical preferences, racism, and therefore race, exists.

Because race is a mutable interpretation, it is an expression. Watzlawick, Beavin, and Jackson (1967) have argued that one cannot not communicate. This is in accord with Husserl's (1962) claim that perception *is* meaning. Whether we like it or not, our physical features communicate. One does not experience discrete stimuli of a particular visual frequency *and then* interpret that spectral array as "moving" and as "coming toward me" and as "a person," and then as a type of person, and so on. Rather than seeing a "blob" of "color," because I am a cultural being, I *see*, I recognize a "friend" or "stranger," a "black, young, male, scary, swaggering, threatening, menacing human being coming at me." And that seeing is passively synthesized. It happens without conscious reflection, and is given instantly. But as soon as a person can speak in terms of "constituting" reality, and interpretation, a deconstruction occurs. One begins to recognize the contingent nature of reality and at that moment one is enabled to evaluate the consciousness structure that constituted that reality and to become free from it.

Racism is culturally inflected reaction. Perception is identification which involves categorization as part of the constitutive process of awareness. "To observe" means to examine, assess, and survey. It also means to say, comment, and remark. Observation is always already valuative. Race is a categorical interpretation born of the primitive distinction between self and Other. There can be no identity, no meaning/experience, without difference. It is natural that a person have "color" and facial features, that people are different. But the interpretation of what those physical phenomena mean (their quality), even when they are always already constituted as meaningful (even at the preconscious level of passive synthesis), is not natural but cultural. This is evident by the vastly differing interpretations of colors, facial features, and by our ability to reevaluate. While all may agree that a person is "black" (presuming that they share the same language which is already a deep bias), few may agree as to what this means.

Because, as Immanuel Kant (1929) demonstrated, consciousness is not passive but active and capable of reflection, interpretations can be reinterpreted, evaluations can be reevaluated, and transvaluated. In short, interpretations can be seen as such (as contingent) and can be evaluated in light of metaphysical and moral criteria which enable one to consciously reject or reinforce them; as Nietzsche (1974) put it, to be "wide awake" and self-reflective about one's "objective" reality. People can change their minds. Despite the pseudoscience of eugenics, race vanishes at the molecular (genetic) level. All DNA is the same color, but this is irrelevant anyway because no one sees the Other's DNA.

Race is a projection. Racial proclamations tell very much more about the person making the proclamation than about the subject described. Correlations of color with sociocultural and psychological traits are even more ephemeral. The correlations social scientists choose to pursue often tell us much more about those scientists than it does about the people they are studying. Multiculturalism is not an ideology or a goal. Multiculturalism is a fact and it has been a defining characteristic of the American experience since before the word "America" was associated with the land masses of the Western hemisphere. Cultural streamlining and global adaptation resulting in a nondistinct amalgam has never existed. Such ideas are figments of the social "scientific" imagination.

NOTES

1. In all Nietzschian honesty, this is a category statement that can reflexively include itself.

2. All page citations refer to the 1985 translation of *Ursprung und Gegenwart*, which appeared as two volumes in 1949 and 1953. The English title is *The Ever-Present Origin*, translated by Noel Barstad and Algis Mickunas.

3. Slavery has been known throughout history and among peoples of every level of material culture. Slavery is not unique to any particular type of economic system. Experts divide the institution into two types: commercial slave societies, where slaves are used as a primary work force as in the southern United States, and slave-owning societies, where slaves are used principally for personal and domestic use such as concubinage.

REFERENCES

Bacon, F. (1937) *Essays, Advancement of Learning, New Atlantis and Other Pieces.* Garden City, NY: Doubleday, Doran & Company.

Barlow, J. P. (1995) "Welcome to Cyberspace." *Time* 145, no. 12 (Spring): 4–11.

Brown, T. (1995) *Black Lies/White Lies: The Truth According to Tony Brown.* New York: W. Morrow and Company.

Chomsky, N. (1968) *The Acquistion of Syntax in Children from 5 to 10.* Cambridge, MA: MIT Press.

Derrida, J. (1974) *Of Grammatology.* Baltimore: Johns Hopkins University Press.

Gebser, J. (1985) *The Ever-Present Origin.* Athens: Ohio University Press.

Gilroy, P. (1993) *The Black Atlantic: Modernity and Double Consciousness.* Cambridge, MA: Harvard University Press.

Husserl, E. (1962) *Ideas.* New York: Collier.

Kant, I. (1929) *Critique of Pure Reason.* New York: St. Martin's Press.

Kierkegaard, S. (1941) *Concluding Unscientific Postscript.* Princeton, NJ: Princeton University Press.

Kramer, E. (1988) *Television Criticism and the Problem of Ground: Interpretation After Deconstruction.* 2 Vols. Ann Arbor, MI: University Microfilms International, no. 8816770.

———. (1992) "Consciousness and Culture." In *Consciousness and Culture: An Introduction to the Thought of Jean Gebser*, edited by E. Kramer. Westport, CT: Greenwood Press, pp. 1–60.

———. (1993a) "Mass Media and Democracy." In *Open Institutions: The Hope for Democracy*, edited by J. W. Murphy and D. Peck. Westport, CT: Praeger, pp. 77–98.

———. (1993b) "The Origin of Television as Civilizational Expression." In *Semiotics 1990: Sources in Semiotics, Vol. XI*, edited by J. Deely et al. Lanham, MD: University Press of America, pp. 28–37.

Kuhn, T. (1962) *The Structure of Scientific Revolutions.* Chicago: University of Chicago Press.

Levi-Strauss, C. (1978) *Myth and Meaning.* New York: Schocken Books.

Marx, K. (1967) *Capital, Vol. 1.* New York: International Publishers.

McLuhan, M. (1967) *The Medium Is the Message.* New York: Bantam.

Merleau-Ponty, M. (1973) *The Prose of the World.* Evanston, IL: Northwestern University Press.

Milgram, S. (1974) *Obedience to Authority.* New York: Harper & Row.

Niebuhr, R. (1976) *Love and Justice.* Glouster, MA: P. Smith.

Nietzsche, F. (1974) *The Gay Science.* New York: Vintage.

Sartre, J. P. (1960) *To Freedom Condemned.* New York: Philosophical Library.

Watzlawick, P., J. Beavin, and D. Jackson. (1967) *Pragmatics of Human Communication.* New York: Norton.

West, C. (1993) *Race Matters.* Boston: Beacon Press.

Wittgenstein, L. (1971) *Prototractatus.* London: Routledge and Kegan Paul.

2

The Importance of Social Imagery for Race Relations

John W. Murphy

THE USE OF SOCIAL IMAGERY

Social Imagery is a part of every theory about social life. Herbert Blumer (1969: 6) referred to these ideas as "root images," while Walter Benjamin (1978: 20) favored the phrase "dialectical images." Their point is that every theory presupposes a tableau of social life, a pictorial of how society is organized. Some of these images are obtrusive, while others are subtle. Nonetheless, these representations are always operative and outline a "framework of study and analysis" (Blumer, 1969: 6).

Throughout the history of sociology, a variety of images have been adopted. For example, writers such as Auguste Comte, Herbert Spencer, and Emile Durkheim popularized the organismic analogy (Stark, 1963). Society, in other words, is compared to a living body, and each institution is treated as a major organ that contributes to the survival of the entire society. Although emphasis is placed on integration, each part is imagined to have some, albeit very limited, autonomy.

Other writers, such as Henri Fayol, Vilfredo Pareto, and Frederick Taylor, opted for imagery that is much more harsh (Callaghan and Murphy, 1983). The machine, in other words, was used to describe society. Each worker in a factory should be viewed as one of a series of gear wheels, claims Taylor. This viewpoint has had enormous impact on conceptualizing and regulating the workplace. Fayol's "scalar chain" of authority, for example, is thought to be a forerunner of the modern bureaucracy. According to the mechanical model, society consists of a balance of forces, statuses, and positions that must be kept in equilibrium.

This style of imagery remained dominant until the 1950s. At that time, increased refinement was desired as social scientists tried to improve their status.

The social sciences became "mathematical, and thus . . . avail[ed] themselves of the enormous wealth of formalized tools for thought" (Gehlen, 1980: 36). Talk about bodies and machines was not precise and scientific enough. If sociology was ever going to be taken seriously, this kind of speculation would have to be avoided. Accordingly, Talcott Parsons (1951) argues that society should be viewed as a system. Appropriate structural imagery was introduced, and thus society was described to be a network of interlocking roles. In the late 1960s, influenced by the work of Norbert Wiener, Parsons combined functional analysis and systems theory to form his now famous cybernetic hierarchy. Social imagery, in short, began to look scientific and technological.

During the past decade or so, these images have been challenged. Specifically, their focus on integration and group solidarity has come to be viewed as stifling. In the field of economics, more individual-oriented imagery has had a long history. Nonetheless, in sociology the perennial concern has been fostering social cohesion. The individual, therefore, has been ancillary to the group. Even Spencer, originally a staunch advocate of *laissez-faire*, gradually elevated the commonweal in importance.

Nevertheless, the recent emphasis on the supply side has begun to influence contemporary sociology. Giving credence to human agency has become quite *de rigueur*. Attempting to merge the so-called macro and micro levels of society has become the latest trend (Alexander, 1987). As a consequence of pursuing their own preferences, individuals are transformed into social beings. Without saying so explicitly, a variant of the standard market analogy has been accepted. Through exchange and rational calculation, individual freedom becomes the basis for maintaining the larger society. Hence the individual is elevated in significance.

THE ROLE OF THESE IMAGES

These images have a unique purpose. In general, they explain how society operates. For example, the status of the individual, the nature of interpersonal relationships, and the extent of social responsibility are illustrated. These and other important messages are conveyed in a symbolic manner. Social reality is thus restricted by certain discursive practices; a particular symbolic realm is allowed to surpass others (Guattari, 1984: 168).

For example, in both the organismic and mechanistic analogies, personal autonomy is downplayed. Rather than individual freedom, attention is directed to supporting society's goals. Social integration, stated differently, is elevated above everything else; societal interests are given primary consideration. For this reason, these two analogies are commonly thought to be indicative of holism. In point of fact, the writers associated with these positions were devoted to averting chaos, which they believed could erupt at any moment. And they believed only repressive imagery could forestall this tragedy.

As opposed to this scenario, advocates of market imagery want to liberate the individual from the constraints imposed by holism. Because of the stress that is placed on the individual, this viewpoint has been characterized as atomistic. Simply put, society consists of concatenated agents. Any social concern, at best, is an afterthought and given little consideration. As persons meet their own needs, the unintentional effect is that society is reinforced. It is assumed that personal fulfillment also results in social gains.

As is suggested, social imagery outlines norms in a way that most people can understand. The average citizen may know nothing about moral theory. Yet when the market is mentioned, an entire theory of social existence comes to mind. Personal freedom, choice, and individual sovereignty are themes that are commonly recognized. In the case of holism, cooperation and allegiance to the nation or state are ideas that are typically mentioned. Almost in a flash, persons are informed of their rights and duties by social imagery.

STRIVING FOR A REALITY *SUI GENERIS*

At first glance, atomism and holism appear to be dissimilar. On closer examination, however, a common theme unites these two descriptions of social existence. To use a phrase introduced into sociology by Durkheim (1983: 86–88), both of these viewpoints incorporate a "reality sui generis." In each case, an autonomous referent is sought to unite society. "Society," argues Durkheim (1983: 68), "always possesses a higher dignity than what is individual." Through this demarche, social order is thought to be secure. Moral order is impersonal and supplies the constraint required for the survival of any civilization.

Some critics contend that the traditional social imagery contains a conservative streak. That is, individuals are not trusted to establish order, even in atomism, because a source of social organization is sought that is uncontaminated by human agency. The coordination of society is the result of autonomous forces, as opposed to personal or collective *praxis*. Therefore, order is believed to have a firm foundation that is unaffected by social or cultural exigencies.

In sociological circles, this way of grounding order has been called social-ontological realism (Stark, 1963; Hinkle, 1980). At the heart of this designation is the idea that not only does the source of order exist beyond the influence of human action, but this site is the most reliable base of society. Fundamentally disconnected from misinterpretation, perceptual error, and other human foibles, an inviolable normative referent is available. A universal standard exists—that is acultural and neutral—for judging the adequacy of behavior.

This base of order is made possible by a theoretical maneuver that is quite old. In the parlance of philosophers, social norms are sustained by dualism. Searching in this manner of an Archimedean point of knowledge and order pervades the Western intellectual tradition. But the separation of subjectivity and subjectivity that is necessary to establish a reality *sui generis* is usually associated with Descartes and the rise of so-called modern philosophy in the seventeenth century.

Essential to Cartesianism is a schism that is accepted to exist between *res cogitans* and *res extensa*, which, in turn, separates opinion from true facts. According to this division, reality transcends the exigencies of consciousness and defies interpretation. Reality is uncontested, while human action is ephemeral and unreliable. To be sure, consciousness can be overcome, so that reality can be directly encountered.

The culmination of this transcendence is the revelation of an ultimate reality. A reality can be invoked, writes Durkheim (1983: 73–76), that is not embroiled in controversy. This reality *sui generis* is neutral, unbiased, and able to adjudicate fairly all matters. As a result, this entity is even more powerful than the state. Due to the presence of this normative framework, society is prevented from devolving into the proverbial "war of all against all," for questions about the meaning of existence are answered in an unequivocal way (Parsons, 1966: 8).

With regard to holism, the influence of realism is obvious. The parts of society are coordinated in terms of some overarching plan. For example, Parsons (1951) contends that order reflects deep-seated "functional prerequisites." These tenets supply the *telos* for society.

The realistic side of atomism is not as obvious, but this tendency is still operative. In this sense, atomists regularly make a nonsequitur. Specifically, on the one hand they value individual freedom, but on the other society is not placed within human control. The market, state, or cosmos is treated as an almost metaphysical entity, and is given the latitude to regulate society. In a subterranean way, control is moved gradually away from the individual.

Until very recently, therefore, sociology has been an exclusively realist endeavor. In Marxist terminology, society has been externalized and reified. Society is thus conceived to be an obtrusive entity that can be systematically probed and scientifically studied. Order is an objective thing. Moreover, society has a status that cannot be reduced to psychology or some other micro-source. Society is unabashedly real and can demand recognition by all of its citizens.

REALISM AND RACE RELATIONS

Social realism has had an adverse effect on the field of race relations. Specifically, discussions about race have been dominated by an assimilationist perspective (Metzger, 1971). This finding has been true even when pluralism has been advocated. In fact, some critics have charged that the thrust of race relations in the United States has been the attempt to eliminate any vestiges of ethnic identity. Hence most people think automatically of America as a "melting pot," which produces a bland concoction referred to loosely as an "American."

Due to the asymmetrical relationship between society and the individual presupposed by social-ontological realism, immigrants are expected to strive to emulate their superiors. The dominant culture represented by the reality *sui generis* is supposed to be internalized. As demonstrated by Sartre (1969: 133) in his discussion of anti-Semitism, a metaphysical justification is present to support assimilation. Through contact with American society, which is considered to embody reality *sui generis*, new arrivals are changed and improved. A version of cultural imperialism has been not only tolerated but honored. Peter Rose (1968: 50) summarizes this trend when he states that supporters of assimilation believed the "immigrant should take off his foreign mantle and quickly adapt himself to *American* ways." In the end, persons are supposed to become very similar.

From the 1920s until the 1950s, the so-called Chicago School, headed by Robert Park and Ernest Burgess, practically monopolized the discourse about race. Their famous cycle of race relations, for example, was used as a blueprint for bussing and other integration policies. Through increasing contact with mainstream society, they contend, skills and traits are acquired that enable immigrants to become *bona fide* Americans. At one juncture, Park and Burgess (1969: 762) equated assimilation with Americanization. As summarized by Stanford Lyman (1994: 71), Park believed that the "various folk cultures that made up its [America's] ghetto enclaves would eventually disappear, the peoples having become fully acculturated to and assimilated within its industrial, civic, and mass society." The burgeoning immigration problem of the time would thus be solved. By stressing assimilation, the moral base of American society would be preserved.

During this period, however, not everyone agreed with Park and Burgess. These self-proclaimed pluralists, such as Horace Kallen, Randolph Bourne, and, later, Nathan Glazer, Daniel P. Moynihan, and Pierre van den Berghe, argued that complete assimilation is not required for society to survive. America might even be enriched by the introduction and cultivation of cultural differences. Vitality may be introduced into American society.

Nonetheless, a complete break with assimilation was not made by these pluralists. Because of the influence of William James, Kallen (1956: 98) believed that an abstract social force bound persons together. Accordingly, Kallen introduced his well-known metaphor of everyone playing a part in a similar orchestra. Bourne, also affected by James, viewed society to be held together in an almost cosmic manner. In the case of Glazer, Moynihan, and van den Berghe, naturalistic tendencies, although not crudely biological, are thought to be at the root of society. Because individualism is tempered by this naturalistic corrective, order is preserved. While these pluralists want to recognize the uniqueness of the individual, human *praxis* is not entrusted to unite society. Order still constrains the human element.

Following this brief respite from overt assimilationism, the focus returned to assimilation in various ways. During the 1960s, Milton Gordon's (1964) work received significant attention. He recommends several areas of assimilation, including social, cultural, and, indirectly, biological dimensions. And throughout the 1970s, 1980s, and 1990s, attention was given to the ranting of Arthur Jensen, William Schockley, and J. Phillipe Rushton. This trend culminated recently with the publication of *The Bell Curve*, which supposedly represents the most scientific treatment of the biological reasons for justifying assimilation. In the end, this fascination with eugenics represents a sophisticated effort to establish social hierarchy (Smith, 1993). And because blacks are identified as inferior, they can never become autonomous and self-directing.

But a host of newer writers, characterized by Omi and Winant (1986) as advancing a "new paradigm," have emerged to challenge the reign of assimilation. Authors such as bell hooks, Cornel West, and Paul Gilroy, for example, maintain that the social totalization and reification required by assimilation is not justified, either theoretically or politically. Central to their position is that realism is passé, and thus the rationale for assimilation is undermined. Homi Bhabha (1994: 42) writes that there is no "master narrative," divorced from interpretive and political *praxis*, that can dictate a person's identity and social position. This exalted ground of order, he claims, can no longer be reached.

In view of recent shifts in linguistics and philosophy, realism is under siege. The dualism that sustains a reality *sui generis* is deemed to be untenable. This collapse of dualism, notes Bhabha (1994: 4), is the hallmark of postmodernism and signals an end to the absolutes that have been used to enforce assimilation and, accordingly, discrimination. Subsequent to the advent of postmodernism, the theoretical maneuver presupposed by realism is illegitimate. Novel ways must be sought to conceptualize order that do not rely on realism, and therefore do not open the door for one group to dominate another through cultural imperialism.

THE POSTMODERN TURN

Jean-Francois Lyotard (1984: xxiv) defines postmodernism as "incredulity toward metanarratives." His point is that ultimate realities, particularly universal explanatory schemes, are no longer tenable. Universal laws, historical trajectories, or religious justifications, in other words, are deprived of their traditional seignorial position. This conclusion is predicated on the realization that nothing eludes consciousness, contrary to what Descartes imagined. Roland Barthes (1985: 52) has this conclusion in mind when he states that "objectivity is only one image-repertoire among others." Everything that is known, in short, is mediated completely by conscious activity. A metanarrative is thus simply another narrative.

In this regard, Edmund Husserl (1975: 13) declares that "consciousness is always consciousness of something." Only in the most analytical way can knowledge be stripped of interpretation. All knowledge originates, therefore, in the *Lebenswelt* or "lifeworld." This is the realm of experience—"the construct of a universal, ultimately functioning subjectivity"—that scientists strive to conceal (Husserl, 1970: 113). The lifeworld exists prior to the invention of dualism and the desire to covet knowledge that is unaffected by the human presence.

While borrowing from the late work of Ludwig Wittgenstein, Lyotard (1984: 9–11) makes Husserl's position more accessible by announcing that reality is mediated by ''language games.'' Lyotard (1984: 10) uses this phrase to maintain that the ''various categories of utterance can be defined in terms of rules specifying their properties and the uses to which they can be put.'' The pragmatic thrust of language, in other words, is united inextricably with what is accepted to be real; language use specifies the contours of reality.

Nothing escapes the exigencies of interpretation, due to the ubiquity of linguistic *praxis*. In Barthes' (1985: 162) words, ''there is nothing real without language.'' Language is a creative capacity to make and continually remake what is treated as real. No longer merely a conduit, or something that points to what is real, language transforms reality into a symbolic dimension. Consequently, truth emerges from language, rather than reality.

The discovery of metanarratives is prevented by language use. Indeed, the only access to knowledge is through the labyrinth of language. Whatever is known, therefore, is denied universal meaning. All knowledge is local, as postmodernists like to say, or shaped by particular interpretive acts. Interpretations may change, but pure vision is never achieved. Facts are thus not simply encountered, as positivists and other empiricists seem to think, but flow from ''historically limited modes of thought and action'' (Fish, 1989: 13). Postmodernists acknowledge this restriction when they say all knowledge is indirectly revealed.

This challenge to dualism poses severe problems for sociologists, particularly relative to conceptualizing order. Norms, laws, and other regulations must emerge from language, rather than from a reality *sui generis*. Social order is thus a human construct; order is an ''imaginary'' phenomenon, as contemporary scholars contend (Sprinker, 1987). There is no core to society other than one that arrives through linguistic discourse. Any base that claims to be central to society is merely an interpretation, which is reinforced through a variety of means. As a result, there is nothing left to which people are supposed to assimilate.

In postmodern jargon, subverting the prospect of erecting a reality sui generis ''decenters'' society. Without the synoptic vision provided by this location, however, the charge is often made that society will devolve into anomie. Without a clear justification for assimilation, cultural differences will erupt into chaos. But, notes Bhabha (1994: 148), there are non-metaphysical modes of order that do not culminate in hierarchy, marginalization, and other forms of repression. Order can be conceptualized in such a way that cohesion is achieved without the repressive side effects of assimilation.

In the absence of a hegemonic reality *sui generis*, ambivalence can be embraced. Actually, without this uncertainty pluralism can never be realized, for true pluralism requires the proliferation of interpretations that can occur only in the absence of an ultimate authority. New social imagery illustrates that an appreciation of difference does not necessarily culminate in tearing society apart. Difference and order are shown to be compatible.

Suggested by the typical realist imagery is that order cannot survive in the absence of cultural hegemony. The parts of society must be subordinated to a seignorial whole. What this asymmetry does is to set the stage for assimilation and domination. Some groups, accordingly, are inevitably placed in a subaltern relationship to others. Most problematic is that this arrangement comes to be viewed as natural and logical. In fact, a society that is not arranged in this manner is labelled utopian and often dismissed as illusory, without any serious discussion.

The non-dualistic, and thus decentered, imagery that is an outgrowth of postmodernism does not require the suppression of difference for order to survive. Quite the opposite, differences are arranged so that their association does not result in an abstract whole. A whole is revealed, instead, that continues to exist without obscuring the integrity of its parts. Discordance and juxtaposition, writes Bhabha (1994: 217), are not necessarily antagonistic to order.

DECENTERED IMAGERY AND ORDER

Because of the pervasiveness of language, postmodernists disperse the traditional core of order. As described by Jean Gebser (1985: 544), "the center is everywhere." This awareness is not new, but is found in the work of artists such as Pablo Picasso, Jackson Pollock, and John Cage. The idea is that because any core is fully interpretive, the usual absolute separation of center and periphery cannot be maintained. This differentiation, instead, is simply an accident of symbolism (Bhabha, 1994: 25). Moreover, the interpretation spawned by symbolism can infect any location and is very difficult to contain. Order can thus begin and end anywhere.

This dispersion of any core is apparent in the imagery chosen by postmodernists to describe order. Gilles Deleuze and Felix Guattari (1983: 10–20), for example, declare that order should not be compared to a tree, another well-known analogy, and thus introduce the rhizome as a substitute. As opposed to a tree, a rhizome does not have a core, grows laterally, and extends concomitantly in several directions. The rhizome, writes Guattari (1984: 258), tolerates the "proliferation of new intensities, [and the] development of new growths." Their point is that order can thrive without a centralized and hierarchical structure; order is not destroyed by the development of new strands.

Paul Gilroy, who is an expert on race relations and works within the postmodern tradition, argues that intergroup interaction could be improved by more fluid social imagery. In this regard, he refers to music, particularly jazz, in his attempt to create "a tradition of ceaseless motion" (Gilroy, 1993a: 122). While relying on the writing of Toni Morrison and Ralph Ellison, Gilroy (1993a: 79) notes that the antipathy found in jazz "symbolizes and anticipates new non-dominating social relationships." Like a jazz ensemble where musicians both play against and with one another, order is possible that is replete with contradictions, oppositions, and innovations. In contrast to realism, formalization is not a prerequisite for the survival of order.

To demonstrate that "unity within diversity" is possible, postmodernists point to the collage, mosaic, and patchwork quilt (Gilroy, 1993b: 116). In each of these examples, order emerges out of juxtaposition and contrast. Differences, in short, illustrate and inform one another. "Collective bonding" is thus fostered, claims bell hooks (1990: 29), as a result of locating order at the nexus of differences. Persons begin to understand that every identity is simply another difference, rather than a potential foundation for all differences. And without the contrast supplied by difference, no identity would be possible. Implied is that persons need one another for any particular identity to exist, thereby encouraging unity. Cornel West (1993: 82) refers to this approach to viewing order as "synechdochical."

This new imagery has encouraged some postmodernists who work in the area of race relations to accept Emmanuel Levinas's (1961: 64–70) portrayal—order without intermediary or abstraction—of society. While rejecting a reality *sui generis*, Levinas believes a base of order is available that has been overlooked. This region is the dialogical or, according to Bhabha, the "intersubjective realm." According to this scheme, order can be constituted in the "form of circulation *in between*" persons (Bhabha, 1994: 206). On the basis of discourse alone, order can be maintained; through a dialogue among differences society can survive.

At this juncture is where Lyotard's (1984: 65) rejection of consensus is relevant. He scandalized many readers when he denounced this idea. They jumped to the erroneous conclusion that he did not care about order. What he was criticizing, instead, was the need for majority rule. In other words, without presupposing the existence of a foundation upon which a consensus can be built, chaos is believed to be inevitable. That order should reflect variegated interests, and nothing else, is not considered to be cogent.

But Lyotard never embraced anarchy. What he did do, however, was to abandon the notion that agreement among persons is a prerequisite for order. Here, again, the principle of sameness is operative, when primacy is given to consensus. On the contrary, Lyotard (1984: 40) writes that the social bond is a "fabric formed by the intersection of at least two (and in reality an indeterminate number) language games, obeying different rules." Similar to Levinas, Lyotard argues that persons can recognize the likelihood of certain differences appearing, thereby facilitating adjustment to these traits. A majority-led campaign to insure the survival of a vital sameness is unnecessary for order to prevail.

Most important is that, again, assimilation is shunned. Consistent with the structure of the rhizome, a direct linkage is sufficient to sustain order. Through immediate contact, empathy, and iteration persons can learn to anticipate each others' actions. Translated into terms used in studying care relations, order is engaged and prevails through the recognition of differences. Order continues in the absence of potentially repressive realist props.

Order without assimilation is thus possible. The model has been broken whereby homogeneity is required for the persistence of solidarity. Therefore, real pluralism does not have to be viewed as a threat to society. This fear is based on old imagery, which may fragment with the addition of more differences. But because the collage is nothing but differences and contrasts, this form of order is not jeopardized by new additions. Instead, the beauty of a montage may be enhanced by this kind of growth.

DEMISE OF PUBLIC ORDER

Just about every politician is lamenting the demise of public order. The United States has become a nasty place to live. The usual litany of problems is cited to account for this breakdown. Schools are failing, family values are eroding, and people are becoming increasingly mean-spirited. A sense of civility seems to be missing from everyday life. According to Walinsky:

We have fled from our cities, virtually abandoning great institutions such as the public schools. We have permitted the spread within our country of wastelands ruled not by the Constitution and lawful authorities but by the anarchic force of merciless killers. . . . We have become isolated from one another, dispirited about any possibility of collective or political action to meet this menace. (Walinsky, 1995: 53)

But how can the public be returned to prominence in a multicultural society? This is the tough question that needs new answers. Who can command the authority to demand that diversity be sacrificed to erect a hollow abstraction, such as the state, to enforce unity? Such an idea is certainly un-American.

But the typical response is that more law and order is needed. In the case of race relations, the old assimilationist strategy is resurrected, only this time with a moral twist. Black enclaves, mostly in urban, inner-city areas, are operating according to moral standards that are at variance with the American ideal. As a result, the inhabitants of these locations are excluded from jobs and other productive activities.

The culture of the ghetto, resulting from the isolation described by William Julius Wilson (1987), must be eradicated. Otherwise blacks are condemned to a life of poverty and despair. Unless these persons learn the ways of white America, and defer to corrupt authority figures and work at menial jobs, their future is bleak. This appears to be the same message conveyed by Israel Zangwill in his 1908 play, *The Melting Pot.*

The Melting Pot

However, now the world is different. For many reasons, multiculturalism has been emphasized to the extent that unanimity is close to impossible to sustain.

Indeed, minority groups balk at demands to assimilate, because they believe this process violates their individual rights. To the chagrin of conservatives, democracy is often cited as a reason for not assimilating. And these modern critics of assimilation make a good point. Why should the suppression of one's cultural identity be required for citizenship? Does the survival of democracy demand that persons relinquish their identies?

But most important: How much time is actually spent talking about a person's obligation to the public? This issue is not addressed in either atomism or holism. In the former, individual autonomy is stressed, while in the later, the social is equated with the state and eschewed. A person's responsibilities to others is unimportant in each case.

Without proper social imagery, public order cannot be restored. In a manner similar to a collage, persons must be informed that they are essentially tied to one another. The individual does not exist without the other; identity presupposes difference. Every individual action, accordingly, implicates others. Therefore, there is no reason to assimilate, for order is constituted by sameness *and* difference. One does not exist without the other. Personal identity and collective solidarity occupy a similar plane, and thus social order is not antagonistic to human action. Because turning to the other does not require assimilation, order does not require adherence to a reality *sui generis.*

Interracial harmony will be difficult to develop until appropriate social imagery is instilled that elevates the public in stature. This new imagery, however, comes into conflict with many currently cherished institutions. The economy, for example, encourages and thrives on hierarchy. Without this sort of social differentiation, capitalism will atrophy. Nevertheless, institutions that are at variance with decentered imagery will have to be reevaluated and, most likely, abandoned. Harsh and difficult choices will have to be made, if primacy is going to be given to the public.

This is the political side of postmodernism that its critics choose to ignore. A non-monolithic image of social life is advocated that contravenes most of modern society. Alternative imagery is proffered that challenges current social arrangements.

What could be more political! But this imagery, notes Lyotard, does not carry the metaphysical baggage of Marxism and other collectivist ideologies. Rather than abstract, the collective emerges at the juncture of discourse. And because this imagery is new and untried, many critics of hierarchy doubt its radical nature.

Yet the implications of this imagery for social relations are clear. Specifically, the usual culture of hierarchy must be jettisoned, along with the institutions that support this tradition. These changes will extend far beyond affirmative action, and thus will likely be pilloried by most mainstream politicians. In this regard, postmodern social imagery has the potential to inspire far-reaching political policies.

CONCLUSION

The key point of this chapter is that social imagery is important for social relations, but is often overlooked. What realism suggests is that ethnicity should be sacrificed to reinforce order. Given this symbolism, authorities and other citizens can request, without embarrassment, that minorities subordinate themselves to an alleged dominant culture. This kind of assimilation is deemed legitimate to reinforce society. Those who do not conform, moreover, can also be openly attacked.

The imagery proposed by postmodernists, on the other hand, conceives order in a different way. In short, order represents a confluence of differences. The message is that pluralism does not destroy culture. Order can be preserved just as effectively by this method as when realism is adopted. The important difference is that ethnicity does not have to be concealed. This is a significant advancement, however, for any society that aims to be pluralistic.

REFERENCES

Alexander, J. C. (Ed.) (1987) *The Micro-Macro Link.* Berkeley: University of California Press.

Barthes, R. (1985) *The Grain of the Voice.* New York: Hill and Wang.

Benjamin, W. (1978) *Reflections.* New York: Harcourt Brace Jovanovich.

Bhabha, H. K. (1994) *The Location of Culture.* London: Routledge and Kegan Paul.

Blumer, H. (1969) *Symbolic Interactionism.* Englewood Cliffs, NJ: Prentice-Hall.

Callaghan, K. A., and J. W. Murphy. (1983) ''Changes in Technological Social Control: Theory and Implications for the Workplace.'' In *The Underside of High-Tech*, edited by J. W. Murphy, A. Mickunas, and J. J. Pilotta. Westport, CT: Greenwood Press, pp. 17–28.

Deleuze, G., and F. Guattari. (1983) *On the Line.* New York: Semiotext(e).

Durkheim, E. (1983) *Pragmatism and Sociology.* Cambridge: Cambridge University Press.

Fish, S. (1989) *Doing What Comes Naturally.* Durham, NC: Duke University Press.

Gebser, J. (1985) *The Ever-Present Origin.* Athens: Ohio University Press.

Gilroy, P. (1993a) *The Black Atlantic.* London: Verso.

———. (1993b) *Small Acts.* London: Serpent's Tail.

Gehlen, A. (1980) *Man in the Age of Technology.* New York: Columbia University Press.

Gordon, M. (1964) *Assimilation in American Life.* New York: Oxford University Press.

Guattari, F. (1984) *Molecular Revolution.* Middlesex, England: Penguin Books.

Hinkle, R. C. (1980) *Founding Theory in American Sociology 1881–1915.* Boston: Routledge and Kegan Paul.

hooks, b. (1990) *Yearning.* Boston: South End Press.

Husserl, E. (1970) *The Crisis of European Sciences and Transcendental Phenomenology.* Evanston, IL: Northwestern University Press.

———. (1975) *The Paris Lectures.* The Hague: Nijhoff.

Kallen, H. M. (1956) *Cultural Pluralism and the American Idea.* Philadelphia: University of Pennsylvania Press.

Levinas, E. (1961) *Totality and Infinity.* Pittsburgh: Duquesne University Press.

Lyman, S. M. (1994) *Color, Culture, Civilization.* Urbana: University of Illinois.

Lyotard, J. F. (1984) *The Postmodern Condition.* Minneapolis: University of Minnesota Press.

———. (1993) *The Postmodern Explained.* Minneapolis: University of Minnesota Press.

Metzger, P. L. (1971) "American Sociology and Black Assimilation: Conflicting Perspectives." *American Journal of Sociology* 76, no. 4: 627–647.

Omi, M., and H. Winant. (1986) *Racial Formation in the United States: From the 1960s to the 1980s.* New York: Routledge and Kegan Paul.

Park, R. E., and E. W. Burgess. (1969) *Introduction to the Science of Sociology,* 3d ed. Chicago: University of Chicago Press.

Parsons, T. (1951) *The Social System.* Glencoe, IL: Free Press.

———. (1966) *Societies.* Englewood Cliffs, NJ: Prentice-Hall.

Rose, P. I. (1968) *They and We.* New York: Random House.

Sartre, J. P. (1969) *Anti-Semite and Jew.* New York: Schocken.

Smith, J. D. (1993) *The Eugenic Assault on America.* Fairfax, VA: George Mason University Press.

Sprinker, M. (1987) *Imaginary Relations.* London: Verso.

Stark, W. (1963) *The Fundamental Forms of Social Thought.* New York: Fordham University Press.

Walinsky, A. (1995) "The Crisis of Public Order." *The Atlantic Monthly* (July): 39–54.

West, C. (1993) *Prophetic Reflections.* Monroe, ME: Common Courage Press.

Wilson, W. J. (1987) *The Truly Disadvantaged.* Chicago: University of Chicago Press.

3

A Brief Archaeology of Intelligence

Eric Mark Kramer and Lonnie Johnson, Jr.

THEMATIC PROLEGOMENA

Modernity (see Chapter 1) is characterized by Western-style individualism. One of its manifestations is the obsession with comparative (actually economically competitive) "intelligence" as a central value. The development of the modern concept of intelligence is related to craniometry and race. Craniometry is the measurement of human skulls as an indication of intelligence. According to Montagu (1975: 146), "What craniometry was to the nineteenth century, intelligence testing has been to the twentieth." In order to understand this statement and the impulse that sustains the modern obsession with "intelligence," we must understand the historical setting immediately before and during the heyday of craniometry.

During this time, the ideology of the Enlightenment was prevalent. Part of this ideology was the preeminence of mental-rationality. While romanticism had valued the individual, it also valued passion and compassion. By contrast, Aristotelian modernity only recognizes the exclusive validity (value) of calculating manipulation and efficiency (technological power). In modern discourse, measurement and accounting came to be the only legitimate ways to establish what is "important," "significant," "true," and "real." Everything else is idle chit-chat, essentially unverifiable and of little ulterior use-value. Friendship, for its own sake, was replaced by "collegiality," which equated being a "good citizen" with conformism and etiquette in the service of organizational goals (almost always the expansion of market share and capital resources).

The drive to "perform," in a measurable fashion (in a way that lends itself to surveillance), continues to intensify. Even elementary school curricula manifest the imperative to generate "intelligent" (meaning skilled and trainable) workers for the labor markets of the twenty-first century. Summer camp is no longer a place to make wallets, take canoe rides, and learn how to shoot a bow and arrow. Increasingly, summer camps teach computer programming, and basic principles of engineering to children as young as eight so that they can get a jump on their competition. Even childhood is conforming to the dictates of market forces, striving to make oneself as profitable to employers as possible. What if this drive to measurably perform continues as populations continue to grow astronomically and resources become more and more scarce? Will we begin to test newborn infants, or even test them before birth? Eventually, the screening process will begin before conception—genetic engineering. In fact, the Cable News Network's *Science and Technology Week* reported on genetically engineered puppies—the parents do not even have to meet (March 3, 1996).

In the twentieth century, war became total so that the line between civilian and combatant was deconstructed. Entire civilian populations became legitimate targets. This was because modern war could not be sustained for long periods of time without entire populations manning the assembly lines. But in "peacetime" too, industrial ordination completely dominates the movements and orientations of "civilian" life. Domesticity has become the servant of industrial organization. So, too, has intelligence. The sense of both has been altered, reduced to the narrow interests of material production and capital concentration. Reason, too, has been truncated, excluding prudence and promoting only technique. It has become instrumental-behavioral. Because it is not quantifiable, "wisdom" may be quaint but essentially irrelevant. The original promise that capitalism would produce surplus, thereby enhancing leisure, is all but forgotten. Instead, as productivity along with profits continue to rise at unprecedented rates and to ever-new levels, people are working harder and harder, taking more years for technical education (usually at their own expense), and less time for reflection (thinking) and conversation. Today, market logic dictates that people work in order to work (when not collapsed before a television), not in order to play.

In the modern industrial age, instrumental reason has become the sole criteria against which behavior and thoughts should be evaluated. And rationality has become a quantity. In the modern Spencerian environment, it is only logical that self-interest take precedence over other-interest, or mutual (dialogical) interests. "Careerism" and "professionalism" are the modern commandments. They are the code words for a mode of life dedicated to the modern social isolate who is at war with all others for time, private space, and money. It is smart to be self-sufficient, self-reliant, independent, and to look out for "number one." According to market logic, this is self-evident. The enhancement and hypervaluation of mobility (an endless search for stimulation) of all sorts, has whittled the village down to the extended family, down to the nuclear family, and now that atom has been "split." Conversation, the core of all relationships (community), is increasingly restricted to the exchange of information in a means-ends utility. Community has been systematized into an aggregate of functional, hence interchangable, agents related only by economic exchange. Time spent on "casual" talk is time "wasted." The daily intercourse of life has become instrumental.

In the modern world, rationality has become identified with the metaphysics of "demonstration" and modern truth. Truth is what "works." Truth is that which is rational, but the rational has been redefined as that which can be operationalized and accounted for (visiocentrism). The absurdity that modern science defines that which gives it its power, mathematics, out of existence (because mathematics is not an empirical thing), is largely ignored. Truth is no longer a process, a Socratic form of communication, but a thing. Truth has been reduced to the empirical contingency of direct personal observation (existentialism), and this manifestation of individualism has hypertrophically expanded to universal status. Science (especially of human behavior) has become the generalizability of opinion (refereed consensus).

Whoever has the political power to control discourse (including categorical definitions) has the power to determine the direction of future research, and thus, of what will become demonstrated and confirmed "reality." Sedimented in the author(ity) of definitions, including operational ones that generate the phenomena they claim to "discover," are interests and prejudices (*doxa*).

A common prejudice manifested in nearly all metaphysical statements, such as operational definitions (which presume *a priori* "by definition," that all entities are "really" quantities), is that the authors of metaphysical claims privilege their own perspective, inflating it to the status of absolute reality. Metaphysics is almost always self-serving. This political aspect of metaphysics is the case with all ideologies including religions, philosophies, sciences, and mythologies. Therefore, one needs to ask why a group at a certain time and place has begun to talk in a certain way. Exposing the contingent nature of "reality" opens up the possibility and potential for action as well as reaction. Making the rules of the language game, or doing an archaeology can reveal the sudden shift in emphasis and which interests are being privileged. When did "intelligence" become so important that the institutionalization and formalization of it became problematic. Of all measures, perhaps only visual acuity and shoe size are as globally generated, but with less institutional interest. Practically everyone is measured for intelligence and these measures are carefully monitored, recorded, and used for distrubution of resources, including labor-power. Knowledge has become labor-power.

When did this obsession emerge? Why? Who benefits? Which interests are served by such widespread comparative and competitive evaluation? Why is intelligence continually correlated with other measures like "race" and "gender?" From the point of view of commercial goals, does it not make sense to spend the most educational resources on those who need them most? Instead, the "smartest" get the scholarships and access to the best educational experiences. This is because knowledge and intellect are seen as exploitable resources so that only those best prepared to take advantage of educational resources get them. The consequence is tracking. In many industrialized countries, tracking begins as early as kindergarten so that those children who initially score best on intelligence tests are privileged with the best educational experiences. Hence, the conveyor belt of tracking becomes a self-fulfilling prophecy. Of all variables, parental involvement in a child's education is by far the best predictor of educational success. When this is combined with rigid linear tracking, children who have family backgrounds that do not give them emotional and instructional support are lost to the system. Families with this "profile" are disproportionately low income, which correlates with racial categorization. The system rationalizes this state of affairs with objective testing.

In the promotion of "objectivity," context is ignored. However, it is well documented that poverty, rates of penal incarceration, and poor educational experiences are highly correlated (Spohn, 1995; Mann, 1993; Walker, 1993; Clarke and Koch, 1976; Langan, 1991; Mauer, 1990). Part of the missing context, which a single IQ score cannot address, is that single-parent families are six times more likely to be in poverty than two-partner families with children (USDCBC, 1993). About 90 percent of single-parent homes are without a father (USCCBS, 1992), and about 30 percent of all child support payments go uncollected (USDCBC, 1993). "Out of wedlock" births often lead to a lack of emotional and economic commitment by the biological father. The number of such births is increasing dramatically. For whites such births rose from 2 percent in 1960 to 22 percent in 1991. Among the African-American population, the change was more profound, increasing from 23 percent in 1960 to 68 percent in 1991 (USDHHS, 1993). In 1991, ten major U.S. cities experienced a single-parent birth rate of over 50 percent (USCHHS). According to a 1993 publication of the United States Department of Health and Human Services, in 1960, 5 percent of all births in the United States were out of wedlock. By 1991, the number had risen to 30 percent (USDHHS, 1993). One out of every five children in the United States lives in poverty. Such children are at risk. Their educational attainment is dangerously threatened not because of genetic "defects," but because of socioeconomic conditions within which they find themselves, through no fault of their own.

Intellectual power has become more valued than nonmodern qualities like justice, temperance, courage, magnificence, magnanimity, liberality, gentleness, prudence, wisdom, the virtues that guided the proper behavior of a citizen from Plato to Cicero and Quintilian, indeed until World War I. Chivalry, that formal disregard for the "bottom line," has vanished. More like animals, modern humans strive to systematically control their movements to conserve energy and maximize productivity. They function according to bio-logic (efficiency). But industrial systematics is producing far more than is necessary to sustain life. Each worker is producing more than s/he needs. Even animals have rest time and expend a great amount of energy in courtship.

Has intellectual prowess ascended because it is presumed to be more measurable? Since the modern has faith only in measurements, has (s)he therefore excluded classical virtues from consideration? Or, have these other qualities simply come to be seen as obstacles to increased productivity and speed? Neither the blitzkrieg nor nuclear attack has time for judgment or mercy. Perhaps it is productivity and speed which are the values that are really driving the modern world, including the obsession with quick minds. Since the advent of the mass, which wedded value with quantity, this logic behooves the profiteer to move as many units as quickly as possible because profit is realized with each unit sale. The value of quality has been compromised by the metaphysics of quantity, which began as a military economic value.

ARCHAEOLOGY

As early as the 1600s, in his *Discourse On Method* (1637/1956), René Descartes emphasized that his ''search for truth'' was equated with reason; method was reason. In classic Aristotelian style, Descartes claimed that his (of course) version of reason also ''distinguishes us from the brutes'' (1637/1956: 2). Thus, to be human, or at least civilized, meant to be rational. According to Descartes' self-esteemed reasoning, those who were not rational were ''accidents,'' and were not even ''of the same species'' (1637/1956). Later, in the 1700s, this prejudice became formalized in the classification systems of Linnaeus and Buffon.

No matter how one manifests one's prejudice, in prose or statistics, it remains. Like almost every metaphysical/ideological prejudice one can imagine, the new science defined ''good'' in its own self-image. It is not surprising that scientists would equate operational definition, classification, and other inventions with truth. They equate their own activities with the highest order of human achievement and even according to ''natural'' criteria. Auguste Comte and Saint-Simone presented their positive ''religion'' as the *non plus ultra* of human development. This is perspectivism, which is the privileging of one's own self-actualization and tiny slice of direct, personal experience with universal validity. Generalizability is guaranteed via control, that is, to make all samples the same and then to proclaim a universal trait.

Modern taxonomies of race are manifestations of privileged perspectives with ''universal validity.'' Linnaeus and Buffon were the two greatest taxonomists of the eighteenth century. Linnaeus was a Swedish biologist who is often considered the founder of modern biology. In his *A General System of Nature Through The Three Grand Kingdoms of Animals, Vegetable, and Minerals* (1806), he created the following classification system of race:

1. Homo. Diurnal; varying by education and situation.

2. Wild Man. Four-footed, mute, hairy.

3. American (i.e., Indian). Copper-colored, choleric, erect. Hair black, straight, thick;

nostrils wide, face harsh; beard scanty; obstinate, content, free. Paints himself with fine red lines. Regulated by customs.

4. European. Fair, sanguine, brawny. Hair yellow, brown, flowing; eyes blue; gentle acute, inventive. Covered with close vestments. Governed by laws.

5. Asiatic. Sooty, melancholy, rigid. Hair black; eyes dark; severe, haughty, covetous. Covered with loose garments. Governed by opinions.

6. African. Black, phlegmatic, relaxed. Hair black, frizzled; skin silky; nose flat; lips tumid; crafty, indolent, negligent. Anoints himself with grease. Governed by caprice. (Popkin, 1973: 248)

In addition to Linnaeus, Buffon was also a central figure in eighteenth-century biology. His major works include *Ethics of Nature* (1778) and *Histoire Naturelle* (1749–1804). Although he had some differences with Linnaeus in terms of methodology, his taxonomy of race was strikingly similar. The following quotes provide an account of his taxonomy and racial views. He describes nonwhites thus:

they are gross, superstitious and stupid (Eskimos); they are gross, stupid and brutal (Tartars); are effeminate, peaceable, indolent, superstitious, submissive, ceremonious and parasitical (Chinese); their indolence and stupidity make them insensible to every (useful) pleasure (the Negroes of Sierra Leone); though some were more savage, cruel and dastardly than others; yet they were equally stupid, ignorant and destitute of arts and industry (the North American Indians). (Popkin, 1974: 135)

In reference to white-skinned people, Buffon says:

The most temperate climate lies between the 40th and 50th degree of latitude, and it produces the most handsome and beautiful men. It is from this climate that the ideas of the genuine colour of mankind, and of the various degrees of beauty ought to be derived. . . . The civilized situated under this zone are Georgia, Circassia, the Ukraine, Turkey in Europe, Hungary, the south of Germany, Italy, Switzerland, France, and the northern part of Spain. The natives of those territories are the most handsome and most beautiful people in the world. (Popkin, 1974: 136)

These initial attempts to provide an account of and for human diveristy were hierarchical. The European populations (from certain parts of Europe, according to Buffon) had superior intellect, customs, beauty, and so on. These classification systems were significant because, from the very onset of systematic racial description, intelligence was presumed as an important variable. Though ''beauty'' and ''temperment'' are no longer considered to be a part of scientific discourse, intelligence remains so highly valued that practically everyone in the industrial world has been measured in this way.

It is evident that description is always already valuated because description requires some principle of division which is defined by the describers. In the case of Buffon and Linnaeus, their values were manifested through their principle of division, and the creation of "intelligence." In this way, eighteenth-century taxonomy "scientifically" established a connection between race and intelligence (Todorov, 1993).

Many philosophers of the Enlightenment also made the connection between race and intelligence. For example, in Hume's (1711–1776) "Of National Characters" (1982), he says:

I am apt to suspect the negroes and in general all the other species of men (for there are four or five different kinds) to be naturally inferior to the whites. . . . In Jamaica indeed they talk of one negroe as a man of parts and learning; but 'tis likely he is admired for very slender accomplishments like a parrot, who speaks a few words plainly. (quoted in Popkin, 1974: 245)

In addition, Voltaire (1694–1778) described Negroes by saying, "If their understanding is not of a different nature from ours, it is at least greatly inferior. They are not capable of any great application or association of ideas, and seem formed neither for the advantages nor the abuses of philosophy" (quoted in Gossett, 1963: 45). Both Hume and Voltaire made it clear that intelligence was a fundamentally important distinguishing factor for racial classification. Once this is juxtaposed with the economic conditions during the period, the rise of craniometry can be understood. Briefly stated, the economic conditions were characterized by the enslavement and colonization of "inferior" races. Not incidentally, this included "inferior" populations within Europe (i.e., see Buffon's description of Germans and Tartars, earlier in this chapter). Now we can understand the impact of craniometry.

If the philosophers were correct, if the taxonomists were correct, if the economic conditions were to be justified, there had to be a method of connecting race with intelligence. It must be kept in mind that the Enlightenment concept of "proof" had taken on the value of an "objective," albeit derived, fact. This was the function of craniometry. It was a way to objectively prove the connection between race and intelligence. Craniometry legitimized the social order. It was a way "To 'prove' that upper-class whites and black slaves were biologically suited to their places at polar ends of the social hierarchy, the craniometrians did not hesitate to manipulate their measurements" (Mensh and Mensh, 1991: 14). Craniometry constitutes the initial steps of a scientifically articulated racism that rendered itself factually infallible, empirically verifiable. Craniometry gradually developed into intelligence testing, which originated with Alfred Binet.

Intelligence Testing—Binet's Project

Binet is commonly identified as a seminal figure in the development of intelligence testing. In fact, public schools still use various forms of his tests in their curricula. However, what is not commonly known about Binet is the entirety of his project, and how it is an extension of the eugenics movement generally, and craniometry specifically. This becomes evident when one studies the two major themes in his works: physiological psychology and intelligence testing.

Binet was an experimental psychologist from France. Before he became interested in psychometry (i.e., measuring intelligence), he focused on the physiological bases of psychology. This was then known as "physiological psychology." Binet acknowledged a debt to M. Ribot of France, saying that Ribot was "The real inaugurator of the psychological movement proper" (Binet, 1896: 1). Ribot founded the Society of Physiological Psychology. The importance of physiological psychology lies in its association with craniometry.

From its inception, physiological psychology has had various interests, one of them being the connection between intelligence and physiology (which is often interpreted as biological characteristics). Franz-Josef Gall (1758–1828), Luigi Rolando (1773–1831), and Marie Jean-Pierre-Flourens (1794–1867) were among the first to advocate and support the idea that different functions of the brain are localized in different areas of the brain. Primarily, it was Gall who advocated that these areas of the brain were innate. However, the influence of Gall was due in large part to Levater's (1775–1778) *Essays on Physiognomy.* In this book, Levater discussed how facial appearance reflects personality (for more detail on the development of physiological psychology, see Murray's *History of Western Psychology*). Levater organized the fundamental elements of Gall's cranioscopy (later termed "phrenology") as the scientific study of character (e.g., intelligence), through analyzing bumps on the head. Thus, craniometry, like Binet's work, has its roots in physiological psychology.

Binet incorporated his experimental psychology with physiological psychology. He wrote several works such as *The Psychology of Reasoning* (1899), *The Psychic Life of Micro-Organisms* (1897), and *On Double Consciousness* (1896), all of which deal with the relationship between psychological states and physiology. It is also at this stage in Binet's work that he cites (and builds on the work of) two of the foremost leaders in the eugenics movement—Sir Francis Galton (1822–1911) and Thomas Huxley (1825–1895) (see Binet's *The Psychology of Reasoning*, 1899).

Galton was strongly influenced by his cousin, Charles Darwin (1809–1882). Darwin (*The Origin of Species*, 1859) advocated biological evolution. In the late 1800s, Galton attempted to further this claim, extending it into the realm of character traits and abilities, specifically intelligence. He advocated the position that intelligence is inherited. He then began to develop measuring techniques for abilities such as sensory acuity and reaction time. Thus, as is commonly noted, Galton was the forefather of modern eugenics.

In addition to Galton, Huxley was also strongly influenced by Darwin. As a social Darwinist, Huxley believed that society was a product of evolution. Therefore, in order to further society, or even sustain it, the weaker tendencies of human traits should, indeed, must be, suppressed. In addition to Galton, Huxley also strongly advocated a eugenics program.

Presuming the ideas of Galton and Huxley as a foundation, Binet proceeded to develop his work in intelligence testing. Two of his primary works in this area are: *Mentally Defective Children* (Binet and Simon, 1914) and *A Method of Measuring the Development of the Intelligence of Young Children* (Binet and Simon, 1913).

The purpose of these tests was to measure the intelligence of the children in the public schools so that mentally deficient children could be selected out. To this end, in 1904 the Parisian municipal government instituted intelligence testing in all of its schools. This was regarded as a cutting edge development in scientific educational reform and as a powerful tool in assessing the placement of children within the system (tracking). Binet (Binet and Simon, 1914: 10–11) claimed that this was a concern for him because the mentally deficient children were not getting an education appropriate to their needs. Therefore, these tests were meant to be "a guide to the admission of mentally defective children to special schools or classes." According to Binet (quoted by Alexander Darroch in the Introduction to *Mentally Defective Children*), the stated purpose of the segregated classes was "every class, every school for defectives, ought to aim at rendering the pupils socially useful. It is not a question of enriching their minds, but of giving them the means of working for their living" (Binet and Simon, 1914: vii).

Manifestations of Eugenic Thinking

As discussed earlier, Sir Francis Galton is commonly called the founder of eugenics. Although influenced by Darwin's biological evolution, Galton attempted to push this theory into the arena of individual characteristics (primarily intelligence). Galton advocated that intelligence was inherited and he strove to develop ways to measure intelligence. This led directly to his assertion of a systematic eugenics program.

Eugenics is a campaign to create (and as many believe, sustain) a superior (initially French) race. One of the most vivid and treacherous examples of eugenic thinking was manifested by the Jewish Holocaust under the rule of Adolf Hitler. Hitler's goal was to create a "master race," a "pure" race of selectively bred Europeans. With this goal, all inferiors had to be exterminated lest they pollute the gene pool. Under this regime, pollution included non-Europeans, the physically handicapped, intellectually deficient, homosexuals, and so on. For this reason, the Nazis had plans to turn on and enslave their "ally," the Japanese people, after victory (conversation with Professor Thomas M. Seebohm of Johannes Gutenberg—Universitat Mainz, Germany, who has studied the pertinent historical documents). However, the Nazi movement is only one manifestation of eugenic thinking.

From this example, we can derive some essential features of eugenics, and

thereby recognize how eugenic thinking has recurred. Eugenic thinking neces-
sitates a distinction among populations based on some standard or principle of
division. Variance must be established. The Nazis were particularly adroit at
systematizing the measurement of variance. In the Nazi movement, this standard
was race. However, the standard can be any number of phenomena, such as
religion, ethnicity, nationality, economic status, and so on. The importance of
division is central because it establishes identity.

Once identity is created, it becomes hypertropic. It becomes all-important.
Other characteristics are rendered irrelevant. But since such measures (which
establish identity) are taken to be ''empirical,'' and as such, inherent to the
object rather than dialogically constituted via difference (see Chapter 6), the
Nazis did not recognize that their own identity as ''superior'' depended upon
the existence of the other as ''inferior.'' In eugenic thinking, the other is not
seen as a co-constitutional manifestation of one's own identity, but rather as an
independent thing, as an obstacle to purifying one's own identity. This is why,
for the systematically minded Nazis, the Other had to be physically exterminated. In the Nazi movement, this denial of existence was usually enforced by
killing those who were labelled ''inferior.'' However, death was not the only
denial of difference. It also included the systematic denial of participation in
society. To be denied the right of expression (which is fundamental to human
life) is much like death. To not have a voice in society is to not exist (Kramer,
1992).

Another denial of existence is assimilation. When others are forced to assimilate to some dominant standard, this is another way of denying their identity,
their existence. We see the world by our own eyes, we hear through our own
ears. Assimilation is the attempt to change these eyes and ears so that they see
and hear (thereby behave) the way the dominant group does. Thus, difference
is denied which supposedly removes all threats to the purity of the ''superior''
identity. In fact, voluntary assimilation may be one of the most powerful manifestations of eugenics. Voluntary assimilation indicates that the individual has
defined his/her own identity as ''inferior'' (based on some standard), and thus
must change. At this point, inferiority is not a label that society has created and
implemented; instead, it has become internalized by the individual (the authors
are employing the same dualisms, such as individual/society and internal/exter-
nal, in order to be consistent with the literature on assimilation).

In light of the essential features of eugenics, it is evident that eugenic thinking
is not unique to the Nazi movement. In fact, eugenic thinking was even made
manifest before Galton's formal campaign. This is evinced by the classification
systems, craniology, and their relationship to the economic conditions. These
historical conditions, therefore, not only constitute the foundations of modern
intelligence testing, but intelligence testing is a recurrence of, or a manifestation
of, the same type of thinking—eugenic thinking.

Institutionalized Eugenics: Schools and Intelligence Testing

Binet claimed that the purpose of intelligence testing was to provide a better or more appropriate education for the mentally deficient. But what exactly did this mean? Binet and Simon (1914: vii) advocated that the education of mentally weak students should "aim at rendering the pupils socially useful [not] . . . enriching their minds." Thus, Binet's concern was in finding a productive place for them within the social system so that their energies could be rendered profitable. The best that could be done for such "feeble-minded," was to make them economically productive. It was presumed that their happiness and fulfillment would be maximized to the extent that they could work.

Where was this socially appropriate place within the system? Binet suggested that some mental deficients should have medical attention and be taken to asylums (Rose, 1979; and Binet and Simon, 1914:76). He suggested that others could possibly be trained for manual labor. At any rate, mentally deficient children were not to be educated and encouraged to think, let alone become future leaders of society. Thus, intelligence testing was a new "rational" scientific way of establishing a meritocracy—a caste system based on "IQ." The fruits of industrial labor, which rewards the organized mind more than the hand, were not to go to the mentally weak.

Adorno's (1992) critique of the "dialectic of the Enlightenment" is applicable to this systematic segregation of the hand and the mind. The dialectic of the Enlightenment separated the mind from the hand. Of course, the workers too have minds, so that the dialectic, like all dialectical relationships, constituted an opposing and even antagonistic relationship. They were to relate henceforth in a hierarchical way, with the hand being subordinate. Modern management and labor relations manifest this artificial segregation of ideas from physical behavior. In the modern assembly system, planning and "supervision" (including the power to evaluate, hire, and fire) takes place in a separate place among an educated and economic elite. They disperse the orders that workers implement. Workers are strongly discouraged from thinking or taking initiative because any change in the routine disrupts the highly structured linear assembly system. Under such a scheme, education and skills (training too) became segregated. Those who were privileged to be educated were further privileged with oversight or supersight. Merit came with knowledge of the "big picture." Access to management was restricted to those who had been educated. Education was reserved for those who could benefit most from it. The latter is in large part determined by intelligence testing. To be a "productive citizen," and a "valued member of the community," meant to be beneficent. "Benefit" was fairly synonymous with productivity (profitability).

This is strikingly similar to what we see happening in the school systems today. Education means training. Workers must be educable. However, machine-language is very often applied to workers who must periodically "retool." In many schools, we have what is known as tracking or ability grouping. Those who meet the appropriate criteria (which always includes test scores) are placed in higher tracks. Research has shown that minorities and lower income children are overrepresented in the lower tracks (Braddock and Dawkins, 1993). In these lower tracks, instruction is often characterized by less experienced instructors, a slower pace of covering material, less content covered, and fewer and less rigid requirements (Oakes, 1985). In short, educational opportunities and resources are unequal. Thus, tracking and ability grouping lowers educational aspirations and attainments. Needless to say, this does not adequately prepare children for a highly competitive job market in a highly specialized, thus education-based, economy.

This situation is also the same for ''special'' education classes. According to Harry and Anderson (1995), low income children and minorities are disproportionately represented in special education programs such as Educable Mental Retardation (EMR), Serious Emotional Disturbance (SED), Specific Learning Disability (SLD), Speech Impairment (SI), and Trainable Mental Retardation (TMR). The consequences of being educated in these programs is just as devastating as those listed above. Among the consequences are decreased motivation, poorer quality resources, teacher shortages, unacquainted personnel, low rates of returning to mainstream education, high drop-out rates, and low graduation rates. Children in these classes are being prepared for punitive institutions or low income jobs. They are being prepared to not have a voice in society.

Why are minorities and low income children overrepresented in the back-waters of our educational system? According to Harry and Anderson (1995), the systematic process of selection is the central problem. One problem with the process is the bias of the selection process. Often, teachers misinterpret the behaviors of students due to a lack of cultural familiarity. Thus, the children are referred to testing. Upon being tested, they face more bias which is embedded in the test itself. Lastly, the categories of mental deficiency are extremely vague. Therefore, the interpretation of the behavior and test scores is ambiguous yet extremely important because life-changing decisions are made based in part on these scores. Inevitably, the instructor's personal opinions concerning the individual (which may or may not have to do with his/her intellectual capacity) influences whether or not the student is placed in a special program.

Eugenic thinking is manifested in the educational programs that we have developed and implemented in the school systems. In fact, the educational system is a eugenic system. From the very beginning of an individual's schooling, his/her identity is redefined in terms of his/her intelligence. Based on this, people are placed in certain programs that have implications for the rest of their lives. Those placed in lower tracks and ''special'' education programs become marginalized, not only within the school system, but eventually from the larger social system. Although in a democracy, the ideal is that marginalized voices are heard, pragmatics makes it obvious that the process of being heard is often expensive. Thus, marginalized voices, which are by definition weak, are not heard. They are rendered non-existent, non-influencial. Rose (1979: 1) advocates that "early work in intelligence testing was closely linked to the eugenics movement." In addition, Selden (1977: 1) claims that the American educational system is a "manifestation of the work and theories of the British naturalist Galton and the Eugenics movement." Buss (1976) adds that the very drive to discover individual differences (differential psychology) and genetics is at the root of eugenic ideology. These concerns are not unwarranted. There has been much research on the critique of intelligence.

BEYOND CRITIQUE—RECONSTITUTING INTELLIGENCE

There has been much research on intelligence and IQ testing. Many themes are recurrent. Major themes have included the inherently biased nature of IQ testing, the nature–nurture debate, and methodological limitations. We will briefly address these issues. However, these issues will be treated as incomplete and symptomatic of a deficiency in our very mode of articulating intelligence. This is not to say that these critiques are not legitimate; instead, we would like to add another dimension to them. At this point, the foundational issue is the mind/body dualism that pervades the sciences. However, we must first address the common critiques in order to provide a foundation for reconstituting intelligence.

Methodological concerns are commonly addressed when critiquing intelligence testing. Other problems exist as well, however; the following are issues that statisticians acknowledge as being potentially problematic. One methodological problem is that of comparison. Analysis of variance (ANOVA) tests are commonly used to establish differences between and among groups. One aspect of the ANOVA is the comparison of group averages. This can be problematic because many times extreme scores can make an average a poor representation of the group. Another essential element of the ANOVA is in the actual comparison of the groups. If the within-group variance is greater than the among- or between-group variance, then very often another grouping is needed to determine any legitimate difference. In addition, most statistical comparisons of intelligence presume a general factor (based on factor analysis) which can capture "intelligence." Many statisticians have argued that a general factor is a statistical phenomenon based on initially unrotated factor solutions, not a naturally occurring psychological phenomenon of "intelligence" (Sternberg, 1995: 257). Another methodological problem is random sampling. How can we obtain a representative sample of any particular "race" that is representative of that race as a whole, especially when the parameters of "race" are problematic. Another methodological problem is that of truthfulness. Gould (1975), in an elaborate discussion of measuring intelligence, has demonstrated that measurements are often inaccurate and even fabricated.

In addition to methodological problems, the nature–nurture debate is a continually recurring issue. Intelligence tests are supposed to measure innate ability—one's potential intellectual capacity. However, many scholars believe that environment has a great deal of influence on one's intellect. Horace Mann Bond (1934) found that blacks and whites from the North scored higher than those from the South. Later, Otto Klineberg (1935) found that blacks from the North outscored whites from the South. In addition, he cited figures concerning the amount that each spent on education; the North had spent more. Ten years later, Montagu (1945) added to this evidence with more states and samples, and concluded that the primary factor in determining IQ test scores was a socioeconomic factor. Thus, the environment was shown to have a profound influence on IQ scores, not hereditary factors.

If such test score distributions were used to redistribute resources to help those scoring lowest, then one might be able to make a moral argument for testing. However, what the scores are used for is quite the opposite. Those who score low are excluded from educational opportunities. This practice perpetuates the inequality that is linked to environmental variance. Thus, the educational system becomes an institutionalized agency whose latent function is to help recycle the culture of poverty.

Another commonly acknowledged critique of intelligence testing is the inherent bias of the instruments used. How do we know when we have a legitimate test? An accurate measure is one that corresponds to our *a priori* ideal of a good student (or an intelligent person). This is also a methodological issue in terms of what IQ measures measure. They measure the test designer's concept of a well-adjusted learner. As Binet originally indicated, an intelligence test determines whether or not a child is up to par in terms of some norm. In fact, Binet advocated (Binet and Simon, 1914: 38, 41) that "a defective child is one who does not adapt himself, or who adapts himself badly, to school life." Intelligence is reduced to adaptation—the recurrence of eugenic thinking. Thus, intelligence testing is biased, from its inception, in favor of social stability, not creativity.

Methodological limitations, environmental influences, and the inherently biased nature of intelligence testing are all legitimate and well-documented critiques of intelligence measurement. However, these limitations are manifestations of a more fundamental issue—the very way in which intelligence is articulated. Therefore, the next issue to address should be: How is intelligence articulated? This is where the Cartesian dualism of mind and body becomes a founding prejudice.

With the mind/body dualism, physical experience is distinguished from mental experience. The problem with this is that it is an unwarranted metaphysical assumption about the world. We do not experience these two things as fragmented and distinct entities. They are always given together. As David Hume (1973) demonstrated, empiricism leads to absurdity because we can only access the world through our senses, the body (which is fallible and cannot be trusted).

Where there is a mind, there is also a body; where there is an object, there must also be a subject. This is the foundation for the problem of intelligence testing.

This is first made clear in the Introduction to *Mentally Defective Children* by Binet and Simon (1914: viii) "The essential thing is for all the world to understand that empiricism has had its day, and that methods of scientific precision must be introduced into all educational work, to carry everywhere good sense and light." Binet (1914: 2) also elaborated on this by referring to science as "pure and disinterested" and beneficial as a means to "play a part in the discussions between capital and labor." Thus, science became a primary feature in policy-making—and intelligence testing became a central tool for establishing and maintaining this ideological system. This becomes ironical when one considers the nature of scientific discourse, and its presumption of the mind/body dualism.

Science has essentially defined intelligence out of existence. Intelligence is intellectual capacity, which means performance or work, especially technical reasoning. It is one's ability to *demonstrate* that one can use information in order to solve complex problems. Intelligence, by definition, does not exist based on the premises of empiricism itself. It is the "ability to . . .", which means that it is futuristic, which is not empirical. Furthermore, as a capacity, it cannot be apprehended directly but only via implication. Thus, in order for empiricists to measure intelligence, they must operationalize it. Herein lies the fundamental difficulty of intelligence.

Once intelligence is operationalized by IQ tests, it is reduced to a spatio-temporal scalar phenomenon. This has several consequences. First, intelligence is presumed to be a spatializable phenomenon so that, second, it can be meaningfully quantified. Third, it is conceived as a variable, a single line running from zero to 200 or so. This presumes that as one approaches one end of the scale (200), by the imperative of ratio, one *must* be moving away from the other end (zero) with equal and opposite measure. Consequently, the instrument can measure only one kind of intelligence. Such an instrument cannot address the possibility that an individual may be brilliant in one way and idiotic in another. Despite its intensely narrow focus, the IQ score is parsimonious and convenient so that its import is greatly inflated to cover intelligence in general. Since it is a record, and a measure to boot, the score has great status conferred upon it by the bureaucratic culture which conceived of it in the first place. In a mass society that organizes itself through the systematics of bureaucracy, a single recorded measure is given great weight in evaluating the worth and identity of individuals.

Furthermore, the process of operationalization transforms intelligence into a behavior (labor). Once this occurs, it is no longer the "ability to" but, instead, it is the interpretation of what is already done. No longer is it the mental capacity, but rather, the manifestation of the students' knowledge and how they have expressed it. If they do not conform or adapt, and do so in an "appropriate" way (according to the prefabricated structure of the instrument), then they are defined as "defective." What is measured is the *techne* of test taking. The classic, preindustrial sense of intelligence, which was *praxis*, and which included the concept of *phronesis* or prudence, is truncated by the instrument. Even modernists like Edmund Husserl (1970) have protested, referring to the narrow definition of intellect in instrumental terms as the ''decapitation of reason.'' Since only doing can be measured, to speak of thinking is considered pure speculative philosophizing. In an environment that is hyperperspectival in its valuation of means-ends pragmatism, thinking is considered a waste of time. This is the source of American anti-intellectualism. Rather, doing is all that ''counts,'' indeed all that is countable. But this presumes that a person has been socialized or taught how to do what is being measured; how to take tests, how to do test taking and certain skills. The IQ instrument is, after all, like everything else, a cultural artifact that articulates the kinds of doing that the inventors of the instrument value. Children do not share a level playing field in terms of life experiences. ''Adaptation'' is not neutral. Only certain kinds of modified behavior are wanted. What we measure becomes fundamentally different from what we claim to want to measure. At this point, behavior becomes a fundamental aspect of ''intelligence.'' Thus emerges the power struggle over what constitutes ''legitimate'' intelligence/behavior. From its inception in military culture, intelligence has always and only been valued insofar as it promotes operational goals. Tests express what kind of doing is *really* ''smart'' behavior. What is knowledge? What is intelligence? Test taking presumes a stock of knowledge including how the information gleaned may be used, how important it may be to one's future. Without such knowledge, the test taker may not even take the exercise seriously, and just fill in the bubbles as quickly as possible so as to return to some other activity, like playing. Intelligence is defined by ''science'' acting as a handmaiden to sociopolitical forces, especially industrial production and military campaigning (Albee, 1988; Alderfer, 1994). Intellect is a kind of doing. What kind it is is determined by the values of those making the instrument, and the goals they have in mind, which conceives of intelligence specifically as a means to those ends.

In addition to the identification of power and knowledge, the operationalization of intelligence becomes a cultural expression. This goes beyond the critique of cultural bias in intelligence testing. This indicates that once intelligence is reduced via spatio-temporal terminology (thus becoming an object), it becomes exclusively perspectival. Perspective is established in the form of written logic (Ong, 1982: 56). Other expressions of intelligence are suppressed and excluded. Intelligence, thus operationally defined, is always already partial and preestablished as a scale. As Binet himself admitted, low scores mean that, for whatever reason, the person has failed to adapt to acceptable standards of expressing intelligence. The test establishes, institutionalizes, and reifies those standards. The test itself is an expression of prejudice, not an instrument that reveals some independent reality within a certain degree of validity and reliability. In order for intelligence to be understood as an eidetic recognition of one's ability, we must bracket the mind/body dualism.

Sui generis, what happens to the concept of intelligence once the mind/body dualism has been bracketed? One implication is that intelligence is not an object that exists "outside" of the "self." In practical terms, this means that intelligence is not determined by focusing on what is not known versus what is known. That which is not known enables us to appreciate and recognize the value of that which is known. This also has implications for the relationship between intelligence and perfection.

Intelligence, as an object "outside of the self," implies that perfection is the lack of mistakes. But this is not consistent with experience. There is something uncanny about absolute perfection defined as the complete lack of flaws. No mistakes is not the same as perfection. Perfection is not the same as simply making no mistakes on a test. Rather, perfection is the ability to see through mistakes. Perfection is not the lack of imperfection. Instead, it is imperfection that enables us to recognize perfection.

In this same sense, intelligence is recognized through what is not demonstrated. This is what Binet and others wrestle with when they define intelligence as potential. Potential, by definition, is not empirically demonstrable. It is an inference based on that which has been demonstrated. Thus, intelligence is recognized through the invisible—it is potential. However, empiricists limit themselves to that which is empirically demonstrable, indeed, that which is already demonstrated. One cannot measure intelligence any more than one can measure the invisible.

For empiricism, this is a problem because if it is not demonstrated, but must be measured, subjectivity is inevitably intertwined with judgments of intelligence (i.e., the *a priori* criteria of intelligence which is manifested as an arbitrarily created norm). However, if we recognize that subjectivity is an essential aspect of the object of intelligence, then we enable ourselves to apperceive prejudices as well as the uniquenesses of particular expressions of intelligence. In practical terms, we enable ourselves to consider what it is about the totality of the individual that makes him/her "intelligent."

This opens to the appreciation of new dimensions of intelligence that are traditionally not recognized as "intelligence." This could be called the polytypic nature of intelligence. Intelligence can take on several different manifestations— not just those typically considered cognitive or mental. Intelligence then becomes embodied. Here, we can recognize the embodied intelligence of the quarterback who knows exactly when and where to throw the football versus when to run. We can recognize the embodied intelligence of the mechanic who can feel the rumblings of an ill engine and precisely diagnose the treatment, or the "gift" an artist has in transforming marble into a vision. We can recognize the intelligence of the child who struggles to mimic the sounds of its mother. Intelligence becomes much more than that of rocket science or analytic philosophy. The brain comes to be seen as integral with the body, not merely a localized organ, isolated in the cranial cavity. The nervous system extends to the finger tips and beyond (McLuhan, 1964). I feel "down there," not "up here.'' To enforce a particular life-path on the basis of a written examination is not rational, but conveniently instrumental. It also cannot take into account time, freedom, change—indeed, all the things which have made humans ''intelligent'' long before industrial values and IQ testing.

REFERENCES

Adorno, T. W. (1992) *Dialectic of Enlightenment*. New York: John Comming.

Albee, G. (1988) ''The Politics of Nature and Nurture.'' *American Journal of Community Psychology* 10, no. 3: 4–28.

Alderfer, C. P. (1994) ''A White Man's Perspective on the Unconscious Processes Within Black-White Relations in the United States.'' In *Human Diversity: Perspectives on People in Context*, edited by E. J. Trickett, R. J. Watts, and D. Birman. San Francisco: Jossey-Bass Publishers, pp. 131–158.

Binet, A. (1896) *On Double Consciousness: Experimental Psychological Studies*. Chicago: The Open Court Publishing Company.

———. (1897) *The Psychic Life of Micro-Organisms*. Chicago: The Open Court Publishing Company.

———. (1899) *The Psychology of Reasoning: Based on Experimental Researches in Hypnotism*. Chicago: The Open Court Publishing Company.

Binet, A., and T. Simon. (1913) *A Method of Measuring the Development of the Intelligence of Young Children*. Lincoln, IL: The Courier Company.

———. (1914) *Mentally Defective Children*. London: Edward Arnold.

Bond, H. M. (1934). *The Education of the Negro in the American Social Order*. New York: Prentice-Hall.

Braddock, J. H., II, and M. P. Dawkins. (1993) ''Ability Grouping, Aspirations, and Attainments: Evidence from the National Educational Longitudinal Study of 1988.'' *Journal of Negro Education* 62, no. 3: 324–336.

Buffon, G. L. L., Compte de. (1812) *Natural History, General and Particular: The History of Man and the Quadrapeds*. London: T. Cadell and W. Davies.

Buss, A. R. (1976) ''Galton and the Birth of Differential Psychology and Eugenics: Social, Political, and Economic Forces.'' *Journal of the History of the Behavioral Sciences* 12, no. 1: 47–58.

Clarke, S. H., and G. G. Koch. (1976) ''The Influence of Income and Other Factors on Whether Criminal Defendants Go to Prison.'' *Law & Society Review* 11, no. 1: 57–92.

Darwin, C. (1911) *The Origin of Species*. London: John Murray.

Descartes, R. (1637) *Discourse on Method*. Chicago: Open Court.

Gould, S. J. (1975) ''Racist Arguments and IQ.'' In *Race and IQ*, edited by A. Montagu. New York: Oxford University Press, pp. 145–150.

Gossett, T. F. (1963) *Race: The History of an Idea in America*. Dallas: Southern Methodist University Press.

Harris, M. (1968) *The Rise of Anthropological Theory: A History of Theories of Culture*. New York: Thomas Y. Crowell Company.

Harry, B., and M. G. Anderson. (1995) ''The Disproportionate Placement of African American Males in Special Education Programs: A Critique of the Process.'' *Journal of Negro Education* 63, no. 4: 602–619.

Hume, D. (1973) *A Treatise of Human Nature*. London: Oxford University Press.

———. (1982) "Of National Characters." In *The Philosophical Works*, edited by T. H. Green and T. H. Groce. London: Aalen, Scientia Verlag, pp. 244–257.

Husserl, E. (1970) *The Crisis of European Sciences and Transcendental Phenomenology*. Evanston, IL: Northwestern University Press.

Klineberg, O. (1935) *Negro Intelligence and Selective Migration*. New York: Columbia University Press.

Kramer, E. M. (1992) "Terrorizing Discourses and Dissident Courage." *Communication Theory* 1, no. 4: 336–346.

Langan, P. A. (1991) *Race and Prisoners Admitted to State and Federal Institutions, 1926–1986*. Washington, DC: U.S. Government Printing Office.

Linnaeus, K. (1806) *A General System of Nature Through the Three Grand Kingdoms of Animals, Vegetables, and Minerals*. London: Lackington, Allen, and Company.

Mann, C. R. (1993) *Unequal Justice: A Question of Color*. Indianapolis: Indiana University Press.

Mauer, M. (1990) *Young Black Men and the Criminal Justice System: A Growing National Problem*. Washington, DC: The Sentencing Project.

McLuhan, M. (1964) *Understanding Media: The Extensions of Man*. New York: Mentor.

Mensh, E., and H. Mensh. (1991) *The IQ Mythology: Class, Race, Gender, and Inequality*. Carbondale: Southern Illinois University Press.

Montagu, A. (1945) "Intelligence of Northern Negroes and Southern Whites in the First World War." *American Journal of Psychology* 58 (April): 161–188.

Montagu, A. (Ed.) (1975) *Race and IQ*. New York: Oxford University Press.

Murray, D. J. (1988) *A History of Western Psychology*. Englewood Cliffs, NJ: Prentice-Hall.

Oakes, J. (1985) *Keeping Track: How Schools Structure Inequality*. New Haven, CT: Yale University Press.

Ong, W. J. (1982) *Orality and Literacy: The Technologizing of the Word*. New York: Methuen.

Popkin, R. H. (1973) "The Philosophical Basis of Eighteenth Century Racism." *Studies in Eighteenth Century Culture* 3, no. 2: 245–262.

———. (1974) "The Philosophical Basis of Modern Racism." In *Philosophy and the Civilizing Arts*, edited by C. Walton and J. P. Anton. Athens: Ohio University Press, pp. 126–163.

Rose, N. (1979) "The Psychological Complex: Mental Measurement and Social Administration." *Ideology and Consciousness* 5 (Spring): 5–68.

Selden, S. (1977) "Conservative Ideology and Curriculum." *Educational Theory* 27, no. 3: 205–222.

Spohn, C. C. (1995) "Courts, Sentences, and Prisons." *Daedaulus* 124, no. 1 (Winter): 119–143.

Sternberg, R. J. (1995) "For Whom the Bell Curve Tolls: A Review of *The Bell Curve*." *Psychological Science* 5, no. 6: 257–261.

Todorov, T. (1993) *On Human Diversity: Nationalism, Racism, and Exoticism in French Thought*. Cambridge: Harvard University Press.

U.S. Department of Commerce, Bureau of the Census. (1993) "Poverty in the United States, 1991." In *National Commission on American Urban Families, Families First*. Series P-60, No. 181. Washington, DC: U.S. Government Printing Office.

U.S. Department of Health and Human Services. (1993) *Vital Statistics of the United*

States, vol. 1, 1991: Natality. DHHS Publication No. PHS 93–1100. Washington, DC: U.S. Government Printing Office.

Walker, S. (1993) *Taming the System: The Control of Discretion in Criminal Justice, 1950–1990.* New York: Oxford University Press.

4

Dialogue and Race

Algis Mickunas

INTRODUCTION

By now, the debates, analyses, and descriptions of dialogue, and its major variations, cover one of the major theoretical trends of this century. At times these trends are confused—intertwined with various systems of dialectics. These trends and their theoretical issues have been analyzed by Martin Buber (1970), Mikhail Bakhtin (1981), Bernhard Waldenfels (1971), and Richard Grathoff (1983). These scholars have summarized the problematic of dialogical thinking and have provided excellent bibliographies. They also point out that dialogical thinking grounds all other ventures. Indeed, other writers posit dialogue as a fundamental theoretical-methodological problematic (Egon, 1990).

Given this plethora of concerns with dialogue, it is imperative to decipher its "priority" over other modes of thinking, without reducing it to some specific interpretation, such as "lingualism," hermeneutics, semiotics, postmodern notions of discursive practices, sociological theses that posit the primacy of society over the individual, or even to claims that individuals possess some inherent drive to form communication with other individuals. These explanations have created various theoretical and ideological "others" who are supposedly oblivious of the true condition of their lives.

Yet what could not, and indeed in principle cannot, be excluded even by ideologies and theories is the presence of the other as a condition for reflection upon one's own positionality. This means that the limits of understanding and awareness are not offered within a given position. They require reflection from a different, an alternate domain that, even if not completely understood, indeed, even if rejected, compels recognition of the other. This suggests that dialogical thinking is granted even in cases of transcultural, transnational, transideological, and even transdisciplinary engagements. Radically speaking, "the other" is affirmed even in its negation.

Every theoretical effort to identify and explain dialogue is already dialogical by virtue of the recognition of other theories. Dialogical awareness, it seems, cannot be limited to other theories and their presumed grounds, such as society, culture, matter, history, biology, myth. Dialogue comprises a domain that must be articulated by some other, not yet obvious means. The effort, nonetheless, is worthy of the reward, especially if the latter compels us to recognize the essential and inevitable affirmation of the other at whatever level the other is encountered. Indeed, the very encounter already grants our recognition of the "sense of the other" that is not absolutely alien, that is different and yet not radically transcendent from some sense of ourselves, regardless of how this "ourselves" is culturally designated. To reach this level of the "sense of the other" requires a scrupulous observance of numerous steps, each presupposed by the building of other steps.

METHODOLOGICAL REQUIREMENTS

In light of the various methodologies in currency, ranging from qualitative to quantitative, from neopositivistic to culturally relativistic, we maintain (despite the postmodern claims that essence is meaningless) that every subject matter requires an articulation of its own access. This is to say, it would be not only inadvertent but also arbitrary to "apply" our favorite method, dogma, or theory on all phenomena as if they are essentially "the same." Since this procedure would be another variant of negation (and thus affirmation of the presence of other methods and dogmas), it would be already within the domain of dialogue. Hence, to access the dialogical requires its own "way." The latter can only be reached through the steps of testing the limits of various methods and theories, regardless of how much these may be established and promoted.

One of the most prevalent views of communicative dialogue is composed of the triad sender-message-receiver, with a variant inherent in the term "message." The latter may be regarded as a channel, and the channel, as in the case of Marshall McLuhan (1964), may be the message. The empirical study of this triad must be quantitative, regardless at what level the study be undertaken. One may count the frequency of specific sounds; one may measure the decibels and the reactions they evoke; one may measure the physiological channels transmitting light waves emitted by a sequence of marks on a page; one may measure the waves emitted by satellite technology, and so on. The utility of such studies is obvious.

However, this triadic model and the empirical method leave some aspects of communication untouched. First, the message is more complex and can be at variance with the channel. Messages are understandable to the extent that they efface themselves in order to signify, point to, delimit some "object." Second, the latter may be cultural, physical, psychological, mythical, science-fictional, and so on, yet all cases require a dialogical focus. In the case of this essay, the focus is dialogue and the other, and specifically the other as different, racially, ethnically, and/or culturally. Third, despite the disagreements that may occur concerning the delimitation of the subject matter, the latter is a required condition for the continuity of communicative engagement. If the common subject matter is lost, the question will arise: Are we talking about the same thing?

The other theoretical side, the rational-logical, with its *a priori* structures, has been shown to be limited to the extent that the connection between such structures and the world of experience is not implied by the structures. Rational structures, such as logic or mathematics, must be applied from some situated and dialogical position. The latter may be articulated as a point of interest, a hermeneutical setting, or available on the basis of tacit prejudgments. In all cases, reason is mediated, and hence cannot take priority as the sole arbiter of human encounters. Specifically, in such cases as race, there is no *a priori* structure that is obvious to all concerned parties. Moreover, cultural others may have a different logic that can reveal the limits of our culture's rationality. Even within one's own culture's rationality, whenever human action is introduced, there arise ambivalences: Human action constantly defies strict rules, and indeed reveals its own, and the contingency of presumed, fixed logics.

These considerations suggest that the requirements to understand dialogue and the other are more complex than typically assumed, and can only be unfolded dialogically. In short, dialogue can only be studied dialogically. While this may appear to be circular, theoretically speaking, some principles that delimit a region cannot be denied without denying the very region through which such principles appear. This is to say, dialogical understanding is a principle which is involved in the very explication of dialogue, and, as mentioned above, dialogue is involved in the acceptance-rejection of the other (Pilotta and Mickunas, 1990). In this sense, any method, any theoretical controversy, any question of the racial other, is dialogical.

What is required, then is (A) a delimitation of dialogical morphology in order to (B) show what types of dialogue attempt to negate the other (even though the other never leaves the dialogical setting), and (C) describe which dialogical modalities (in principle) affirm the other. It is important to note that even the modes of denial are revelatory of the elevation of the other's importance, and, in cases of race, even the exaggeration of the other is status (Fanon, 1963: 50).

DIALOGICAL WORLD

At the outset, it must be emphasized that the world is dialogical, intersubjective. As Ludwig Wittgenstein (1958) noted, there is no such thing as a private language/world. This realization disposes of the protracted controversy as to the foundational priority of the individual over society or vice versa. In the first instance, society is regarded as a sum of separate, and indeed, solipsistic individuals having solely antagonistic relationships, while in the second, the individual is a conjunction of social events wherein society (at times interpreted in the form of institutions) is the defining dimension. It will be noted that institutions, such as science, may in fact lead to the negation of the other and promote racism (see Chapter 3). Meanwhile, the composition of dialogue has to be understood as prior to, and pervasive of, any claims to individualism and collectivism (Waldenfels, 1971: 132ff).

First, in dialogue the other is not present as an object, a given entity, a mind inhabiting a body, but as a copresence engaged in a common venture. Before regarding the other as other, one speaks with someone about something, some topic, concern, or subject matter. The commonality, here, is a subject matter in which *we* are engaged, which *we* confront, dispute, or agree upon. There is granted an orientation toward something prior to an orientation of a self to the other.

Second, the notion of sender-message-receiver must be modified away from a sequence of activity-passivity, where the sender acts while the receiver accepts the message. Rather, it is a complex process of the establishment of both sender and receiver in a way that they both are contemporaneously active-passive as a mutual articulation and interrogation of a subject matter. Each partner founds the dialogue and, in turn, is founded by it. There is neither the priority of the individual, as the ultimate foundation, nor of the dialogical *we* as the more encompassing. They are mutual and can be regarded (analogously) as a melody: each note is an individual and without it there can be no melody, but the melody also allows a note to have its say as position in the melody. Change in either one is change in the other.

Third, the dialogical partner is not merely the currently copresent other, but others whose orientations toward the world (their perceptions of the topic, the subject matter) are equally copresent. The books I have read, the conversations I have had with others—perhaps long forgotten—comprise an extension of my perceptions and constitute a polycentric dialogical field. I perceive with the perceptions of others, perceptions that contest, extend, and modify my own regard of a given subject matter. The same is true of my current dialogical partner; she too is founding of, and founded by, a polycentric field. And in our dialogue we mutually involve our polycentric awareness and hence extend our polycentric participation (Pilotta and Mickunas, 1990). This also constitutes the basis for the transcendence of one's own limitations and for openness and freedom. Without the other, and without our being copresent to a polycentric field, we would lack the transcending movement.

Fourth, polycentric dialogue defies traditional notions of sequential history. Dialogue constitutes a field of temporal depth wherein ''past'' dialogical partners are not passive, but participate equally in articulating, challenging, and interrogating a specific issue, topic, or subject matter. Thus, it is quite normal to say, for example, that for ancient Egyptians, humans were not articulated in terms of some presumed racial features, but in accordance with hierarchies of social positions and tasks. Of course, the focus of our dialogue is the human, while the others (the Egyptians) open and extend our perception by showing our own limitations and positionality on the topic. Here, their perceptions actively contest with our own perceptions. At the dialogical level, even when we would reject the other's perceptions of a given subject matter, we are constantly decentered from our limitations. Indeed, the very preoccupation with rejection, the efforts to demonstrate the inadequacy, the mistaken understanding, and downright error, shows the extraordinary credence and copresence of the other. Thus, the copresence of the other is the condition of transcendence.

Fifth, the dialogical copresence of the other not only decenters mutually absolute positionality, but also constitutes the initial awareness of human situatedness as well as a reflective self-identification each through the other. It could be argued that dialogical processes comprise the domain of interpositional reflexivity, such that one recognizes oneself only by way of differences from the other. This is the transparency principle: I know myself to the extent that I reflect from the other. I see myself through the different perceptions offered by the other that connect us by way of a common theme, task, subject matter, which allow us our recognition of our own positions.

Another aspect of this dialogical morphology must be mentioned in order to avoid misunderstandings inherent in the efforts to objectify the other. Even if we engage in a dialogue about the other, we shall find that she cannot be understood apart from her perceptions of something, of some concerns inherent in her world. We shall understand her only to the extent that she is engaged in some task or concern, as an aspect of our own polycentric field. After all, to discuss Virginia Woolf is to discuss her views about something and thus to introduce her as our dialogical partner. Even if we are so crude as to intrude into her ''private feelings,'' we could still understand them as ''feelings about something.'' She as well as we are comprehensible only with respect to the world we address, contest, and share in our different ways.

An all-encompassing, undifferentiated, homogeneous thesis is not recognizable, cannot possess an identity. It ceases to be dialogical. At the moment it ceases to be intersubjective, speech says everything and nothing. Without the copresence of the other there is no sense. Monadology is a denial of the other's existence as copresence through difference. That such divine positions are assumed is obvious from numerous examples across cultures and even within specific cultural institutions. It behooves us, therefore, to explicate such positions which, while dramatically paradoxical (due to their emphasis on the other), they attempt to abolish the other's existence.

We know that there are numerous institutions in cultures, such as scientific and theological ones, that purport to ''explain'' everything and specifically the other. Not all such theories need to be explored; however, what is required is to articulate their common principles that will inhere in such explanations. In turn, we shall not rank such theories with respect to their ''higher'' status in a given culture (not because we wish to insult the adherents to such theories) because our effort is to comparatively elucidate essential commonalities.

To speak in principle, all theories that posit inevitable causes for, and outcomes of, human actions engage in homogenization, and thus, a denial of human
presence as a diversity. In the final analysis it is the will of divinities, universal
laws, forces clashing in the cosmic night, childhood violations, historical market
forces, and even cultural habits that speak. Here one cannot claim a situated,
responsible, dialogical, contesting, limited but open human presence. For instance, Newt Gingrich once announced that the welfare system was the cause
of a woman's death in Chicago. She died during a botched abortion attempt,
but the "real" cause, according to Gingrich, was the anonymous welfare system.
The same can be said of the many claims (including Robert Dole's) that entertainment media force people to do what they do. In principle, this is an abolition
of the subject in favor of an object as a product of causes, an engagement in
monological and all-encompassing presence that attempts to silence the other.

In such cases, the situated, dialogical individual is replaced by an abstract set
of factors: The human is subject to the force of institutions (such as mass media)
that are deemed to be in a position to posit the individual as an object and to
determine her course. In brief, the other does not exist as a dialogical other, but
is an object without any situational perception or dialogical (differential) identity. What is of note is that such speakers proclaim these theses—even if for a
moment—(ex catedra) form a homogeneous position. But, their own dialogical
differentiation is dependent on other positions. Objectivists and other theologians
claim to be unsituated, apart from, and untainted by the very institutions which
they posit as grounds for all explanations. This is their dramatic paradox: Peoples are dominated by institutions, but our proclamations are from a position of
unaffected privilege. We are the subject and our discourse is homogeneously
absolute. The other, here, does not exist as a speaking, dialogical subject. One
specific result of this homogeneity is the tacit assumption that the other cannot
be held responsible; he is naive. Indeed, in some discourses, he may be defined
as an innocent victim.

An unavoidable dialogical reflexivity comes into play, and in principle. The
very claim to innocence and victimization is a position, differentiated from other
positions in a dialogical field of claims and counterclaims, accusations and ex-
cuses. The first moment of such a dialogical interplay is the pointing out that
the objectifiers of the other must either belong to the same explanation (and
hence cannot claim to be responsible subjects), or are cynical (Sloterdijk,
1983: 33). In all cases, the second moment appears when the victimized proclaim
their innocence and accuse the other as the victimizer. The victimized joyfully-
sorrowfully exhibit the scars of being "crucified" and oppressed and, therefore,
of having a greater moral authority, by dint of their suffering, to judge all others.

This is the syndrome of the "colonized" other as (s)he appears around the
globe, regardless of the circumstances of oppression. In the current breakdown
of major empires, the other, the third world, minority "nationalities," are vying
for the privilege of being the greatest sufferers, the most violated, and hence,
the most qualified to judge and demand of the other all sorts of retribution

(Shafarivic, 1991: 389ff). What is characteristic of such claims (as a third moment) is equally an abstract universal posture: The Germans did this to us, the Soviets have crucified us, the Japanese owe us an apology. Eurocentrism is a neocolonial, privileged invasion. The fourth moment shows that the other, the colonizer, the oppressor, is not another at all, not a dialogical partner, but a monstrous object, an anonymous blind force bereft of human features—even beyond being a "blue-eyed satan."

The denial of the dialogical other, in the other's very forceful presence, takes on a dual abstraction. The oppressor sees the other as a lesser being, and if this view is pushed to the limit, the other is denied human existence. The other belongs to a race that cannot be characterized as human; she is on a lower level of evolution and per force is best suited for subservient tasks. Here the oppressor, the racist, denies her own positionality and dialogical situatedness and regards the other from a divine position. The other may offer her deeds, achievements, trajectory of her life, but the racist has presumed the sole and true standard, such that the other can never offer adequate evidence that she has a right to human existence. If her deeds, history, and achievements are excluded, then she is left as a pure body, an entity that does not resemble anything human.

But the ethnically or racially oppressed are equally exposed to the same logic. They must regard the oppressor in terms of decontextualized abstraction. The oppressor (the racist) is equally lacking in human characteristics. He lacks conscience, is a brutish barbarian and, as all lower creatures, is a predator. Moreover, he is incapable of providing for his own needs; all his possessions stem from theft. All his deeds, his life's achievements, do not belong to him but to those he oppresses and exploits. He is a body bereft of significance, a greedy biochemical mechanism. This too constitutes a non-dialogical attitude and establishes a divine gaze toward the other. On both sides, dialogical transcendence and human situatedness as decentered freedom is abandoned. This is the grand consequence of deconstructive reversal. Only the names (persons) change positions, but the structure remains unchanged. This is the status quo of diacritical reversal, the endless eye-for-an-eye until, as Gandhi noted, everyone is blind.

Such a dual abstraction, indeed disembodied reification, is extended to include various moves toward liberation from racism, ethnocentrism, and their modes of oppression. In this case, those to be liberated must be passively ideal, voiceless. They cannot have any faults; any faults are the result of oppression. In this sense the oppressors are completely faulty, corrupting, and immoral. Unless one grants the oppressor a status of pure reification, one will have to lend him a position of subjectivity, intentionality, and responsibility for his morally unjustifiable (racist) activities. The ideal oppressed, the colonized, the exploited, has to surrender the status of subject, the being of intentionality, of making decisions. In order to retain their purity and innocence, they have to parade their passivity, their life as death as the ultimate virtue. It is an ideality that is as equally without position as the oppressor, although it may proclaim that it is the highest bearer of moral virtues. For example, when the Baltic tribes declared their independence from the Soviet Union, they also took the status of being victims and thus the bearers, exemplars, and teachers of unconditional universal morality. As perfection no situated human appeared, and no dialogical positionality and differentiation could be offered: no human presence. They disappeared into divine pronouncements (pure, universal objectivity). This self-abolition of their situated dialogical transcendence had the consequence of abolishing their humanity.

The denied presence of the other, in a racist and ethnically antagonistic world, appears quite frequently in institutionalized styles of rhetoric. Scientific research, as one of the major institutional practices, purports to offer truths that are impartial, objective, and universal. Such discourse seeks, and claims to offer, the most basic explanations of human events. Thus, recent investigations in genetics, and uses of the genetic model, result in such defining texts as *The Bell Curve* (Herrnstein and Murray, 1994), which "demonstrate" the "truth of failures" of some minority groups: of the other. Failures of the other are obvious from the institutionalized, universal discourse of science. As such, society is exonerated because it is not at fault with respect to racism and the failure of the other. The other is equally not at fault with respect to his limited capacities. Both the scientific institution and the other are subjected to a non-dialogical universality, such that scientific discourse is regarded as valid under all conditions, while the other, as an incapacitated body (not yet human), must also be understood with respect to the laws advanced by science. What is of essence, here, is that scientific institutions themselves define the social functions which are deemed to be human.

In a technocratically militaristic world, each human activity is subjected to calculated functional requirements and efficiencies, which are regarded as universal expressions of human intelligence (see Chapter 3). This decontextualization strips away all dialogical partnerships in correlation to tasks and their varied significations, and reduces them to a system of discrete signals, to a necrophilic body that cannot have any slack. Each body part is a function reacting to, and inserted into, a system of functional parts. Each part is equivalent to, and replaceable by, other parts. Those bodies that retain slack, deviate from efficient use of energy, time, and motion in the technocratic world, are regarded as irrational. The other, the minority, the ethnically different, is thus the one who bears the very traces of inefficiency, and indeed, irrationality in his very comportment. This irrationality, then, is discovered by scientific institutions to be, in Reality, built in by the very metaphysics of universal geneticism.

By definition, racism is universal, and the very technocratic functions of this society must equally support racism, not for economic reasons, but for the very legitimation of the denial of the other as human, denial of the other's right to exist. Thus, as unfit, the other is exorcised from the functional system and punished by numerous disadvantages. Obviously, the institutionalized scientific version of reality will always prove its case, since the social functions that it requires are its own invention—technical. Only those who subject themselves to such a functional society will be regarded as "human." Paradoxically, to become "human" in this sense requires that they cease to function dialogically, and become a system of homogeneous and interchangeable parts. They too accept racism as a universal necessity—as "natural."

This type of institutional racism is, at this level, now regarded as a universal logic. It is a standard that determines the other's status as belonging to either a race or an ethnic group that is inadequate. The inadequacy may be regarded as either a scientifically demonstrated fact or a result of social, cultural superstitions. Thus, for example, the women of the others have no intelligence concerning their sexuality, overproductivity, and ability to use scientific means for birth control. To speak functionally, they are inefficient with respect to the good life. If it is not their intelligence, then at least their cultures are flawed. Thus, they must be extricated from their "irrational superstitions" and made to function in a technocratic, truly "objective" environment, constituted by the racially superior intelligence. Their culture will have to be surrendered as a faulty system of irrational, subjective beliefs that has hindered the entrance of the other into objective "world history." Of course, surrendering the faulty culture is not a guarantee that the other (exorcised from her dialogical setting) is adequate to function in the non-dialogical context of institutionalized science and social technocracy. At best, the other will be placed in tasks requiring no intelligence. The racist will have to be benevolent, have some pity on the lesser others, so well paraded in *The Bell Curve* (Herrnstein and Murray, 1994). There is proffered *universal evidence* as to the objective embodiment of material inferiority of the racial other. In this sense, the denial of employment, education, and the "normal" social amenities will be the denial of a woman's right to existence, will be equivalent to her death. Institutionalized racism and ethnicism do not regard these denials as violations, but as objective necessity: There is nothing you can do for, or with, these others.

The proclamation, in principle, is this: Neither institutionalized racism nor the other can do anything about objective, genetic facts. The latter legitimate the tacit assumption of the superiority of racist institutions. The very fact that, through our technology, "we discovered" the ultimate explanation of all human capacities is proof that we are not only the best, the presence of true humanity, but also that we have a "manifest destiny" to manage the affairs of others. This very claim confirms the racist regard that the other is, *a priori*, dysfunctional, inefficient: an irrational child.

But, as noted above, this racist attitude, vis-à-vis the scientific, technocratic social world, is equally bereft of the dialogical human presence. Indeed, he too is a result of the same genetic laws that rob him of any claim to humanity. He is a subjected subject, equally explainable by such impartial universal laws, which leave no room to claims concerning *his* achievements. After all, genetic rules have no "personalities" and ply their trade without any regard to the dialogical, intersubjective human world. What this suggests is that the racist, pegging himself on institutionalized science, abolishes his right to claim any superiority.

There are also the components of institutionalized cults, tacitly legitimating racism by proclaiming *the truth* of chosen peoples. Regardless who makes such a proclamation, the other must be outside of the exclusive circle and, minimally speaking, on the verge of evil. This holds despite the fact that there are numerous cults, such as fundamentalist Christians, Muslims, Jews, Hindus, who vie for outdoing one another's claim to supremacy and cultocentric racisms. Each holds its position to be the sole and ultimate truth and may, at times, hold members of other, similar cults, as racially inferior, suited, at best, for conversion, subservience, or extinction (Hazel, 1992: 192ff). Numerous confrontations today occur among cultic groups, each intent on converting all others to its own proclamations and imposing the latter on all publics. This is well-known under the essential rubric of *holy war*, ranging from war with words, "divinely inspired" murder. The suggestion, here, is that despite surface variations among cultic groups, the murder of the other is an extension of attacking and killing, by words.

We must remind ourselves that, for cults, words are not discursive, dialogical, but rather magical deeds, identical with creation and destruction. A prayer, after all, is a power for the unleashing of events (Gebser, 1985). In this sense, murder of the other is not an individual act, but an embodiment of divine speaking, of carrying out the "word" of a god. Indeed, the other, the enemy of the word, is radically important as the worthy enemy, as the embodiment of evil itself, calling one to destructive acts against the other. The current language of those who carry out *the word* is replete with the terminology of good and evil, with demonization that calls for a cleansing of the other from the world. Such speechacts blatantly exclude the other from consideration as a dialogical partner. This constitutes the presumption of monological speech, which is coextensive with the ultimate word of a cult's divinity.

REGARDLESS OF RACE

At the outset, the above delimitations suggest an inevitable "logic." In their exclusion of the other, monological abstractions and universalities constantly revert to the positionality and specificity of including the other as the most important aspect of their logic. While denying the other, these logics allow the other's freedom and indeed transcendence of racist claims to universality. What is meant by freedom is the resiliency, the constant requirement to deal with and include the other as never completely subjectable to racists universality. The history of racism reveals diverse, devious, cunning, banal, sublime, and "scientifically sober" efforts to ban, kill, destroy the transcendence of the other. Hence, even institutionalized modes of racism, that spread their message among collectivities, do so precisely at the level which admits the uncontrollable other, the impossibility of subjecting her completely to institutionalized racism. The spread is a general attitude which sees in every black all blacks, in the lynching of him, a lynching of all of them. Here, the dialogue is reversed, such that the universal rationality of an institution, claiming to dispel the darkness of cultural superstitions, becomes a promoter of another superstition, of an aura that surrounds an entire group. Hence, when the racist reacts to an individual, he does not do so rationally, reacting to this individual, but to a "black, much too black" other.

What enters here initially is the notion that racism, such as white racism, is a white problem in the white dialogue. The term "dialogue" can no longer be avoided, because the white constantly addresses questions concerning the solution of "black problems." The latter cannot be solved by blacks since, by institutional definitions, they do not possess sufficient human intelligence. Hence, they must be saved from themselves. The white, in this racial context, cannot be offered salvation. He can either help, destroy, or get out of the way of, the black; yet at the end no contemplated option exists for the white. Even in cases of white persons seeking racial justice for the other, (s)he knows intimately that racial justice is not for herself/himself, since (s)he invented this problem of justice. In this sense, to be a white racist is either to be condemned by the other, or to condemn oneself.

Condemnation is a white dialogical issue. Before white racism, black peoples were not black. They had no ontological reason to regard themselves as such. To become black requires the conditions set up by whites that were external to the other. This is correlative to the notion that the other, in order to become human, must enter history—the white definition of history. The other, therefore, need not have history; this lack is not an issue for the other, but for the white. In turn, the universal history of the white is itself dialogical, and by drawing the other into its wind, it demands that the other be copresent as an unavoidable player in this universal history. The above-mentioned technocratic world is white history, premised on "progress" and hence posited at the head of all others: others who lack such progress, and either do not have history or must look up to the "advanced" peoples for guidance and mastery. History, while demanding the degradation of the other, is also the dialogical "elevation" of the other to the status of positioner of white people as superior.

The result of racism for the racially other is not only constant attention, a constant exclusion through overstudy and overcodification, but above all of singularization. While the other is black, any black, a black, the black, he is also noticed, harassed, called upon to justify himself, prove his humanity, masculinity, prove her femininity, beauty, and hence to be the one who must constantly be situated, dialogical, and therefore transcendent. Every decision of this other is a risk, an exposure to indeterminacy, chance, and freedom. The institutionalized racist is subject to his racism without notice, as something natural, requiring no unique and singular moment of transcendence. Things take their normal course, society and economy are events to which one is subject to, subjected to, and even determined by. Indeed, one could even pridefully admit

to this subjection: I do my duty. But, for the racially other, the gaze, the institutional look, the surveillance is upon him. Consequently, his decisions are not
for his race, not to beat the institutionalized racism, but to face, day after day,
his unique situation, its demands to transcend the constrictions, and to demonstrate this transcendence under a constant gaze.

If we take historical black figures, we discover that despite their autobiogra-
phies, they reveal specific lifeworlds of the United States. Their situated transcendence constitutes relationships to moments of the history of institutionalized
racism. The writing by Frederick Douglas is a recognition of his former situation
as a slave. It was *he* who was a slave, and it was *he* who, by dint of his
autobiography, became a historical figure in the world of racism. But, there was
a Frederick Douglas who was not a historical figure, who was the singularized
person deciding to escape from Maryland. At that moment of *his* black lived-
history, he was no hero. He had to recognize that the real options available to
him were materially overwhelming and foreboding, but his choices were not.
This is to say, his options were given as historical, institutionalized racist facts,
facts created and defined by racism; but his choices were direct, positioned, and
transcendent of the options. No doubt the powers against him were facts beyond
his control, yet *his* freedom could only be gained by *his* singular choices and
actions.

In the face of institutionalized options, *he* was in dialogue with them and he
extended them by introducing the human, situated, dialogical transcendence
premised on a singular position and choice. This is to say, *his* transcendence of
institutionalized racism was enabled by dialogue to the extent that it is a transcendence of the sequential, non-dialogical history of the succession of such
institutions. Douglas, the other, is the confirmation of dialogical engagement
(even under the most dire racist conditions). This is not to say that racism is
thereby condoned. To the contrary, the point is that even under racism, the non-
dialogical racist is compelled to recognize dialogue in the other, who must live
and act as a positioned-positioning singular: as situated transcendence and a free
human.

The dialogical situation for the racially other is unique in the following variations. Fanon (1963: 135) points out the authors, writing about black experience, would have to be incognizant of their *historical* location in order to liberate
themselves (not as black, but as humans) and to be dialogical. Such writers had
to understand themselves, not just as subjects to this history, but as willing and
positioning-positioned, passive-active processes in dialogue. Yet, as soon as
these writers confirmed their position in history, then they also confirmed a
history which made them black and allotted them a position of non-being, of
death. According to Fanon (1963), there is a recognition that while black liberation is necessary, it cannot be a liberation to be black. The black, as the other,
is, of course, thrown into a setting as a total and concrete being; such a setting
escapes the racist. The latter, like the bourgeoisie who claim that there are no
classes, can claim that there is no racism. This claim, according to Fanon (1963:

112), is possible because the racist is not simply the dialogical other, but the monological master, as a pervasive, institutionalized gaze.

And yet, one must also understand that the institutions and the gaze that comprise the history of the racist are contingent, indeed transitory. This is to say, the loss of all "ultimate" explanations has forced the racist to posit his superiority as historical, as the most advanced and progressive. But, this history is not a given. It is the result of temporary, contingent *human* activity. History, including racist history, is a factual situation that has become a tool to subject the other to racist demands. But once this is recognized, the other, who has demanded and maintained his humanity by his transcendence of conditions through choices, reveals his own, and the racist's, humanity. He draws both into a dialogue by showing the situated transcendence of both, and the need of each for the other as dialogical humans.

As Fanon (1963: 229ff) proclaims, "I find myself suddenly in the world and I recognize that I have one right alone: That of not renouncing my freedom through my choices. . . . I, the man of color, want only this: That the tool never possess the man. That the enslavement of man by man cease forever. . . . That it be possible for me to discover and to love man, whoever he may be." The tool of history is an invention, an institutionalized racism. Liberation from it must be a human-dialogical liberation. Any other option is racist. The black person, by dint of his situation, is a human who transcends (by his choices, and not factual options) racist history, and constitutes the "space" where dialogue is maintained. He is already beyond racial color, and cannot demand to remain black without returning to the white racism imposed on him by contingent history.

POSTSCRIPT

Other variations on racism and ethnocultural centrism may be offered. Our focus, nonetheless, had to be on our own situation, our own self-illumination of the constant shift toward "divine," unsituated, universal monologues that pretend to explain our humanity, our being with (and even against) one another. Yet such efforts constantly reveal the heightened significance of the other, her presence as a background across which such monologues play out their destiny. In the case of modern racist monologues, under various guises such as science, theology, history, and functional efficiency, the other is the final dialogical bulwark, the ultimate, situated transcendence that, against all odds, manifests the dialogical essence of being human. Yet, the other will fail if she allows herself to become an all-encompassing, universal voice, the clarion call of unsituated morality, and finally, an institutionalized racist. It is not enough to pronounce a tolerance of the other in order to liberate a race from a racist society. One must discard race as an irrelevant residual of monological thinking.

REFERENCES

Bakhtin, M. M. (1981) *The Dialogic Imagination*. Austin: University of Texas Press.

Buber, M. (1970) *I and Thou*. New York: Charles Scribner's Sons.

Egon, G. (1990) *The Paradigm Dialogue*. Thousand Oakes, CA: Sage.

Fanon, F. (1963) *Black Skin, White Masks*. New York: Grove.

Gebser, J. (1985) *The Ever-Present Origin*. Athens: Ohio University Press.

Grathoff, R. (1983) *Sozialitsaet und Intersubjektivitaet*. Muenchen: Wilhelm Fink Verlag.

Guba, E. G. (1990) *The Paradigm Dialog*. Newbury Park, CA: Sage.

Hazel, C. V. (1992) "Multicultural Wars." In *Black Popular Culture, a Project by Michele Wallace*, edited by G. Dent. Seattle: Bay Press, pp. 189–197.

Herrnstein, R. J., and C. Murray. (1994) *The Bell Curve: Intelligence and Class Structure in American Life*. New York: Free Press.

McLuhan, M. (1964) *Understanding Media: The Extensions of Man*. New York: Mentor.

Pilotta, J., and A. Mickunas. (1990) *Science of Communication: Its Phenomenological Foundation*. New York: Lawrence Earlbaum.

Shafarivic, I. (1991) "Rosafobia." In *Jest Li U Rossii Buduscheje*? Moscow: Sovietskij Pisatel, pp. 383–406.

Sloterdijk, P. (1983) *Kritik der Zynishen Nernonft*, Frankfurt am Main: Suhrkamp.

Waldenfels, B. (1971) *Zwischenreich des Dialogs*. Den Haag: Martinus Nijhoff.

Wittgenstein, L. (1958) *Philosophical Investigations*. Oxford, England: Basil Blackwell & Mott.

5

Symbolic Violence and Race

Karen A. Callaghan

MODERN SOCIAL ORDER AND CONTROL

Modern forms of social control must appear to be unobtrusive, politically neutral, and clearly lacking any brute coercion. In other words, societies that purport to practice pluralism can justify only forms of control that appear to preserve the integrity of individualism and personal freedom. However, modern social arrangements are also underpinned by social ontological dualism, which is best illustrated by the Cartesian understanding of truth and reality (Murphy, 1989). Truth is defined as a pure (objective) view of reality, a perspective that is void of any temporal, relative, or personal characteristics. Furthermore, truth or factual knowledge can result only from the conceptual and analytical techniques commonly known today as scientific inquiry. In the modern worldview, then, knowledge derived from the application of scientific methodology must be granted primary or centered status. Other forms of expression are relegated to a marginal or peripheral status, since they lack the validity and truthfulness of "objective facts." Hence, a hierarchy of knowledge and expressions is established.

In the modern view, human agency as a "subjective experience" is considered suspect, too easily contaminated with misperceptions or personal interests to serve as a legitimate basis for social arrangements. Human perceptions can be made reliable only through the medium of scientific methodology. Only science can be trusted to provide a clear view of right and wrong, the reasonable and the irrational.

Modern sociological theories have typically stipulated the need for identifying an objective, and hence stable basis of social order. According to such social realist theories, stability and order are associated with supraindividual interests and concerns. Durkheim (1938), for example, suggested that society is a reality *sui generis*. Norms, customs, roles, institutions, and other social phenomena should be understood as social facts, forces that exert legitimate and necessary constraints on individual thought and action. Durkheim assumed that without such restrictions on the "insatiable and bottomless abyss" of human emotions, society would collapse (1951: 247). For Durkheim, then, social integration is possible only if society's "members have their eyes fixed on the same goal, concur in the same faith" (Durkheim, 1993: 91). The legitimacy of the "same goal," however, must be validated via social facts. In other words, social cohesion or collectivity is possible only if intersubjectivity is understood as a mere conduit for social forces.

In a similar fashion, Talcott Parsons (1966: 5–29) proposed that "functional prerequisites" must be satisfied for social order and stability to exist. For Parsons, social order is predicated on the assumption that human choices and decisions cannot be self-legitimating. Thought and action must be validated externally, neutrally, preferably on a standard that has been established as objectively legitimate. Furthermore, Parsons (1966: 14) also notes that a tension or "exigency" exists between society and the "personalities of its members." The needs and demands of society expressed via a "central value pattern" must take precedence over the interests and desires of people (Parsons, 1966: 14). In the social realist worldview, human agency as well as social differences are considered anathema to order and stability.

Consequently, an ontologically dualist model of social order results primarily in a hierarchical-supremacist worldview. All forms of thought, expression, action, identity, and hence persons are understood, and scientifically legitimated, in terms of the center/periphery bifurcation. As marginal phenomena, persons are subjugated to a hyperreality (Baudrillard, 1993: 70–76) of natural and social laws which must be revered and respected if chaos is to be avoided. Human agency is viable only within the confines of social, political, economic, and biological parameters which are assumed to originate from an external reality. As a result, domination and subordination are established as the natural, functional prerequisites to social order.

This hyperreal social model implies that conformity to the external and extra-human "reality" of the social and natural worlds is the act of reasonable, mature, and civilized persons. Hierarchical social arrangements are justified as the outcome of market forces, genetic superiority, historical antecedents, and/or other supraindividual dynamics. Modern domination, then, is rarely discerned as the exercise of mere self-serving power and privilege, but rather as the manifestation of regulatory criteria. Furthermore, individuals who fail to recognize the primacy of deterministic thinking and hierarchical relations are viewed as jeopardizing the smooth functioning and productivity of society. Such failures may also appear as if persons are out of touch with reality, a problem for which modern societies have numerous remedies. According to the modern worldview,

Durkheim's bottomless abyss is the fate of people who refuse to accept the limits of reality.

SYMBOLIC CONTROL AND LANGUAGE

In modern hierarchical societies, social relations are legitimatized on the basis of what Lyotard (1984) calls "metanarratives." As metanarratives, specific deterministic principles and values are promulgated as the products of scientific inquiry and supplied with unquestionable validity. Rational persons are those who recognize these metanarratives as a neutral and inherently unbiased view of reality. These views and images of human nature, social order, and the possibilities for social change are used by persons to "normalize" their own thoughts and actions (Murphy, 1994). No longer subject to the crude, barbaric coercion of the past, individuals are rational, free agents now able to discover the social, biological, historical, and economic demands to which self-concept and self-determination must comply. Aberrant and non-conforming thought can be self-identified for remediation, as mature and reasonable persons engage in activities that create integrated societies, free from the subjective irrationality of special interests and political partisanship.

As many postmodern writers have emphasized, modern social control is accomplished, in part, through language. The discourse constructed by modern metanarratives reproduces power and domination through symbolism. Hierarchical control is established and maintained through the use of ideas, images, and information. A monolithic view of reality is produced and reproduced as the only viable form of social exchange. As Bourdieu (quoted in Thompson, 1984: 44) notes, a "linguistic market" is established as the only acceptable context within which persons can exchange what are recognized as legitimate expressions and ideas.

The modern, scientific, technological worldview dominates the current linguistic market. To engage in meaningful exchange, persons must utilize images and expressions that reflect a hierarchical and deterministic understanding of human action and social arrangements. This "linguistic unification" creates a homogenized view of social order that reflects existing power relations (Thompson, 1984: 45). Those who have knowledge of and access to the dominant expressions are able to control the "market," and can circumvent others whose expressions or social identities are not affirmed by the rhetorical context. Hence, persons participate in linguistic markets that inferiorize and oppress certain social identities, forms of expressions, and ideological perspectives (Turner, Singleton, and Musick, 1984). Consequently, this form of symbolic exchange is coercive and violent. To gain social legitimacy and exercise a rational voice, persons must exchange images and ideas that continuously disempower and oppress themselves and others. They must "euphemize" their expressions to comply with prevailing market demands (Thompson, 1984: 57). In essence, the modern linguistic market forces all human action to be euphemized as merely the medium through which universal laws are manifested. Intersubjectivity is degraded to an instrumental status; a medium of regulation and regimentation.

The term ''symbolic violence'' may appear to trivialize the seriousness of physical violence. However, both play an equally effective role, through intimidation and neutralization, in undermining challenges to hierarchical power. Symbolic violence reproduces power by silencing the voice of opposition, and by violating the sense of self-worth, collective power, and integrity of individuals.

SYMBOLIC VIOLENCE AND RACE

Symbolic violence allows systems of domination and inequality to exist within a discourse of social pluralism and individual autonomy. Social exchange is dominated by symbolic images of reality that reify the status quo. Individuals become self-policing and self-defeating as intersubjectivity is predicated to an objective hierarchy of social relations. As bell hooks notes, ''A culture of domination demands of all its citizens self-negation'' (1992: 19). In this modern discourse, individualism is embraced as a liberating concept, but is manifested only as a dualistic and bifurcated notion of human autonomy. Although individual merit and achievement are lauded as the hallmarks of a progressive, democratic society, characteristics such as race, gender, age, and class are defined as ''centering'' persons' identities. That is, these traits have been designated as ontologically significant, as determinants of individual ability and character. In the modern discourse, the linguistic market is comprised of symbolic referents to the primacy of race, ethnic, age, and gender statuses. They are the boundaries of normality within which rational social exchange is to occur.

As one centering identity, race (and ethnicity to an extent) has been sustained as ontologically viable chiefly through scientific significations. Race has been defined as a physiological state, a genetic configuration, and/or a cultural imperative. Science, natural and social, has been used to establish also a racial hierarchy. In America, past and present, numerous attempts have been made to portray whites as socially, intellectually, and physically superior to other racial-ethnic groups. In modern hierarchial societies, scientific proof of such superiority legitimizes the right to exercise power and control over others. Those with superior intellectual capacity are considered best able to understand the demands and prerequisites of society, and therefore are believed to be the agents who should be charged with maintaining social order.

This form of legitimation sustains domination, not as the result of historical or current power struggles, but as a naturally evolving condition. White domination is understood as a fair and ethically neutral arrangement. When portrayed as the result of an inherent superiority, no underhanded scheming, deception, or coercion appear to be required to establish and maintain this power. Hence, white supremacy seems apolitical and unintentional. In fact, within this discourse efforts to establish racial and social equality are defined as irrational and unnatural. Claims of the system's unfairness or exclusiveness can be dismissed as sentimental, emotional, idealistic, and frivolous. Issues and concerns regarding real, live, breathing persons are peripheral within a metanarrative that is based on social ontological dualism. Hence, alterations of the system cannot be justified on an intersubjectively derived desire for justice or equality. Change is acceptable, that is, objective, only as long as social disruption is avoided, and the underlying dynamics of racial order and stability remain intact.

The linguistic market of a white-dominated society idealizes racial supremacy as an inevitable and desirable state. As part of the linguistic and hence cultural context, these ideals are institutionalized as the status quo, the duly normal ways that persons should view and interact with one another. Certain forms of thinking, acting, speaking, looking, and so on, which reify white superiority, dominate the linguistic and social arenas. Since these symbols are usually sustained through scientific techniques, they are imbued with the authority of natural law. Accordingly, persons of color are relegated to a peripheral status, and therefore legitimately the subject of heightened suspicion and control. To engage in the white-dominated, symbolic market, persons of color must euphemize their expressions, biographies, appearance, and identities as similar to, if not the same as, white experiences. They must display acceptance of the prevailing social world or risk even further exclusion and discrimination for engaging in what the linguistic market defines as irrational, disruptive, and uncivilized behavior.

The symbolic violence of these dynamics is clear. Race and racism are defined as the unintentional by-products of various abstract forces. Hence, identifying villains or victims is portrayed as an oversimplistic and naive analysis. Symbolic violence results in persons of color being subjected to the most cruel contradictions. Intentional racism and white supremacy are proclaimed fiction, despite the overwhelming reality of acts such as slavery, massacres, unfair hiring practices, housing segregation, striking differences in overall health and welfare, and so on. The system is described as a meritocracy, yet persons' abilities and skills are regularly stereotyped according to race, as well as gender and class identities. When attempts are made to organize the collective interests or power of specific racial-ethnic communities, this strategy is decried as undermining the fabric of meritorious individualism.

Symbolic violence, like physical violence, results in diminishing the strength, vitality, and personal power of the other. In social and political terms, symbolic violence can be devastating. Persons are not only violated by the portrayal of their social positions and identities as inferior, but they are also required to collaborate with those who control and perpetuate the system. While collaboration is often rewarded (although sometimes only as the absence of further marginalization), this is not the only or perhaps most desired effect of symbolic violence. The ultimate and more powerful result of control through symbolic violence is to continually produce and reproduce the social and political differences of the racial hierarchy. Persons who collaborate and succeed are recognized as exemplary members of their group. Those who cannot or will not comply serve as proof of their inherent inferiority on which the system is supposedly based.

FORMS OF SYMBOLIC VIOLENCE

Symbolic violence, as noted above, is manifested in a myriad of forms. Language, including ideas, images, and other kinds of information, is used to construct the superiority of whites and the dehumanization of persons of other racial identities. The racial discourse of white-dominated society is multifaceted, complex, and resilient. The discourse adjusts and adapts to changing social and political trends, without, however, losing the power to dominate and control.

Violent Science

The most straightforward form of symbolic violence is to portray, via scientific "proof," that certain persons are simply inferior to whites. The basis of the inferiority is usually identified as what can be termed either biological or cultural universals. That is, specific abstract forces, such as genetics or social phenomena, are assumed to have a determinate effect on human interaction, to operate as universal laws of human association.

As Gould (1981) has well documented, numerous attempts have been made to construct a physiological basis for racial domination. The nature of the biological universal, however, has undergone many transformations as scientific knowledge has changed. So while the images of differences in cranial shape and brain size are passé, major efforts are now underway to reconstruct the connections between physiology (and hence race) and scores on standardized educational tests.

Cultural universals are also employed to assure that domination is justified. Social scientists such as Oscar Lewis (1959, 1961, 1966) and Daniel Patrick Moynihan (1967, 1986) contributed to the racial discourse by suggesting that poverty is symptomatic of behavioral maladjustments. Lewis made the claim that a "culture of poverty" might actually pervade racial and ethnic distinctions. However, his theories were used, especially in the United States, to reify the notion that lack of economic success is indicative of certain cultural (and hence racial) deficiencies, such as an inability to delay gratification, lack of value for education, and disinterest in civic pursuits.

In Moynihan's discussion of the causes of poverty he points directly to a "tangle of pathology" that permeates the black family and community. The images created by such analysis portray, for example, lack of mainstream involvement and diminished earning potential as characteristic of an inferior cultural framework, rather than the effects of long-term discrimination and racism. White supremacy, of course, is constructed only as an underlying and inevitable outcome, the indirect consequence of the cultural shortcomings of others.

More recently, the conjectures of Charles Murray and Richard Herrnstein

(1994) represent a conflation of biological and cultural universals. Their work resurrects the debate regarding the relationship between genes, social environment, and intelligence quotient (I.Q.). Interestingly, Murray and Herrnstein (1994) attempt to couch their arguments within the discourse of multiculturalism and pluralism, thereby avoiding the overt use of racist or deterministic language. In fact, the authors repeatedly emphasize that individual differences in IQ scores are "far greater than differences among groups" (Murray and Herrnstein, 1994: 27). However, a good portion of their analysis involves discussion of the "black-white" differences in mean IQ scores, addressing claims of culturally biased tests, and "the deep-seated sense of ethnic inferiority" that is common among some "clans" (Murray and Herrnstein, 1994). Hence, while race-ethnicity is disclaimed as a significant variable, their discussion of IQ is underscored with assumptions about racial identities and race relations.

Murray and Herrnstein (1994: 34) also attempt to present the understanding that IQ is the result of an assumed interplay between physiological and cultural factors. They state that, "As of 1994, then, we can say nothing for certain about the relative roles that genetics and environment play in the formation of black-white differences in I.Q.. All the evidence remains indirect" (Murray and Herrnstein, 1994: 34). However, the willingness to give credence to an environmentally shaped IQ is nonetheless deterministic. Cultural or environmental phenomena are described as a social fact by Durkheim. Naturalistic analogies, such as comparing the social environment to a "desert" or "fertile field," are used to describe the effects of social interaction on cognitive and social development (Murray and Herrnstein, 1994: 31). As a natural phenomenon, the social environment is little affected by human agency, as Murray and Herrnstein (1994: 34) note, "that what matters is not whether differences are environmental or genetic, but how hard they are to change."

The most precise thrust of the symbolic violence of the IQ debate is reiterating the idea that racial identity, and the accompanying sociopersonal characteristics are physiologically fixed. Hence, the obvious social inequalities linked to racial identity must also arise naturally. The symbolic purpose of Murray and Herrnstein's analysis is to construct white supremacy as unintentional, and therefore, the possibility of identifying any persons or actions responsible for the domination and oppression of others is implausible.

Violent Language

In addition to scientific images of racial inferiority-superiority, symbolic violence is also manifested in language use—including specific word and phrase choice and the use of passive voice. Moore (1992) illustrates the racist effect of using words that either reify a white-centered perspective/experience, or symbolically deny the existence of an actor as the source of specific deeds. Moore (1992) cites, for example, descriptions of American slavery that include terms which tend to depoliticize and dehumanize the struggle, brutality, and pain involved in the forcible capture and imprisonment of persons. Words such as slave, master, system, cheap labor, bondage, and so on obviously omit any references to the tangible, historic, racial/racist intersubjectivity. Formal and bureaucratic language can help to create the image that racist acts originate from abstract sociohistorical forces, rather than the everyday actions and decisions of human beings. Furthermore, the use of passive voice allows actors to remain "hidden and unrecognized" (Moore, 1992: 335). Passive voice is a verb form in which "the subject is acted upon" while the "doer of the action" is not emphasized (Troyka, 1993: 218–219). Racism, past and present, can then be referred to without implicating or alluding to those who are responsible for perpetrating such actions.

Examples of the use of apolitical language and passive voice can be found in numerous descriptions of race and race relations. A recent undergraduate text, for example, includes the following passages in reference to American slavery (emphases mine): "whereas blacks, following *enslavement* in Africa and the brutal middle passage, *were dispersed* and *purged* of their native cultures" (Marger, 1991: 224). And again, "The *evolution* of slavery in the United States was most simply a *consequence* of *economic rationality* prompted above all by the demand for *cheap labor*." (Marger, 1991: 225). As another example, Murray and Herrnstein (1994: 34) citing the work of anthropologist John Ogbu refer to (emphases mine): "immigrant minorities . . . and castelike minorities such as black Americans who *were involuntary* immigrants or otherwise *are consigned* from birth to a distinctly lower place on the social ladder." Finally, an article that appeared in the *National Review* discussed the college experiences of African Americans as follows (emphases mine): "Blacks have difficult experiences on campus: high chances of being on academic probation and *feelings* of alienation from the larger community." (Williams, 1989: 38).

Each of these quotations reflects a racist linguistic market, regardless of the intended message of the authors. First, in the above passages, the role of human action is ambiguous. Actions, whether brutal, violent, rational, or logical, are noted, but their origins are mysterious. Who purged African cultures, or realized the economic efficiency of refusing to pay fair wages? Second, the egregiousness of racism for people's lives and welfare is presented rather nebulously. "Involuntary immigration" and "feelings of alienation" convey fairly indistinct images of the exploitation, devaluation of personal worth, and brutality of white supremacy.

Violent Images

According to bell hooks, "From slavery on, white supremacists have recognized that control over images is central to the maintenance of any system of racial domination" (1992: 2). The violent representation of people of color has been common in Anglo-American literature, film, and television programs. Slick, attractive images that appeal and conform to prevailing hierarchical thinking are presented for mass consumption. Modern media allow the dominant linguistic market to be dramatized and embodied within the audiences' consciousness. Images of domination can be affirmed and comfortably, enjoyably consumed. Even the most flagrant stereotypes and fabrications can be imbued with "documented authenticity" (Churchill, 1992: 28).

For control of images to produce and reproduce the power to dominate, the content of these representations must symbolically reflect prevailing views and practices of racial domination and social control. Symbolic violence is effective when existing forms of white supremacy are reified but denied, when individual autonomy is praised but reduced to mythology. Segregation is deemed fiction, and the social progress of multiculturalism is extolled. Consequently, crude racist stereotypes of the past have been replaced with hip, more stylish images of people of color. Nonetheless, white supremacy is reinforced when these images fail to critique the hierarchical, deterministic thinking that underpins modern human relations.

Several examples of this fusion of traditional racist themes with supposedly more progressive and sensitive representations are found in the animated film *Pocohontas* (Walt Disney Pictures, 1995). As a Disney product, the images of Native Americans and Europeans circa the early seventeenth century, which appear in the film, can also be found adorning fast-food restaurant drinking glasses, hair accessories, school supplies, greeting cards, and even candy bar wrappers. Young children are, in other words, inundated with Disney's version of the people who experienced and perpetrated the European conquest of North America.

As the title character, the image and demeanor of Pocohontas are pivotal to creating a plot with a violent, racial discourse. Interestingly, the Disney animators have been praised for producing an authentic representation of Native American features (Dowell, 1995: 28). However, when viewed with a more critical gaze, Pocohontas embodies the traditional white supremacist view that people of color signify primitive, wild, and uncivilized entities. Hooks writes that white culture is disposed to see the bodies of others "as epitomizing this promise of wildness, of unlimited physical prowess and unbridled eroticism (1992: 34). In the film, Pocohontas exhibits superhuman athleticism while scantily clad in a clinging outfit. Her dress and demeanor reveal an exaggerated voluptuousness. With oversized breasts and buttocks she is no ordinary young woman, but obviously the embodiment of the white fantasy that women of color are more earthy, sexually available, and accessible (hooks, 1992: 65–66). Indeed, Pocohontas' seductiveness saves her from John Smith's murderous intentions when her appearance entices him to hesitate and then refrain from shooting her.

Smith's effect on Pocohontas is equally intense. Although she is depicted as feeling constrained and misunderstood by her own community, Pocohontas is instantly overwhelmed by Smith's presence. At the same time, she rejects her father's choice of suitor, Kocoum, as he is "too serious." Is that too serious as opposed to the fun-loving Smith? Kocoum also represents the only death displayed in the film. This character's demise symbolizes that Native American lives are easily expendable, and that the sexual competition for women is part of the racial discourse. The film purposely depicts a sexualized relationship between Smith and Pocohontas. Kocoum loses Pocohontas' affections, and is killed after responding violently to the sight of Smith and Pocohontas embracing.

Disney producers may feel that their portrayal of the Europeans is more sensitive and accurate historically, since, for example, they represent Smith, Governor Ratcliffe, and the crew openly voicing racist sentiments and murderous intent toward Native Americans. However, these attitudes seem to result mainly in transgressions against the environment rather than the people of the Americas. The Euro-invaders are shown randomly and wantonly destroying the land in a heated search for gold. A logical inference from this film might be that Native American deaths from the European conquests were due primarily to habitat destruction.

Overall, the film's discourse on contact between people of different racial-ethnic identities is especially pessimistic and violent. As the plot develops, the European attitude of race hatred and race supremacy is soon reflected by the Native Americans, primarily in response to Kocoum's death. In several alternating scenes, Europeans and Native Americans prepare for battle, their images and voices become merged and juxtaposed with one another. In a climactic scene, a confrontation is staged as spears and arrows are poised to battle muskets and canons. The racial discourse underpinning these scenes is powerful. First, contact between different groups is assumed to result in conflict, usually violent conflict, precipitated by competition over scarce and valuable resources (land, gold, food, and so on). Second, the outcome of this conflict will usually be decided by superior fire power. So, while the film appears to be a rare example of an indictment of European colonialism, the dynamics which underpinned these actions are reified as a natural consequence of human agency. The discourse is: The Europeans are not different in character or philosophy from any other group. They cannot be held accountable for exhibiting what is part of the human condition, but simply for superiority in military technology.

The depiction of Smith and Pocohontas as young lovers trying to transcend the discord of their respective communities is an attempt to create a gentler, more intimate dimension to the grisly nature of genocide and warfare. But their relationship is doomed; it will not work no matter what their intentions, implying that love and affection cannot characterize difference (hooks, 1994: 53). In this regard, Ward Churchill's comments regarding the film *Lawrence of Arabia* are applicable to *Pocohontas*. Churchill writes that *Lawrence of Arabia* "put a 'tragic' but far more humane face upon the nature of Britain's imperial pretensions . . . making colonization . . . seem more acceptable—or at least more inevitable" (1992: 245). These representations of intimacy allow the conclusion that even when individuals are willing and able to surmount racial divisions, the outcome is still the same. The racial hierarchy is portrayed as unassailable, always dominating the intentions and sentiments of mere individuals.

Finally, Disney's decision to focus on a historical episode rather than contemporary people and issues also reinforces a hierarchical racial discourse. The *Pocohontas* story line is basically fiction with a few allusions to real persons participating in the 1607 encounters between Europeans and Native Americans. While an opportunity for education is lost, this is to be expected. Few films portray historical events accurately. However, when racial struggles are presented only in historical contexts, symbolically the message is: The problem is in the past, too bad about what happened, but what can be done about it now? How can people living today be held accountable for the actions that occurred hundreds of years ago? As Churchill comments on the film *Dances With Wolves*, "It's all in the past, so the story goes; regrettable, obviously, but comfortably out of reach" (1992, 245). The "it's-all-in-the-past" representation of oppression symbolically denies the myriad of policies and actions that have occurred since the fifteenth century to produce the existing American racial hierarchy. No matter how enlightened or sensitive revisionism may be, focus on historical events alone reinforces the discourse that current power arrangements are beyond the scope of human agency. If racial-ethnic struggles and inequities are understood as merely remnants of the past, then once again racism can be assumed to originate from a mysterious, abstract source, an inviolate ground over which persons can enact no influence or sway.

CONCLUSION

A key theme in this chapter is that racism, white supremacy, and all forms of domination are sustained through social-ontological dualism. Dualism allows for the justification of oppression by degrading all human agency as impotent, a mere conduit for universal laws and forces. Social hierarchy and domination are, then, assumed to reflect the natural, inevitable essence of the human condition, and not the interests or position of any particular group. Modern social control is accomplished, in part, through discursive practices. Symbolic methods are used to reify the idea that power relations are the result of *a priori* biological, historical, and social demands. The linguistic market is dominated by hierarchical images, and everyday discourse is imbued with violent and degrading depictions of intersubjectivity.

The subversion of dualism reveals the political nature of social order and social control (Kristeva, 1986a). This maneuver allows the society/individual bifurcation to be demystified. Social order can be understood as a product of intersubjectivity, an ongoing discursive exchange; or as Cornel West says, a "dialogue with others" (1993: 155). Jettisoning social-ontological dualism will not automatically demolish hierarchical relations. However, without dualism no form of social arrangements can claim *a priori* authenticity or legitimacy. Existing social arrangements may have negative consequences for some persons,

and involve coercion, manipulation, and power differences, but they are nonetheless created and sustained on the basis of intersubjectivity, or to use Kristeva's term, "intertextuality" (1986b: 37). A linguistic market that reflects the
intersubjective basis of social order facilitates the questioning, review, and debate of any and all phenomena. Furthermore, such exchanges symbolize not a
risky venture into possible chaotic disorder, but rather the dialogical nature of
human agency within a politics of authentic democracy and participation.

REFERENCES

Baudrillard, J. (1993) *Symbolic Exchange and Death*. Thousand Oaks, CA: Sage.
Churchill, W. (1992) *Fantasies of the Master Race*. Monroe, ME: Common Courage
    Press.
Dowell, P. (1995) "Immaterial Girl." *In These Times*, July 10–23, pp. 28–29.
Durkheim, E. (1938) *The Rules of Sociological Method*. New York: Free Press.
———. (1951) *Suicide, A Study in Sociology*. Glencoe, IL: Free Press.
———. (1993) "Individualism and the Intellectuals." In *Readings in Social Theory*,
    edited by J. Farganis. New York: McGraw-Hill, pp. 88–96.
Gould, S. J. (1981) *The Mismeasure of Man*. New York: Norton.
hooks, b. (1992) *Black Looks, Race and Representation*. Boston: South End Press.
———. (1994) *Outlaw Culture, Resisting Representations*. New York: Routledge.
Kristeva, J. (1986a) "Revolution in Poetic Language." In *The Kristeva Reader*, edited
    by T. Moi. New York: Columbia University Press, pp. 89–136.
———. (1986b) "Word, Dialogue, and Novel." In *The Kristeva Reader*, edited by
    T. Moi. New York: Columbia University Press, pp. 34–61.
Lewis, O. (1959) *Five Families: Mexican Case Studies in the Culture of Poverty*. New
    York: Random House.
———. (1961) *The Children of Sanchez*. New York: Random House.
———. (1966) *La Vida: A Puerto Rican Family in the Culture of Poverty*. New York:
    Random House.
Lyotard, J. F. (1984) *The Postmodern Condition*. Minneapolis: University of Minnesota
    Press.
Marger, M. N. (1991) *Race and Ethnic Relations*, 2d ed. Belmont, CA: Wadsworth.
Moore, R. B. (1992) "Racist Stereotyping in the English Language." In *Race, Class
    and Gender in the United States, An Integrated Study*, 2d ed., edited by P. S.
    Rothenberg. New York: St. Martin's Press, pp. 331–341.
Moynihan, D. P. (1967) "The Negro Family: The Case for National Action." In *The
    Moynihan Report and the Politics of Controversy*, edited by L. Rainwater and W.
    L. Yancy. Cambridge, MA: MIT Press, pp. 39–132.
———. (1986) *Family and Nation*. San Diego: Harcourt, Brace, Jovanovich.
Murphy, J. W. (1989) *Postmodern Social Analysis and Criticism*. Westport, CT: Green-
    wood Press.
———. (1994) "Symbolic Violence and the Disembodiment of Identity." In *Ideals of
    Feminine Beauty*, edited by K. A. Callaghan. Westport, CT: Greenwood Press,
    pp. 69–78.

Murray, C., and R. J. Herrnstein. (1994) "Race, Genes and I.Q.—An Apologia." *The New Republic*, October 31, pp. 27–37.

Parsons, T. (1966) *Societies*. Englewood Cliffs, NJ: Prentice-Hall.

Thompson, J. B. (1984) *Studies in the Theory of Ideology*. Berkeley: University of California Press.

Troyka, L. Q. (1993) *Simon & Schuster Handbook for Writers*, 3d ed. Englewood Cliffs, NJ: Simon & Schuster.

Tuner, J. H., R. Singleton, Jr., and D. Musick. (1984) *Oppression*. Chicago: Nelson-Hall.

West, C. (1993) *Prophetic Reflections*. Monroe, ME: Common Courage Press.

Williams, W. E. (1989) "Campus Racism." *National Review*, May 5, pp. 36–38.

6

What Is a "Japanese"? Culture, Diversity, and Social Harmony in Japan

Eric Mark Kramer and Richiko Ikeda

WA AS MAGIC AND MYTHIC HARMONY

Wa is usually translated as "harmony." When non-Japanese scholars attempt to explain the "miracle" of Japan's economic success, they often refer to *wa* as the source of Japanese postwar economic achievement (e.g., E. G. Vogel's *Japan as Number One*). The Japanese seem to agree with this analysis. The translated versions of such books as *Japan as Number One* have sold well in Japan. Japanese highly value the virtue of *wa* (Umehara, 1981: 348). According to Umehara (1981: 348), politicians who do not appreciate *wa* are usually disqualified by public opinion. Is the concept of *wa* unique to Japanese? What does *wa* signify? We must begin at this point in order to unfold the relationship between "harmony," "power," "fidelity," and racial "integrity."

Prince Shotoku's Seventeen Article Constitution,[1] the first constitution compiled in Japan around 600, stated the importance of *wa* in the first article.[2] It says: "Wa o motte tattoshi to shi, sakaraukoto naki to seyo" [Harmony is to be valued, and an avoidance of wanton opposition to be honored] (translated by William Aston, 1956, in *The Nihongi*). According to Umehara (1981: 348), this phrase has had more influence than any other on the Japanese people. Prince Shotoku was the first Japanese official to send a mission to China. He also studied Buddhism extensively. The Seventeen Article Constitution was based on the Buddhist principle of compassion. The second article denotes that one must respect the Buddha, his teachings, and the ones who preach them.

At the end of the 6th century A.D., several clans competed with each other to obtain power. Prince Shotoku resorted to the Buddhist principles of *wa* and compassion in order to rule the country (Umehara, 1981). Many scholars of Japanese history have pointed out that Prince Shotoku's idea of *wa* synthesized and instituted the Confucian notion of harmony with Buddhist ideals (see Ume-hara, 1981). In his scheme, however, Buddhist compassion was expressed and practiced as an integral part of the imperial system. This is not unusual, since Buddhism, from its inception, has ventured to advise rulers on how to govern. Given Prince Shotoku's perspective and interests, however, compassion did not extend beyond the system. Compassion was to be instituted and systematized. As part of the system, by definition, it could not be extended to those "outside." Conversely, the sacred system was to be kept uncorrupted, pure, (uniformally consistent) and coherent. The rest of Article One reinforces this scheme by articulating the importance of maintaining the system based on Confucian pa-triarchal principles. It says:

All men are influenced by partisanship, and there are few who are intelligent. Hence there are some who disobey their lords and fathers, and who maintain feuds with the neighboring villages. But when those above are harmonious and those below are friendly, and there is concord in the discussion of business, right views of things spontaneously gain acceptance. Then what is there which cannot be accomplished? (Aston, 1956: 41)

Articles Three, Four, and Twelve explicitly state the superiority of the emperor's system and his duty to maintain the system, as well as the peoples' duty to maintain the system. The duty of maintenance implies obedience to the rules. According to Prince Shotoku, compassion and harmony are identical with the imperial system. Since his constitution *established* this order, order and orders (articles) are identical. Order is made, as if by magic.

The concept of *wa*, or harmony, that Prince Shotoku had in mind was more specifically a state of "order" manifested as the imperial system. He required that people pay respect to the emperor so that the "order," or the hierarchy of the system, namely, *wa*, would be maintained. In this system, people must blindly follow. Any other path of action could only lead to disorder, disharmony, and suffering. "Egoless" self-effacement is the prerequisite for such a structure (Gebser, 1949 Ger./1985 Eng.). Peace and tranquility exist when contention is absent. In other words, harmony is sustained through egoless souls. Japan, as the egoless extended family of *ie*, with the emperor as head, was first articulated by Prince Shotoku's Seventeen Article Constitution. This constitution instituted a "perspectival," legal articulation of order. It is essentially a Confucian version of proto-perspectivity.

Ego, or awareness of self, is irrelevant to members of *ie* (Ikeda, 1992). The purpose for each member of *ie* is to preserve *ie*, not to express or achieve individual desires. "Political" marriages are, for example, not "sacrifices," but necessities in the "mythic" world. Mythic people simply accept arranged mar-riages. Jean Gebser (1985) characterized mythic consciousness as an egoless world. According to Gebser (1985: 9), "The unperspectival [mythic] world sug-gests a state in which man lacks self-identity: he belongs to a unit, such as a tribe or communal group, where the emphasis is not yet on the person but on the impersonal, not on the 'I' but on the communal group, the qualitative mode of the collective.'' Mythic Japanese people belong to a communal group, the emperor's family. The imperial system was (perspectivally) perceived not as an arbitrary ''ideology'' that required rationale, but as a living world of familial relationships and obligations. In summary, *wa*, or harmony, which Prince Shotoku's Seventeen Article Constitution established, cannot be understood without appreciating the magic and mythic consciousness structures expressed by the emperor's system.

CREATION OF "OUTSIDERS"

In the mythic world, solidarity of the inside is strong. But, communal solidarity creates and excludes ''outsiders.'' People ''inside'' (*uchi*) work together in order to maintain their harmony and protect their communal benefits and resources. Consequently, they exclude others (*soto*) that do not deserve such benefits. The notion of *uchi/soto* (inside/outside), which is the beginning of one's separation from the outer world, is vitally essential in the mythic world. A community, like a village, manifests a finely woven cloth of mutual support. Conformity is the price for such security. The village does not however, give much help to outsiders. Even within a village, once members of a family are defined as outsiders for some reason, they are isolated from the rest of the village people (*mura hachibu*). In order to solidify and maintain the harmony of the insiders, the existence of outsiders as scapegoats may seem necessary.

The Japanese authorities have offered scapegoats as internal feedback mechanisms to maintain the system. The ''outsiders'' are actually an integral part of the system. Scapegoats, or ''others'' were created in the process of Japan's becoming a political unity. For example, during the *Yamataikoku* dynasty (which flourished in the middle of the third century), there were slaves called *geko* and *nuhi*. By the latter half of the fifth century, the clan of the present emperor's ancestor unified Japan. Although no class system, as such, was yet formally delineated, the record of resistance by oppressed groups indicates the existence of intergroup consciousness (Inoue, 1993: 10). In the early seventh century, Prince Shotoku attempted to establish a strong state with the emperor at its center. He did not succeed in realizing this during his lifetime. However, in the latter half of the seventh century, his scheme was instituted as the state law called *Taiho Ritsuryo*. The distinction between *ryomin* and *senmin* classes was then explicitly defined. *Ryomin* were ''those who were ranked close to the top, and thus were close to the Emperor, who were considered good'' and *senmin* were ''those on the lower rungs of society who were considered base'' (Neary, 1989: 13). *Senmin* were mainly slaves and other marginal groups. In order to stabilize the system by solidifying the social order, the authorities created, by law, a group of ''outsiders'' or ''others.''

What is evident is the emergence of a perspectival world which is marked by an emphasis on vision (visiocentrism) as the source of metaphysical certitude

(Kramer, 1992). Vision synthesizes space. Vision posits a conical "scope" of interests and awareness. Form is a spatial phenomenon. Prince Shotoku presents a consciousness mutation from a predominantly emotional mythic world to a predominantly perspectival world of rational order. He set into motion the formalization of a conical state structure with himself (the emperor) at the top and center. Because only the cone of vision is attributed the mantle of truth (rudimentary empiricism), nothing outside the conical perspective *real*(ly) "matters." To use a spatial metaphor, those on the "fringe" of the conical form were less real (marginalized), and as Ralph Ellison (1952), in a different context, noted, practically invisible. To be able to be visible as one wishes (in a perspectival world) is to have power. To have one's own voice, to have "a presence," is to be powerful.[3]

Defining a group of people as "others" is, therefore, closely linked to the formation of a unified group consciousness. During the Japanese "Middle Ages" (from the latter half of the eleventh to the end of the sixteenth century), authorities also created "others" to maintain social order. During the period of the Civil Wars (1467–1580), a group of people called *hinin* emerged and came to be identified with human "pollution." Although the law did not define them as "others," as in ancient times, they were socially and politically defined as "others." *Hinin* literally means non-human. *Hinin* was originally a general term for those who were forced, for various reasons, to lead the poorest lives. *Hinin* included lepers, prisoners, those who dealt with human and animal carcasses. They had been considered "those who performed the conduct which people usually refrained from," and, as such, were discriminated against (Aomori, 1993: 72). With time, the *Hinin* became the *de facto* lowest class. This was reinforced and clarified by law (by those who had the power to define and resolve) (Aomori, 1993: 30).

In the early modern period (from the end of the sixteenth to the middle of the nineteenth centuries), the connection between the idea of pollution and those who were discriminated against was intensified, and their social status became permanent. Toyotomi Hideyoshi ended the civil wars, which lasted about 100 years, and began to form a centralized nation. In order to do so, the Toyotomi administration conducted a nationwide land survey between 1585 and 1598, which resulted in the identification of certain kinds of people, with certain locales, as the lower class. The spatial emphasis is obvious. Modern perspectivism is articulated by spatial segregation and a reservation mentality which has a distinctly administrative style. Modern means mental-rational, or put differently, "legal-official." The logic of organization can be very helpful to insiders, but it enables the manifestation of a focal point of power that can be directed at those who fall out of grace with the group, or are outsiders. Examples are the power "vested" in judges, and negotiators. Un- and pre-perspectival people may not be so well organized. They may not present such a clearly defined "point-man." If you say "take me to your leader," they may be hard pressed to determine the exact individual to whom you refer. And due to their relative "disorganization" (which makes it difficult to identify a singular leader with whom to negotiate), they often do poorly at intergroup negotiations (defense against) with groups that are more organized, meaning groups that present a more centralized focus of power. Administration has the advantage in competitive negotiations. This has been borne out innumerable times around the globe when mythic and magic groups confront perspectival modern interests. Indigenous peoples must struggle to learn the rules of this game or be beaten before they even know that they are in a game.

The surveys conducted by the Toyotomi administration solidified the definition (the identity) of the *buraku* people, vis-à-vis their position relative to other different positions. They became the "Japanese" outcast group. Because of Hideyoshi's land survey, people were tied to the land and their status became permanent. During the mid- to late *Tokugawa* period (1700–1868), control over such outcast groups was strengthened. They were strictly isolated from the rest of the community and considered racial/spiritual pollution. As Gebser (1985) has demonstrated, for magic consciousness, blood is the medium of spirit and race, the essence of identity. It's fidelity (or integrity) must be guarded from contamination. It was during this period that Japan stabilized and solidified as a centralized nation-state system. Gebser's notion of "plus-mutation" helps to explain how legalistic administration presumed and used magical blood identity to rationalize its order.

In the modern period, the authority's effort to legally create "others," and to confine them, was strengthened. Legal definition became a far less permeable barrier than older normative distinctions had been. Since the *buraku* look like everybody else, before spatial segregation and legal documentation, they could take new occupations and blend in. But after administrative definition was imposed, this identity flexibility disappeared. As the Jews discovered in Nazi Germany, record keeping is equal to identity keeping.

Modern "typographic" (to quote McLuhan, 1962) humanity seeks security in the stable system, which is established by histories and bureaucracies that survey and keep track of individuals. For most predominantly mythic societies, the first indication of perspectivism is manifested by a rising emphasis on literacy and record keeping, which almost always involves a small intelligensia that are usually religious scholars, because they are the only people who can read and write (report). For instance, many European medieval paintings depict inquisitorial punishment and judgment-day proceedings, including a scribe dutifully recording the confessions of the condemned and consulting the book of the dead. Recording fixes identity. You are what you do, and although your actions pass, your identity does not. For instance, once someone is identified as a felon, a dishonorable discharge, or "bad credit risk" in a bureaucratic world, it is very difficult to escape such an identity (see Chapter 3 about "IQ" and educational tracking).

Modernity expresses anxiety in the face of change (time) by systematizing and fixating relationships. It makes them "legal," and law transcends or "arrests" (criminal) time. The Nazi and Soviet systems are good examples of centralized drive to create the "new modern industrial man." Their bureaucracies and feedback surveillance channels are legendary. Empire relies on information storage and transmission.

Homogeneity Equals Stability

The histories of the *buraku* people, Ainu, and Koreans in Japan demonstrate the power of administrative systematization combined with blood-based prejudices. The myth of Japan as a homogeneous society is a fiction created to promulgate the "uniqueness" of "Japanese" culture. Such a fictitious story has hidden Japan's cultural history of borrowing (especially from China and Korea), and also its racial/ethnic problems, from the rest of the world. Even many "Japanese" people do not know the racial/ethnic problems of their own country. They may think the problem of Koreans in Japan is somehow different (less sinister) than racial problems in the United States. Although they may be aware of "class" or "status" discrimination against *buraku* people, they regard it as different from racial/ethnic problems generally. Many "Japanese" do believe that they are unique and special, even in their way of being unique. This attitude is manifested in the speeches of the ex-prime minister Yasuhiro Nakasone, and the remarks of other politicians.

For example, Nakasone has expressed the claim to superiority by reference to the racial homogeneity of Japan (Dower, 1986: 315). His remarks offended Japan's minority groups, especially the Ainu. Nakasone denied the existence of minorities, and therefore the possibility of discrimination in Japan. Furthermore, he was severely criticized by Americans when he associated America's minority populations with inferior intellectual, qua educational performance. Japan is not immune to racial/ethnic problems. Discrimination against *buraku* people is, for instance, a manifestation of power which defines a group of people as inferior.

The existence of legal "others" is a necessity for perspectival social order to exist. Such an order embodies a linear ratio (like a variable) whereby the lower one goes the farther one is from power. Along a single axis, one cannot lose Japanese identity and yet keep power. Perspectival authority offers the "others" as a "reason," as a rationale, for maintaining the order. In the modern world, authority offers "reasons" why "others" should be discriminated against.

CONTROL OF "OTHERS"

The early modern period of Japan was characterized by an explicit (exteriorized logic) and rigid class society. While the class system included some flexibility in the Middle Ages, it became solidified by explicit law in the Edo period (1603–1867).

Control of *Buraku* People in the Edo Period

Once people were categorized or "cast" as the lowest in the community (so-called *buraku*) based on their occupation, their family lines could not escape. The occupational line and the family line were inseparable. The lowest cast consisted of two branches according to occupation: *eta* and *hinin*. *Eta* included those who dealt with animal skins and dead people.[4] *Hinin* were criminals, vagabonds, or beggars. Under the rigid system of status control, the number of *hinin*, who violated the order of status and therefore had their status lowered as such, increased (Suginohara, 1982: 132). *Eta* and *hinin* were considered to be outcasts by the Tokugawa administration. That is, as outside of the formal "cast" system (warriors, farmers, artisans, and merchants), and as such, as "non-humans." And yet, their status as outcasts depended on the existence of the cast system. Thus, they were defined by, and were part of, the system.

The Tokugawa administration forced them to live in certain areas by systematically segregating them from the rest of the community. This class system was established in order to rule the majority of people, mainly farmers, who supplied the bulk of the labor force for the economy. The "other" is an opiate, and so long as the farmers believed that someone was less human than they, the farmers were willing to participate, even proudly, in the very system that exploited them. The government knew the psychology of the farmer cast, and deluded them into believing that they were not the "bottom" of society, and to feel "better."

Eta and *Hinin* were necessary components of the system. The Tokugawa government used them to alleviate the dissatisfaction and complaints of the masses (mainly farmers) and to avoid revolt by removing the pretense (Suginohara, 1982: 12). Manipulating powers have long understood that satisfaction is a relative phenomenon.

The Tokugawa administration utilized Buddhist sects in order to strengthen the feudal system (Matsushita, 1985: 128; Taniguchi, 1985: 230; Teraki, 1984: 57). In 1664, the Tokugawa Shogunate ordered feudal lords to compile the *Shumon-cho* (sect book) every year. Sect books constituted cybernetic feedback mechanisms in the system, enabling control. Such bureaucratic tools helped the government monitor the population, including the group status of individuals. These survey instruments also tied people to certain Buddhist sects. People had to belong to their *danna-dera* (family temples) and register as its *terako* (children of the temple). In the middle of the Edo period, control over the *buraku* people was strengthened. In 1712, "each feudal clan eliminated them [the *buraku* people] from the *Shumon-cho*' (sect book). All the villagers where registered in their *Danna-dera* (family temples), and began to prepare a separate book for registering the 'humble people' exclusively" (Suginohara, 1982: 15–16).

Buddhist sects not only helped the government promote discrimination against the *buraku* people, but also organized themselves to facilitate the system. Each Buddhist sect built distinctive temples for the *buraku* people and drove them away from other temples (Taniguchi, 1985: 232; Teraki, 1993: 141–144). The *buraku* temples were called derogatory names such as *eji* (a polluted temple) (Taniguchi, 1985: 232–233; Teraki, 1993: 141–144). Even after death, the Buddhist temples discriminated against the *buraku* people by giving them derogatory *kaimyo*, or posthumous Buddhist names (Taniguchi, 1985: 224). Government authority and religious authority were organized into a mutually supportive (harmonious) system of control and maintenance.

The Tokugawa government justified the formation of the *buraku* people as "outcast," by using the Buddhist/Shintoist concept of "pollution," which was a widely held belief among "Japanese" people (Teraki, 1993: 96–97). Since the Ancient period, when Buddhist beliefs spread through "Japanese" society, contact with death was to be avoided. Buddhist teachings prohibited people from taking any life. Prior to the Nara period (A.D. 645–794), the location of the imperial capital was frequently moved due to the emperor's death. In Buddhism, death was associated with pollution. The Buddhist notion of pollution was then combined with Shintoist notions of *imi* (taboo) and *kegare* (pollution) which were also related to human death. "Japanese" people believed the Buddhist/Shintoist doctrine of "pollution," and avoided contact with death, and by association, the *buraku* people. This faith was also manifested as elaborate purification rituals.

The notion of pollution came to include the avoidance of contact with the bodies of dead animals. This idea further extended to the belief that leather work and eating meat constituted pollution (Neary, 1989: 13). Thus, *eta*, the name for leather workers, came to denote "polluted" and "inferior." Until the Tokugawa period, however, such people were not systematically separated from the rest of the people as a policy. Although people who dealt with "death" tended to be inferiorized before the Tokugawa period, it was possible for them to move out from such communities and engage in different occupations. However, the Tokugawa administration made people believe that "being polluted" was an inherent characteristic of the *buraku* people. In other words, the administration utilized the myth of pollution in order to create and control the *buraku* people as instruments of social order. The Tokugawa administration perspectively transformed a *de facto* status into a *de jure* status which was recorded and thus fixated and rationalized "by definition."

NATURALLY INFERIOR

The Buddhist/Shintoist belief in the doctrine of human "pollution" came from the fear of death. People fear the uncontrollable. Death is inevitable and uncontrollable. Death is a part of nature. Civilization is born as a struggle to control nature (Gebser, 1985). When humans came to believe that nature was something different from themselves, the "perfect" harmony between humankind and nature (identity) was disturbed. Prior to the emergent consciousness of nature, the world is spaceless and timeless. The universe has no distinctions.

For instance, the difference between the sea and sky, is not clear in the story of Chuang Tzu's fish, K'un, which becomes a bird "P'eng," and heads for the Lake of Heaven.

In the Northern Ocean there is a fish called Kun which is many thousand li in size. It changes into a bird named Peng whose back is many thousand li in breadth. When it rises and flies, its wings are like clouds filling the sky. When this bird moves across the ocean it heads for the South Sea, the Celestial Lake. (Chuang Tzu, 1974, p. 5)

Gebser (1985) called this spaceless/timeless world the archaic structure of consciousness. Archaic consciousness is one of such profound and simple identity that the "harmony" of man and the cosmos is not conceivable as such, but simply is the case. "Harmony" cannot be realized until "disharmony" is experienced.

With the awareness of the difference between humans and nature, human beings begin to struggle. This is the beginning of power in the human sense. This struggle is articulated as control of cosmic forces (division between the natural and supernatural is not manifested until the perspectival mutation). Once humans try to control nature, the wholeness of the world begins to fragment. "The more man released himself from the whole, becoming conscious of himself, the more he began to be an individual" (Gebser, 1985: 46).

For magic people, nature is not yet separated from culture and so neither exist as such. The additional fracture between nature and supernature is an expression of the modern world. Magic people struggle to control the world by using magic (Gebser, 1985). Perspectival moderns use technology (material magic). Magic people try to manipulate (usually by appeasement) the forces (later called "laws") of the world by conducting rituals. During the magic ritual, a magic person identifies him/herself with "nature." He or she experiences point-like-unity, in which an aspect of the world "possesses" him or her, or vice versa. But "possession" (which is a unidirectional modern idea) is a not a totally satisfactory concept for describing magic at-onement. Magic is expressed audially. Chants and magic "spells" must be spoken to call into being, to make things happen. Gebser (1985: 46) has traced the shared etymology of "make," "might," "machine," and "magic" to "mag(h)," a Greek word of Persian origin, which means "power." Definitions call into being (concerning operational definitions, see the Preface in Gebser, 1985). Auditory vibrations merge with the hearer and are not so directional as sight. One can look away but not hear away (McLuhan and Fiore, 1967: 111; Gadamer, 1975: 454). While the archaic person does not divide the senses into descreet types of data, they stress touch and smell. Mythic people stress audition, while the perspectival stresses vision.

Vision generates space and separation leading to nature as "other," available for indiscriminate conquest. A magic person does not "conquer" an external and opposing "nature," but influences natural forces by identifying his or her will with them. They move together as one. In the hunt dance, the magic person who dons the skin of the antelope and eats its flesh becomes the antelope. Even modern technologists recognize that the laws of nature are unbreakable, and so one must conform to them in order to manipulate them. In the case of the Pygmies' hunting rite, a "real" buffalo and one painted on a cave wall, as well as a ray of sunlight and an arrow, merge as a unity, fulfilling the magic cycle of killing in order to live. When the first ray of sunlight strikes the painting, the buffalo is already dead. The hunt is a process of sacred gathering. The hunting rite is sacred and very emotional because the buffalo is, if not a superior, at least an equal to the human. They are "brothers" (Campbell and Moyers, 1988).

In the mythic structure of consciousness, separation between humans and nature is more obvious. The mythic universe consists of complementing polarities such as day and night, man and woman, and so on. The distinction between mythic polarities is not clearly resolved or defined. Mythic polarities are ambiguous, not distinctly oppositional as in modern dialectical "positions." For example, the Chinese symbol, *Tai-Ki* or *Tai-Ji*, indicates that polar "differences" include each other. Polarities articulate mythic harmony. Harmony with, not conquest of, is the mythic way. But, mythic harmony is possible only because magic identity has dissolved somewhat. Disharmony is an ever-present potential.

In the mythic world, death is "pollution," but it is still intertwined in a cycle with life. Death can be controlled through such mythic rituals as *oharai* (purification).

Myth does not disappear in the perspectival world, but manifests in a different form, according to the structural criteria of mental-rationality. In the modern perspectival world, myth can be used as a tool in a calculated strategy for the purpose of control. An idealogue need not believe in, or identify with, a narrative (reality) to use it masterfully. In the Western world, the magic of "blood" is superceded (not eliminated) by mythic tradition, which in turn is superceded by genetics in the age of the Enlightenment. Vision is emphasized (Kramer, 1992). The Enlightenment is a discursive formation of redefinitions which do not eliminate but alter the meaning of magic and mythic modes of being. They are newly positioned as mysticism, superstition, and blood-based power legitimation. With the emergence of modern arbitrariness, legitimation of aristocratic power via blood is superceded by dialogical politics and the rhetorical merit of policy deliberation. In the modern world, some mythic and magic phenomena are reduced to mere contingencies, and erroneous ones to boot, thus stripping them of their ontological force. But the sacrality and emotion of blood is not so easily redefined.

The emerging awareness of the individual self has not enabled people to escape entirely from the "natural" fatalism of blood-based power legitimation. It merely redefined it as genetic fatalism, which is even more powerfully convincing since it is rational. Individualism clarified and freed the self from collectivistic traditionism, but entrapped it in a structure of meritocracy and isolation (see Chapter 3).

A different perspectival version of responsibility emerged. It has descended upon the slim shoulders of the lone self with devastating consequences. Materialism has deployed the embodied self in space, giving birth to the related problems of communication and alienation. Existentialism is an essentially modern doctrine. A "new" social order, democracy, was established based on the mental power of the rational individual. In such a society, the more rationally one thinks, the more (s)he can gain power. Knowledge is equated with power. A new definition of competence emerges. A competent person, in modern (post-feudal) Japan as elsewhere, has brain power and thinks rationally, meaning systematically (by the rules). A "new" hierarchy was built based on the ability to think this way. In the West, this social order initially defined blacks, orientals, women, children, and the handicapped as irrationally incompetent, excluding them from access to power.

Since modern power is based on rule-guided thinking, if one is not educated in the rules, then one cannot think ("well"). Mental-rational power is unlike brute force, which is not dependent on access to institutional structure. Since education (or socialization into the rules of thinking) is equated with power/privilege, then education is both the source and result of privilege. The resources of education are not wasted on those deemed unable or unfit. If one cannot get an education, then one cannot become capable (smart), and since one is not smart, one cannot get an education. This is the vicious circle of modern technocratic power, especially in the Third World where gaps in power are very pronounced. The "unwashed masses" are regarded as "subhumans." Responsibility for their condition is shifted, via the ideology of individualism, to the self. They are blamed for their plight. Blaming the victim is a common rationale for maintaining the modern order. But a fallacy arises here. While the rich and powerful like to take responsibility for their own good fortune, at the same time they like to consider the poor as inherently deficient ("bad seed"). But, according to the ideology of genetic superiority, the rich cannot claim responsibility for their good fortune because they acknowledge that they had no control over the selection of their own genes. And yet they blame the poor for somehow being responsible for their "deficient" genetic makeup.

Thus is born the decontextualized bootstrap theory of innate power/privilege. "They" are subhuman because "they" are subhuman, and because they are subhuman they will never change. This is the tautological reasoning of genetic determinism. Those who know how to, or have the characteristics that enable them to pull themselves up by their own bootstraps, are already "up." By dint of their innate superiority, they have bootstraps (the ability to rise by themselves). They have "grit," "character," "drive," "aggression," "appetite," "shrewd instincts," and so forth. But the superior are always already superior, so the bootstraps are never used, and those who need the bootstraps (the innate drive, grit, talent, intelligence) do not have them. Bootstrapping is an innate quality. Some have what it takes and others do not. Yet those who are at the bottom of the system are continually told: (A) you are down there because of innate inadequacy, you have no bootstraps, and (B) I, the superior one, will only hurt (spoil) you if I help you, so use your bootstraps (which I just told you that you do not have). In order to justify and engineer such a "new" social order based on the individual, the scientific discourse of genetics continues to be used. The Enlightenment scientists rationalized that "subhumans" were genetically inferior, and behaviorally irrational (of course, according to the criteria they devised). They created intelligence/power in their own image (see Chapter 3). How convenient. And through the discourse of science and law, what they have created by legal-rational and operational definition appears "natural," and as such, beyond question.

The idea of human "pollution," based on occupational behavior, is a vicious circle, but apparently not pure or vicious enough. In feudal Japan, *buraku* identity was tightly defined, as only *buraku* dealt with corpses and they did so because they were *buraku*. But this identity was still escapable, still loose, for it existed only at the level of *de facto* identity. However, by the end of the seventeenth century, Japan was centralized and stabilized as a national system. In the process of clarifying and legalizing life (tightening up identities and definitions) the *de facto* identity of the *buraku* became *de jure*. *Buraku* characteristics became legally defined (rationalized) *as inherent*. Thus, the plus-mutational veneer of mental-rationality was laid over the magic of blood-based identity. To stray from one's ghetto or occupation became punishable by law. The power of state organization was brought to bare on the enforcement of identity. What had been custom was reinforced by state power.

As the Tokugawa authority authored the new reality (the new order) and daily life was organized, discrimination against the *buraku* people became formalized, instituted as an integral part of the new social hierarchy. As such, their condition became fixated, condemning generation after generation of *buraku* to the bottom of social space. Japanese modernity, like Western modernity, relegated entire groups to occupying niches in a naturalized structure. The Tokugawa government achieved this by creating a "new" myth that the *buraku* people were *genetic* (no longer spiritual) pollution. Since modernization was threatening the old rationale, a new, more powerful one was established. So it is that years later, Japanese fascists and Nazis would be soul mates.

This myth created an atmosphere of strong, newly corroborated and legitimized (via Western objective method) discrimination which added to "Japanese" people's previously dominant magic notion of protecting the purity of their blood lines and mythic hatred of *buraku* as "traditionally" evil. The Tokugawa government outlawed intermarriages between *buraku* and non-*buraku* people. Even *buraku* people tended to believe the new bureaucratic (systematic) discourse about themselves and others. Bureaucracy is "objective," because once established, it is "disinterested." It is automated, running unconsciously. Faced with such organizational might, the *buraku* people internalized this legitimation and "regarded themselves as impure, not quite human, not deserving equal treatment" (Neary, 1989: 26). The perspectival intent of manipulation was apparent in the dualistic and legal-rational structure of oppression at the end of the Edo system.

It was only when the imperial system was ruptured from the outside (by its defeat in the Second World War) that new rules, definitions, language games, were privileged. The consequence has been that the *buraku* have since been able to leave their traditional (not innate) occupations and ghettos. And because they look just like "other Japanese," they are practically undetectable. Nevertheless, to this day this disturbs many "Japanese," fearful that *buraku* blood will find its way into their families. The same sort of prejudice exists in the United States, especially concerning interracial marriage, and in Europe with regard to gypsies.

Ainu as Indigenous "Japanese"

In the middle of the Civil War period in Japan, the dualistic structure of oppressor and oppressed was exported to Hokkaido, the most northerly of Japan's four main islands. Suppression of the Ainu people[5] extends back to the middle of the fifteenth century when the Matsumae clan moved to Hokkaido after being defeated by a rival clan elsewhere. The leader of the Matsumae clan became the ruler of Hokkaido. Prior to this, none of Japan's ruling class had settled in Hokkaido, although some "historical" stories (e.g., *Kojiki, Nihonshoki*, etc.) reported that Japanese troops conquered the Ainu people in ancient times. Even though prewar "Japanese" history textbooks included such stories, there is no evidence to support them (Sarashina, 1970). These textbooks were made for the purpose of glorifying Japan as the emperor's family (Sarashina, 1970).

The history of the Ainu is somewhat similar to that of Native Americans. At first, the Ainu resisted the new ruler. Some Ainu oral stories, and the Matsumae clan's documents, recall and record several severe battles between the Ainu people and the invaders. After loosing several battles, the Ainu people were enslaved.

The Tokugawa government did not show much interest in Hokkaido until the end of the seventeenth century, when it began to govern Hokkaido directly in 1799. In terms of productivity, Hokkaido was not an attractive land to the Tokugawa government. However, Russian battleships appeared in the coastal waters of Hokkaido, motivating the Tokugawa government to establish a strong sovereign presence there in 1800. Since direct rule of the Ainu people by the Tokugawa administration, the Ainu people have been forced to live like "Japanese." They were forced to engage in farming. The sudden shift from hunting to agricultural culture, however, threatened their ability to survive.

Besides this, the Ainu people were subjected to various kinds of oppression, such as being cheated, being forced to engage in hard labor, and so forth (Kayano, 1994; Sarashina, 1970). As a result, the number of the Ainu dropped dramatically in the early 1800s (Sarashina, 1970: 116–117). The attempt to force the Ainu to adapt to Japanese ways nearly exterminated them, not only in terms of their cultural identity, but physically. Adaptation is either demanded by environmental forces or cultural domination, and the difference between ethnic and "physical" difference is erased. To exterminate one means to exterminate the other.

CONTROL OF "OTHERS" IN THE MODERN PERIOD

After the Meiji Restoration in 1868, the Ainu and *buraku* people were legally considered *heimin*, or commoners. Under the new imperial system of Meiji, all "Japanese" people became the emperor's children. Theoretically, the statuses of *eta* and *hinin* were abandoned and the Ainu people became "Japanese citizens." However, discrimination against such people did not disappear. For instance, *buraku* people were called *shin-heimin* (new commoner) or some other terms, which were used to segregate and ridicule them (Kuboi, 1993: 12; Nadamoto, 1991: 100–110). The wording of the Ainu "protection law" (established in 1899) itself expresses discrimination against the Ainu ("Hachiju Yonin Ga," 1995). The law is called *kyu dojin hogo ho* (Indigenous Persons Protection Act). *Dojin* (indigenous persons) implies savage, uncivilized, and connotes inferiority. Furthermore, this law was established without any consultation with the Ainu (Kayano, 1994: 30). The law was enacted in 1995.

In the process of forming a "strong" nation, minority groups were forced to lead "less-than-human" lives. In order to compete with Western nations, Japan used these minority groups as labor to "westernize" and capitalize Japan. The Ainu people were forced to engage in agriculture so that arable land in Hokkaido could expand. The new capitalistic system made "minor" and "poor" people unable to escape from oppressive conditions. Imperial Japan ignored minority groups, legally confining them to the status of "minority." This legal status supposedly gave the Ainu "nominal emancipation." After "emancipating" them, the authorities denied their existence.

Koreans in Japan

Through the process of imperial expansion, Japan created another minority group, Koreans in Japan. By the end of the nineteenth century, Western countries competed with each other for domination in Asia. As an emerging nation (economically and militarily), Japan wanted to become one of the world's "great powers." In order to fulfill its wish, Japan annexed Korea in 1910. Because of Japan's success in the Sino-Japanese war (1894–1895) and the Russo-Japanese war (1904–1905), Japan succeeded in establishing its sovereignty over Korea without experiencing much resistance. The imposition of a colonial economy destroyed the traditional Korean agricultural life. Weiner (1994: 43) writes: "With the introduction of new market relations and the incorporation of Korean agriculture within the wider economic system of the Japanese empire, the subsistence agriculturalist came under intense pressure.'' When a large-scale land survey was conducted, many illiterate farmers lost their land. Also, many farmers increased their debts because of their inability to cope with the new monetary system. In order to survive, many Koreans moved to Japan and engaged in low-wage industrial labor. From 1928 to 1936, Koreans working in manual labor in Japan increased steadily from 171,031 to 289,727 (Pak, 1957: 13; Weiner, 1994: 128). During the same period the number of unemployed Koreans in Japan increased from 43,901 in 1928, to 241,369 in 1936, and Koreans in prison also increased from 323 to 2,341 (Pak, 1957: 13; Weiner, 1994: 128). Virtually no Korean held a salaried, let alone professional position.

Originally, most Korean immigrants did not speak Japanese; thus, they were at a great disadvantage and were easily exploited. They were inevitably forced to take jobs that Japanese did not want. They also received lower wages and sometimes even no payment (especially those who were brought to Japan to alleviate the labor shortage under the war regime) (Michell, 1981: 115; Nakatsuka, 1991: 107).

Koreans in Japan have also been used as scapegoats. Government annual reports from 1933 to 1942 describe Koreans as an inferior ethnic group (Michell, 1981: 113). The 1933 report, for example, states that most Koreans coming to Japan had no skills, were illiterate in both Japanese and Korean, were vulgar and emotional, and liked arguing and fighting (Michell, 1981: 113). The report concluded that the increased crime rate had been a result of an increase in Korean immigration (Michell, 1981: 113). The 1933 annual report reveals that the Japanese government had intended to place Koreans in a lower position than Japanese, and to use them as scapegoats to alleviate complaints from poor Japanese citizens. In those days, the lives of most Japanese people were not easy. They, too, were severely exploited in order to make a ''strong'' nation. The government needed a scapegoat in order to stabilize the country. In Japan, stability has meant harmony. Harmony exists when everyone stays in his place within the system. Harmony has been the key to national strength. Neither stability nor harmony necessarily has anything to do with justice.

From the beginning of the annexation of Korea, the Japanese government initiated the policy of *doka seisaku* (assimilation). It was apparent that the Japanese government wanted to control Koreans by denying their traditional culture and attempting to eliminate their Korean identity by imposing upon them a new, but also less than, ''Japanese'' identity. Ueda (1995: 196–197) called Japan's colonization policy ''the spiritual genocide of their ethnicity.'' Although Koreans were forced to be Japanese-like, they could never be the same. They were legally distinct from Japanese. They were registered in Korea, even if they lived in Japan. It was illegal for them to transfer their registration (*koseki*) to Japan. They did not have the right to vote. In short, they did not have full citizenship in either Korea or Japan. The Japanese government justified this situation under the policy of assimilation by promulgating the idea that Koreans constituted an inferior ethnic group (Iguchi, 1991: 74). Weiner (1994: 211) called this policy of assimilation a manifestation of "Social-Darwinist assumptions of empire and colonial expansion." Equilibrium, or status quo, was maintained through the feedback mechanisms of bureaucratic surveillance.

The policy of assimilation was strengthened during World War II. At that time, a series of policies called *naisen ittai* (Unity of Japanese and Koreans) was implemented to facilitate control of Koreans. The Japanese government had to make Koreans the children of the emperor (*kominka seisaku*) in order to fight against the Allied Forces. They were forced to have Japanese names, visit shrines and pay respect to the emperor, bow to the emperor's residence, and so forth. But they remained the stepchildren of the Japanese family.

Under the slogans of *daitoa kyoeiken* (co-prosperity of East Asia) and *hokko ichiu* (unity of the whole world), Japan invaded other Asian countries. Perspectival mentality was manifested in slogans that justified the military expansion and colonial conquests of the era. These slogans were effective in uniting the "Japanese" people and deluding them into trying to make the world a single family under the emperor. The mythic awareness of *wa* was thus used for this perspectival purpose, which is consistent with the notion of *wa* used in postwar Japan.

UNIQUE RESPONSIBILITY: "*WA*-ISM"

Since World War II, the prevalent notion that Japan is a "unique" country has blurred Japan's sense of responsibility for the war (Yamaguchi, 1994). The uniqueness of Japan is often associated with the concept of *wa*, or harmony. World order (unification) was equated with "harmony." One of the definitions of *wa* is "Japan." Harmonious unity came to be seen as a cultural response to Western duality (Kato, 1990). Kato (1990) has proposed "*wa*-ism" as an alternative modernism to the Western ideology of dualism. Many of Japan's leading scholars, including Umehara (1990), Saeki, Hirakawa, and Miyata (1990), present a similar perspective as Kato (see Yuasa, 1993). Kato (1990) argues that "*wa*-ism" (the Japanese ideology of harmony) is superior to Western culture. But, as pointed out, this form of harmony presumes disharmony, which, ironically, must be suppressed. The cause of harmony justifies the other, and at the same time, justifies seeing difference as dangerous.

"*Wa*-ism" is not new. Furthermore, it, too, is dualistic. The idea that Japan should unite the rest of the world, to make it over in its own image, coincides with the slogan, *hakkoichiu* or the principle of co-prosperity. *Wa*, or harmony, is (in this sense) a manifestation of deficient mythic consciousness. It presents a duality between Japan and everyone else. And like most ideological proclamations, the home culture, religion, metaphysic, science, whatever, is almost always privileged as the best, if not only, true and good version of Reality. The promotion of *hakkoichiu* is similar to the ideologies of Afro-centrism and pan-Africanism promoted by many Westernized black nationalists (usually left Hegelians). The perspectival intent to conquer and assimilate others is obvious. It is a rationale for the oppression of the weak by the strong.

After World War II (theoretically), Japan was no longer a single family under the divine emperor. Japan mutated from a predominantly mythic to a more perspectival country (Ikeda, 1992). This mutation from a feudal world to a modern world is striking. According to Taylor (1983), even though Japan proudly claims the world's longest unbroken line of hereditary monarchs, very little privilege is now inherited. Taylor (1983: 44) notes, "This transformation in a little more than 100 years from a society of strictly hereditary privilege to one where class differences now hardly exist is an astonishing achievement." However, most hereditary monarchies around the globe have been toppled in a matter of days. Taylor continues, "It would be tempting, therefore, to say that *all* ''Japanese'' are now born equal. They are not. Hierarchy begins at birth in the sense that age and sex are important determinants of rank within the family."

Confucianism is deeply sedimented in Japan. But more than this, the residue of mythic consciousness is also still alive (Ikeda, 1992). Mutation of consciousness is not ''minus,'' but ''plus''—it is an incremental expansion of consciousness (Gebser, 1985; see Chapter 2). The concept of *wa* is an example of how a fundamental prejudice can mutate and be manifested in a variety of discursive formations. Mythic group consciousness is still dominant in modern Japan. In order to maintain the privileged (dominant) culture within Japan (harmony), the distinction between inside and outside functions to discriminate against Koreans, foreigners, Ainu, Okinawa people, the handicapped, and so on.

After the war, Koreans in Japan expected that they would be treated as an emancipated ethnic group and as a member of the Allied Forces (Michell, 1981: 130). In the early days of the occupation, however, the Supreme Commander of the Allied Powers (SCAP) did not establish a policy regarding Koreans in Japan. While the Japanese government cautiously avoided expressing its policy on this matter, the ''Japanese'' people renewed their condemnation of Koreans in Japan for supposedly increasing the crime rate, spreading epidemic disease, and so on. (Michell, 1981: 131). Koreans, according to Michell, remained a favorite scapegoat. SCAP also helped to suppress Koreans so that it could carry out its operations smoothly, and reestablish social order in Japan (Michell, 1981: 133).

During the Allied occupation, SCAP admitted that Koreans in Japan held Japanese nationality. But at the same time, they enacted the Alien Registration Law, and proclaimed Koreans in Japan to be aliens. After the San Francisco Peace Treaty was concluded in 1952, Koreans in Japan were deprived of their Japanese nationality. They were, therefore, excluded from any compensation for war damages which ''Japanese'' received. Furthermore, even though a number of Koreans were born in Japan and spoke fluent Japanese, they were treated as foreigners, and to this day, they do not have basic citizen rights such as the vote. The freedom to choose their occupation is limited. They are excluded from most governmental and official jobs (including teaching in public schools). It is extremely difficult for them to work at prestigious corporations. According to a survey conducted by *Osaka Zainichi Chosenjin no Jinken o Mamorukai* in 1984, 173 out of 251 companies refused to answer the question inquiring as to the number of Koreans they employ (Pak, 1991: 216). The researchers concluded that most of the companies that did not respond are first-rate ones, and that it could be assumed that these companies have a policy of not recruiting Koreans (Pak, 1991: 216).

Discriminatory treatment of Korean people in Japan is mirrored by the treatment of foreign workers, whose numbers increased sharply during the latter half of the 1980s. Since many foreign workers are illegal, they work at very low wages and without any protection. They are widely discriminated against. For example, they have had difficulty securing accommodations because landlords hesitate to rent to foreigners. Also, some political rhetoric is quite discriminatory against foreigners. For instance, the mayor of Kawasaki joked that dark-skinned Asian immigrant workers pose a danger because they are "difficult to see at night" (Oblas, 1995). Concerning the problem of foreign prostitutes in Tokyo, the justice minister equated prostitutes with black Americans and alleged that they both destroy good neighborhoods (Oblas, 1995). Foreigners are "others" or "outsiders" in Japan. "Others," including the *buraku* people, the Ainu, and Koreans in Japan are not widely appreciated in Japan. However, an indication of integral consciousness has emerged through the process of demythologizing the faith in pure-blood identity in Japan.

DEMYTHOLOGIZING BLOOD

At the end of World War II, Japan's unconditional surrender changed the identity of the "Japanese" (Ikeda, 1992). One of the conditions of the surrender was the requirement that the emperor renounce his "divinity." Until the end of the war, the emperor was a god who blended "in his person its [Japan's] power and its mercy" (Nitobe, 1905). At a fundamentally magic level, the emperor, Japan, and *wa* were identical. All *true* "Japanese" were the children of the emperor. They identified themselves only in relation to the emperor. After the war the emperor was no longer a god/father-of-the-country. Japan lost the foundation of its mythical and magical unity. "Japanese" began to abandon their faith in blood. At the same time, the perspectival awareness of individual ego has emerged. But perhaps Ainu and Koreans in Japan have not.

Resistance by minority groups against oppressive authority has become much stronger than it had been before the war. Everywhere, the call for individual rights has dramatically increased. In the latter half of the 1960s, many "Japanese" began to be more sympathetic toward Koreans in Japan, the *buraku* people, the Ainu, and others. This new awareness emerged along with a more liberal attitude toward the environment and social problems caused by rapid economic growth and industrialization. People began to realize that rapid capitalization and modernization were not without drawbacks. According to Yun (1987: 14–

15), around 1970, various citizens groups began to push anti-discrimination issues. In the 1970s, the number of publications about Korea increased dramatically. A "Korean boom" resulted (Yun, 1987: 15). Also, around the same time, many universities began to offer Korean language courses ("Chosen-go Towa," 1984). In the 1970s, Japan was pressured by international opinion into accepting "boat people," which led to legal reforms concerning the status of foreigners (Tanaka, 1995: 155–174). The immigration law enacted in 1982 guaranteed the status of "permanent resident" for Koreans in Japan, and helped to stabilize their situation. In 1992, the law admitted that Koreans in Japan were exempted from mandatory fingerprinting. However, other alien residents who stay in Japan for more than a year still have to have their fingerprints kept on file.

After 1982, Koreans were able to receive various welfare benefits including pensions. However, their situation is not exactly the same as that for "Japanese" (the *fukushi nenkin* or welfare pension, for example, is not applicable to Koreans in Japan). In the 1990s, an increasing number of people have begun to argue that Koreans should be given the right to vote, and that they should be able to participate in national athletic competitions.

The United Nations pronounced 1992 the "year of indigenous peoples." This helped advance human rights for the Ainu. *The Asahi Shimbun* reported on December 3, 1995, that more than 70 percent of the congressmen in the National Diet realized the necessity for a new law governing Ainu affairs (instead of the old "Indigenous Persons Protection Act").

Discrimination against *buraku* people was reduced as a result of the new legislation. However, *buraku* communities still suffer from higher crime and poverty rates than other communities (Kristof, 1995: A1, A8). In some opinion polls, almost two-thirds of *buraku* people answered that they have never experienced discrimination; about 73 percent currently marry non-*buraku* people; and most of them deny the possibility that the *Japanese* police might treat *buraku* people unfairly (Kristof, 1995: A1).

With increased numbers of foreign workers, general interest in foreigners has heightened.[6] For example, in the Gifu prefecture, the town of Nakatsugawa welcomed many "Japanese" *Brazilian* workers, and people in Nakatsugawa showed great interest in learning Portuguese (Personal communication, November 2, 1995). However, this may be because they see them as *really* "Japanese," by blood. Foreign workers from India and the Middle East are not so well received.

In the past, the Japanese educational system was notorious for being closed and exclusive. Although there is criticism that "Japanese" people only show sympathy, not empathy, and that their interaction with foreign workers is "one-way," they have begun to enjoy interacting with "something different," on an everyday basis. Since 1988, the Ministry of Education has been extending one-year contracts to non-licensed teachers, to teach in elementary, junior high, and high schools. These teachers include non-Japanese teaching English, French cooking, music, painting, and other subjects from a distinctly foreign perspective. Such teachers numbered over 2,000 in 1994 ("Menkyo nakutemo," 1995: 31). Universities and colleges are also gradually changing. They have begun to accept faculty who have obtained advanced degrees in foreign countries. The Japanese educational system is changing into a more flexible system (Yun, 1987: 41). Also, the number of intercultural marriages is steadily increasing, which shows a shift in attitude regarding race and ethnic purity. From 1965 to 1991, the number of Japanese men married to non-Japanese women increased from 1,067 to 19,096, and for Japanese women married to non-Japanese men it rose from 3,989 to 6,063.[7]

However, enthusiasm for what seemed to be progress in racial and ethnic tolerance during the 1970s and 1980s is tempered by the fact that according to Japan's Health and Welfare Ministry, the divorce rate among marriages between Japanese men and Chinese, Filipina, and Thai women rose sharply from 2,322 in 1992 to 2,843 in 1994—a 22 percent increase (Barr, 1996: 8). According to Mizuho Matsuda, director of a church- and city-sponsored shelter for Asian women in Tokyo called "HELP," many of the men involved in "foreign marriages" were looking for women who were willing to perform "traditional roles" and were presumed to be "more docile" than Japanese women, "who are becoming very strong," including becoming more economically independent (quoted by Barr, 1996: 8; also see *The Outnation: A Search for the Soul of Japan* by Jonathan Rauch, 1992; and *Pink Samurai: Love, Marriage and Sex in Contemporary Japan* by N. Bornoff, 1991). By 1990, roughly 25,000 Japanese were marrying foreigners every year, with Japanese men outnumbering women 3 to 1 (Barr, 1996: 8).

Since the "foreign-marriage boom" of the late 1980s, women's shelters throughout Japan are having their resources strained by an increasing number of "foreign" wives seeking to escape abusive husbands. Their plight is exacerbated by the fact that very few foreign residents are ever granted citizenship, including ones married to Japanese. Consequently, for foreign wives, no matter how long they may have called Japan "home," divorce means the loss of a sponsor so that visas are not extended or renewed. Even if the offspring of such marriages are citizens, the mothers almost never are. Thus, they have little access to governmental benefits. Women in this situation find themselves confronting not only a broken marriage but the state as well. Misao Hanazaki, founder of the Friendship Asia House Cosmos, a "safe house" for women in the suburbs of Tokyo, claims that many of the foreign wives suffer from racial and ethnic bigotry even from their husbands. According to Hanazaki, "The most important thing is to remove Japanese people's prejudice against Asian women" (quoted by Barr, 1996: 8).

Despite this disturbing trend in divorces, "Japanese" society has become more open toward integrating "non-Japanese blood" than it was just fifty years ago. There is a postwar trend of demythologizing blood as the foundation of an innate and immutable identity. Japan is slowly acknowledging that it has always been multicultural.

Interest in Asian countries has also been increasing in the 1990s. Asian films and other arts are enjoying greater global exposure than ever before. Fifty years after World War II, Japanese officials are publicly admitting at least partial responsibility for that conflagration, while new relationships with other Asian countries are being explored. For instance, Ritsumeikan University will open a new branch in Kyushu in 1998. The university announced that it would accept many students from other Asian countries.

In the Kobe earthquake, *The Mainichi Shimbun* reported the heartwarming conduct of Koreans in Japan: a Korean school provided both ''Koreans'' and ''Japanese'' with shelter and food (Sorano, 1995: 136). Although there were some rumors that slandered Koreans, they did not spread widely (Sorano, 1995: 136; Ueda, 1995: 119–120). In the Kanto earthquake, which occurred in 1923, there were rumors that Koreans had poisoned wells, looted, started riots, and so on. The result was that Japanese attacked them. It was estimated that 6,400 Koreans were killed (Ueda, 1995: 119). Compared with such a situation, the Kobe earthquake revealed a major shift of attitudes toward Koreans in Japan. Today, most Koreans in Japan are second and third generation Japanese-born Koreans. Most do not speak Korean. They are said to be confused about their identity. Under such circumstances, an increasing number of them have come out to reveal their Korean identity, by publicly using their Korean names. Koreans in Japan usually have both Korean and Japanese names. In the past, most of them used Japanese names in everyday public life in order to avoid discriminatory treatment. Many younger Koreans, however, are now willing to declare their ethnic heritage.

HARMONY AS APPRECIATING DIFFERENCES

Harmony is also a musical concept. Chords are made up of different complementary notes. The whole sound is constituted by simultaneous differences, or, put differently, by systatic relationship. In other words, different modes of relationships constitute the integral world. Difference is recognized and appreciated only through the relationship of one to the other. Each comes into being only through difference, and difference renders uniqueness and meaning. Systatic relationships include both process and effect, and all modes of time and statements co-exist. Put differently, they are integrating in systatic awareness (see Chapter 1). However, systatic awareness does not give us only joy. It gives us pain as well. ''Awaring'' differences are to understand or appreciate the co-existence of joy and pain, just like the joy and pain that Koreans experience when they ''come out,'' or the joy and pain we (you and I) experience when we are ''concretizing'' harmony.

NOTES

1. Some scholars disagree that Prince Shotoku's Seventeen Articles should be translated as a ''constitution,'' because it does not include any penal code (Sidney Brown,

Personal Communication on December 28, 1995; Umehara, 1981). They consider this to be a moral book.

2. We thank Dr. Yuasa, who suggested that we should examine Prince Shotoku's Constitution for the analysis of *wa*.

3. For instance, the "homeless," in the latter part of the twentieth century in the United States, are practically invisible. When floods ravaged the northwestern part of the country in 1996, the government paid thousands of property owners to rebuild their homes (even in known flood plains). But the homeless who lived along the banks of the rivers were hardly noticed. They received nothing.

4. The term *eta* came to be used toward the end of the Kamakura period (1192–1333) (Aomori, 1994; Suginohara, 1982). It was "an appellation for those people who made a living by slaughtering oxen and horses and skinning them, and therefore lived on river beaches and received discriminative treatment" (Suginohara, 1982: 131).

5. The current number of Ainu is estimated to be 50,000 (Burger, 1995; Kayano, 1994: 29).

6. After the 1970s, new emerging fields of social science (international politics, comparative politics, international studies, etc.) began conducting research on identity, multiethnicity, minorities, and so on, and to explore the way different ethnic groups live together (Yun, 1987: 35).

7. The source for these statistics is the Japanese Ministry of Health and Welfare, which has offered such data every year since 1965.

REFERENCES

Aomori, T. (1994) "Chusei" [The Middle Ages]. In *Buraku no Rekishi*, edited by B. K. Kenkyujo. Osaka: Kaiho Shuppansha, pp. 25–75.

Aston, W. G. (1956) *Nihongi: Chronicles of Japan from the Earliest Times to A.D. 697.* London: Allen & Unwin.

Barr, C. W. (1996) "Failed Foreign Marriages in Japan: Boom or Bust?" *The Christian Science Monitor*, March 14, pp. 1, 8.

Bornoff, N. (1991) *Pink Samurai: Love, Marriage and Sex in Contemporary Japan.* New York: Simon & Schuster.

Burger, J. (1995) *Zusetsu Sekai no Senjumin* [The Gaia Atlas of First Peoples: A Future of the Indigenous World]. Tokyo: Akashi Shoten.

Campbell, J., and B. Moyers. (1988) *The Power of Myth.* New York: Doubleday.

"Chosen-go Towa Donna Kotobaka" [What Kind of Language Is Korean?]. (1984) *Kikan Sanzenri* (May): 38.

Chuang Tzu. (1974) *Inner Chapters.* New York: Vintage.

Dower, J. (1986) *War without Mercy.* New York: Pantheon.

Ellison, R. (1952) *Invisible Man.* New York: Random House.

Gadamer, H-G. (1975) *Truth and Method.* New York: Seabury Press.

Gebser, J. (1985) *The Ever-Present Origin.* Athens: Ohio University Press.

"Hachiju Yonin Ga 'Shinpo Hitsuyo' " [84 Diet Members Agreed that "A New Law Is Necessary"]. (1995) *The Asahi Shimbun*, December 3, p. 34.

Iguchi, K. (1991) "Kindai Nihon Ni Okeru Chosenkan No Kozo" [Structure of Images of Koreans in Modern Japan]. In *Zainichi chosenjin—Rekishi To Genjo*, edited by T. Yamada and C. Pak. Tokyo: Akashi Shoten, pp. 63–84.

Ikeda, R. (1992) *Ie to kazoku: A Shift in the Communication Pattern of the Japanese Family*. Master's thesis, University of Oklahoma.

Inoue, M. (1993) "Kodai" [The Ancient Period]. In *Buraku no Rekishi*, edited by Buraku Kaiho Kenkyujo. Osaka: Kaiho Shuppansha, pp. 1–24.

Johnson, L., Jr. (1993) "Race and Enlightenment: Situating the Concept of Race." Paper presented at the Seventy-ninth Annual Meeting of the Speech Communication Association, Miami Beach, Florida (November).

Kato, E. (1990) "Wa-ism no Teisho" [Proposal of *Wa*-ism]. *Chuo Koron* (November): 80–85.

Kayano, S. (1994) "The Current Situation of the Ainu in Japan." In *Gathering in Ainumoshir, the Land of the Ainu: Messages from Indigenous Peoples in the World*, edited by Nibutani Forum Organizing Committee. Tokyo: Eikoh Educational and Cultural Institute, pp. 15–35.

Kramer, E. (1992) "Consciousness and Culture." In *Consciousness and Culture: An Introduction to the Thought of Jean Gebser*, edited by E. Kramer. Westport, CT: Greenwood Press, pp. 1–60.

Kristof, N. D. (1995) "Japanese Outcasts Better Off than in Past But Still Outcast." *New York Times*, November 30, pp. A1, A8.

Kuboi, N. (1993) *Kindai no Sabetsu To Nihon Minshu no Rekishi* [Discrimination and Japanese People's History in the Modern Era]. Tokyo: Akashi Shoten.

Matsushita, S. (1985) *Kyushu Hisabetsu-burakushi Kenkyu* [Research on the Oppressed Buraku People in Kyushu]. Tokyo: Akashi Shoten.

McLuhan, M. (1962) *The Gutenburg Galaxy*. Toronto: University of Toronto Press.

McLuhan, M., and Q. Fiore. (1967) *The Medium Is the Message: An Inventory of Effects*. New York: Bantam.

"Menkyo Nakutemo Kyodan De Kirari" [Without Licence, Brilliant in Classroom]. (1995) *The Asahi Shimbun*, November 31.

Michell, H. R. (1981) *Zainichi Chosenjin no Rekishi* [The Korean Minority in Japan]. Tokyo: Sairyusha.

Miyata, N. (1990) "Tashinkyo Bunka no Jidai" [The Era of Polytheistic Culture]. *Shokun* (December).

Nadamoto, M. (1991) "Sabetsugo To Ikani Mukiauka [How One Should Face Discriminated Terms]. In *Buraku no Kako Genzai Soshite*, edited by K. Henshubu. Kyoto: Kyoto Burakushi Kenkyujo, pp. 100–137.

Nakatsuka, A. (1991) "Zainichi Chosenjin no Rekishiteki Keisei" [Koreans in Japan Created in History]. In *Zainichi chosenjin—Rekishi To Genjo*, edited by T. Yamada and C. Pak. Tokyo: Akashi Shoten, pp. 85–115.

Neary, I. (1989) *Political Protest and Social Control in Pre-war Japan: The Origins of Buraku Liberation*. Atlantic Highlands, NJ: Humanities Press International.

Nitobe, I. (1905) *Bushido: The Soul of Japan*, 10th ed. New York: G. P. Putnam's Sons.

Oblas, P. B. (1995) *Perspectives on Race and Culture in Japanese Society: The Mass Media and Ethnicity*. Lewiston, NY: The Edwin Mellen Press.

Pak, C. (1991) "Zainichi Chosenjen no Shakai Keizai Seikatsu" [The Social and Economic Life of Koreans in Japan]. Edited by T. Yamada and C. Pak. Tokyo: Akashi Shoten, pp. 209–243.

Pak, K. S. (1957) "Nihon Teikokushugi Ka ni okeru Zainichi Chosenjin Undo" [The Korean People's Movement in Japan under the Rule of Japanese Imperialism], part 1. *Chosen Geppo* 2, no. 4: 6–36.

Rauch, J. (1992) *The Outnation: A Search for the Soul of Japan*. Boston: Backbay Books.

Saeki, S., S. Hirakawa, and N. Miyata. (1990) ''Tashinkyo Bunka no Jidai'' [The Time of Polytheism]. *The Shokun* (February): 54–65.

Sarashina, G. (1970) *Ainu To Nihonjin* [Ainu and Japanese]. Tokyo: Nippon Hoso Shuppan Kyokai.

Sorano, Y. (1995) ''Hanshin Daishinsai To Zainichi Chosenjin no Jinken'' [The Kobe Earthquake and Human Rights of Koreans in Japan]. In *Zainichi Chosenjin no Seikatsu To Jinken*, edited by Y. Sorano and C. Y. Ko. Tokyo: Akashi Shoten, pp. 135–139.

Suginohara, J. (1982) *The Status Discrimination in Japan—Introduction to Buraku Problem*. Kobe: The Hyogo Institute of Buraku Problem.

Tanaka, H. (1995) *Zainichi GaikOkujin* [Foreigners in Japan]. Tokyo: Iwanami Shoten.

Taniguchi, S. (1985) ''Buraku Sabetsu To Shoukyo To Jinken'' [Buraku Discrimination, Religion, and Human Rights]. In *Koza Sabetsu To Jinken* (vol. 2), edited by E. Isomura, Y. Ichibangase, and T. Harada. Tokyo: Yuzankaku Shuppan, pp. 223–257.

Taylor, J. (1983) *Shadows of the Rising Sun: A Critical View of the "Japanese Miracle."* New York: Quill.

Teraki, N. (1984) ''Hisabetsu-buraku no Rekishi'' [History of the Oppressed *Buraku* People]. In *Koza sabetsu To Jinken* (vol. 1), edited by E. Isomura, Y. Ichibangase, and T. Harada. Tokyo: Yuzankaku Shuppan, pp. 15–59.

———. (1993) ''Kindai'' [The Early Modern Period]. In *Buraku no Rekishi*, edited by B. K. Kenkyujo. Osaka: Kaiho Shuppansha, pp. 171–265.

Ueda, T. (1995) *Zainichi Kankokujin no Sokojikara* [Power of Koreans in Japan]. Tokyo: Nisshin Hodo.

Umehara, T. (1981) *Shotoku Taishi II, Kenpo 17jo* [Prince Shotoku, the Constitution of 17 articles]. Tokyo: Shogakukan.

———. (1990) ''Isshinkyo Kara Tashinkyo e [From Monotheism to Polytheism]. *Chuo Koron* (February): 84–90.

Weiner, M. (1994) *Race and Migration in Imperial Japan*. London: Routledge.

Yamaguchi, Y. (1994) ''Futatsu no Gendaishi'' [Two Modern Histories]. In *Senso Sekinin, Sengo Sekinin*. Tokyo: Asahi Shimbunsha, pp. 221–265.

Yuasa, S. (1993) *Nippon Wa Naze Koritsusurunoka* [Why Is Japan Isolated from the Rest of the World?]. Tokyo: Taiyo Shuppan.

Yun, K. (1987) *Ishitsu Tono Kyozon* [Co-existence with Differences]. Tokyo: Iwanami Shoten.

7

Community Control, Base Communities, and Democracy

Woo Sik Chung and John T. Pardeck

Democracy has become a very prevalent topic in both socialist and capitalist countries. Participation in the democratic process is thought to result in greater equality in both the political and economic life of citizens. In many societies, rightly or wrongly, a host of social problems are assumed to abate because of democratization.

Why is democracy so greatly valued? Most social theorists would suggest democracy is highly valued because it allows new ideas to proliferate, peoples' abilities to expand, and the maximum feasible participation of all citizens. To use the imagery supplied by John Locke, the most effective proposals will emerge from the marketplace of ideas. The assumption is that in the absence of any *a priori* restriction on creativity, the full productive capacity of a society is unleashed (Murphy, Pardeck, and Chung, 1992).

Unfortunately, none of this will occur by merely outlawing structural barriers to political involvement and participation. However, it is suggested that removing barriers to political participation is an important step, but not enough. For in final analysis, what is important is the kind of input that can be introduced. All the structural openness in the world will prove to be irrelevant, if certain topics are censored and certain citizens are not allowed to participate in the democratic process, especially oppressed minorities.

The point is that most discussions of democracy have been inadequate. Usually, this form of government is equated with the existence of a market economy and parliamentary procedures. Voting and free enterprise are considered to be the cornerstone of democracy. But these issues are merely structural considerations (Murphy, Pardeck, and Chung, 1992).

A number of critics have argued that this focus is insufficient to insure that democracy will work (Murphy, Pardeck, and Chung, 1992). Feyerabend (1978)

captured the thrust of their argument when he noted that openness is very different from allowing all persons to participate in the political system in a particular way. Everyone may be permitted to vote, including oppressed minorities;
however, the options that are available to all may be unduly truncated. In short,
true democracy is far more than the adoption of a few political practices. Mannheim (1971) recognized this issue when he distinguished between political democracy and the democratization of culture. Mannheim's work may prove
helpful in providing insight into why all must be active participants in democracy in order for this kind of political system to thrive.

Mannheim (1971) viewed democracy as a political system that should not
only be limited to removing structural barriers to voting, encouraging economic
self-sufficiency, or obtaining office. In fact, none of these aims may insure that
the government receives direction from its citizens. If the purpose of democracy
is to foster the self-governance of citizens, attention should be given to more
essential factors. Most important is the spirit (*Geist*) of the population. In essence, the spirit of a society must be democratized so that all citizens can participate in a meaningful fashion. This is what Mannheim (1971) had in mind
when he centered on the democratization of culture in his work.

DEMOCRATIZATION OF CULTURE

Culture is often viewed as an autonomous entity. This abstraction results in
culture being treated as the last defense against barbarism. As suggested by
Freud (1948), culture must be able to exert the necessary force to constrain
human passion. Culture, in essence, is transformed into an object that can with-
stand most threats and assaults (Murphy, Pardeck, and Chung, 1992).

This reification of culture obscures the true essence of culture. Culture,
through the reification process, is seen as a system that can be easily rearranged.
Enhancing democracy through various structural changes thus makes sense.
Overlooked by this view of culture, however, is an important issue. Raymond
Williams (1989) concluded that such a view of culture means the ''informing
spirit'' of culture is dismissed as unimportant.

Williams (1989) argued that culture does not consist solely of visible artifacts,
such as art objects, dwellings, or institutions; these activities are a product of a
much more profound dimension. This perspective supplies the justification for
the more obtrusive features of culture. Weber (1958) referred to this subtle
source of legitimacy as a ''comos.'' Weber concluded that culture is underpinned by various assumptions about reality. These presuppositions, moreover,
reflect particular values and beliefs (Murphy, Pardeck, and Chung, 1992).

Jean Gebser (1985) illustrated how this underlying realm supplies a proper
context for understanding culture. He argued that empirical entities do not have
inherent meaning. In essence, the physical features of an object gain their significance from the social milieu that is created through human action. Art work
begins to make sense, for example, once certain conceptions of space, time, and

individual identity are understood. These ideas are an outgrowth of the mind and provide the spirit of a culture (Murphy, Pardeck, and Chung, 1992).

Often this underside of culture is overlooked. The reason for this omission is self-evident: Western philosophical tradition is manifestly dualistic (Murphy, 1989). Dualism means a distinction is made between subjectivity and objectivity. This distinction suggests that the most reliable source of information is based on objective criteria, while subjective information is not highly regarded as a source of reliable knowledge. This means that maintaining culture becomes a structural problem. Valid knowledge is divorced from the human element (Murphy, Pardeck, and Chung, 1992).

Through the objectification of culture, there is little wonder why the human side, or spirit, of democracy does not receive much focus. Clearly, this hidden facet of a democratic polity cannot be ignored for long without unfortunate consequences. Unless democracy is simply going to be the culmination of a *tour de force*, the assumptions of this style of political reality should be instituted, widely endorsed, and enforced. If such is not the case, democracy will become merely a shallow exercise of complying with structural mandates (Murphy, Pardeck, and Chung, 1992).

Democracy will rapidly wither without the enthusiastic support of all citizens. Within the United States over the past thirty years, legislation has been passed that removes traditional structural obstacles to political participation. Despite these changes, political participation is at an all-time low. Furthermore, persons report that their opinions are not actively sought and the political system is seldom responsive to their political expectations (*Citizens and Politics*, 1991). This chapter argues that these deficiencies will not be corrected unless the spirit of democracy is renewed. In essence, meaningful participation by all will have to occur before the spirit of democracy is promoted.

SUCCESSFUL DEMOCRACY

What is central to a successful democracy is not simply measuring voting statistics, the demographic traits of officeholders, or the frequency of election. Rather, more importantly, democracy means a political system must be receptive to new ideas and information, and allow meaningful participation by all citizens. In order to achieve this level of democratic participation, the following issues must be considered.

Knowledge

Traditional views of democracy appear to overly value scientific kinds of information; specifically, information that is grounded in objectivity. Typically, this kind of information is seen as data that promote fairness because science is seen as objective and value free. What this means is science is supposedly not affected by political motives.

Science is popularly seen as an approach that improves social life. Science would appear to hold high promise for promoting democracy; however, it may well be counterproductive to this political system. The rationale for this conclusion is quite evident: Particular sources of information are deemed more valuable than others. In effect, a hierarchy of knowledge is created.

This situation has tremendous implications. Gradually, select citizens may come to dominate the planning process because of their access to information and data that is believed to be more reliable and valid than other sources of information. Before long, a very narrow range of options is considered to be worthy of serious attention. In political terms, opinions that lack a scientific basis are treated as meaningless and pushed to the periphery of any discussion. Ordinary citizens may begin to sense that their views are not highly regarded. In essence, science emerges as an instrument that is counterproductive to democratic participation.

Science traditionally is highly regarded in Western societies. As noted earlier, science is seen as a strategy for analyzing data that is value free. According to Mannheim (1971), this perspective results in science becoming anathema to democracy. In order to diversify input and increase the number of new ideas, the status of science must be challenged within democratic societies. In other words, science should not be viewed as more objective or correct than other approaches used to understand and interpret the social world.

This realization is not necessarily a novel idea and has been endorsed by a number of social critics of science. Specifically, Thomas Kuhn (1970) suggests science should be viewed as value-based and not objective. Kuhn's (1970) work means that scientific data are not pristine, and thus objective, but reflect the subjective interpretation held by scientists. As postmodernists conclude, interpretation and reality are intertwined in science (Barthes, 1985). This notion challenges the dualism upon which science is based; in other words, science is simply another source of knowledge that is no more valid than other worldviews.

Science should be placed on equal status with other sources of knowledge. Making reference solely to scientific data in a political debate implies that science has greater value than other perspectives. Furthermore, adhering to a conflicting standard is not necessarily indicative of non-rationality, for elevating one value base over another is a matter of personal judgment and choice. Citizens using other worldviews are thus able to express their opinions, without the fear of having them seen as automatically uninformed.

Social Reality

Citizens are often told that they must work within the structures imposed by the system or order will be destroyed. Consequently, when citizens challenge prevailing political reality, it is seen as impractical. Pragmatic approaches to political issues are highly valued, whereas novel, risky, or innovative strategies are disregarded. Ideas that challenge conventional wisdom are brushed aside, in favor of more workable approaches. In the end, however, what is possible comes to be seen as synonymous with current social reality.

Democracy has no room for such realism because social arrangements are supposed to receive their legitimacy from citizens. Authority, law, and order, for example, should not be viewed as an outgrowth of some abstract, meta-physical principle; however, when such a view is endorsed, citizens are stifled by an imposed reality and rendered impotent. The human spirit is undermined, along with the ability to think critically, and the freedom to self-govern is lost. In essence, citizens are systematically inferiorized.

If realism is not challenged, totalitarianism rather than democracy may well be endorsed. Intolerance is demanded because differences of opinion are seen as contaminating social reality and, ultimately, the stability of society is at risk. Normalcy is thus seen as critical to a well-functioning polity.

Realism is incompatible with democracy. Consequently, realistic portrayals of acceptable ideas or behavior should be abandoned. What is especially critical to avoid is the reification of social reality. This is only possible if reality is seen as a social construction by citizens (Berger and Luckman, 1966).

For at least thirty years, theories have been advanced that stress the contingent nature of social reality (Morris, 1977). Nonetheless, the political importance of a socially constructed social order has not been examined in great detail. This analysis is critical to the creation and survival of democracy. Citizens in a de-mocracy must realize that social reality is merely a modality of interpretation that is accepted until further notice.

Social reality is simply a possibility that has become ingrained. Like other themes, a paramount social reality can be reconsidered and changed. This shift in theory means reality is a social construction that can be changed through new interpretations by citizens. Politically, this suggests citizens can define social reality as they see fit and, thus, control their own destinies.

Technocrats

Social life in advanced societies is thoroughly bureaucratized; this results in a highly developed division of labor dominated by technocrats. Under these conditions, specialization is highly regarded (Guba and Lincoln, 1982; Nam, 1986). The more rationalized a task becomes, the more efficient and productive the organization is believed to be (Boden, 1977). Extolling specialization in a democracy may well be problematic because the political process becomes dom-inated by technocrats.

This issue is critical as numerous societies become bureaucratized and tech-nocratic. Due to the emphasis placed on the mastery of technique, specializations have proliferated (Freedman, 1973). Technicians have become prominent in practically every aspect of social life. The government is no exception, for con-sultations, academics, and other specialists monopolize most political discus-sions (Macauley and Heubel, 1986). Since these individuals have honed their special talents, their input is considered to be crucial to making sound political decisions. Such experts are thought to be effective in processing information and detecting germane issues (Fitzsimmons, Schwab, and Sullivan, 1979). The result is that they often become key advisors to government officials (Murphy, Pardeck, and Chung, 1992).

Technocrats are antagonistic to democracy because most citizens are not viewed as capable of making informed decisions (Macauley and Heubel, 1986; Marlett, 1988). Technicians epitomize the motif of specializations that pervade modern society. This outgrowth of bureaucracy is devastating to the democratic process, due to the gradual narrowing of knowledge, assessment models, and solutions that are seen as workable (Murphy, Pardeck, and Chung, 1992).

This tendency can only be counteracted by reversing the increasing rationalization of the social world. Presently, a number of social critics have concluded that formalization and centralization is not necessarily efficient (Murphy, Pardeck, and Chung, 1992). As Kanter (1984) has concluded, the entrepreneurial spirit may be extinguished by this kind of concentration of power. Innovation and decentralization must be undertaken to make democracy work effectively.

In conclusion, specialization must be understood as effective within a controlled social system. In a multicultural society, specialization is particularly counterproductive because it creates insensitivity and resentment which will inevitably create a lack of trust in government by citizens. If pluralism is to thrive within a democracy, the views of technocrats must be seen as being on equal basis with the opinions of all citizens.

Social Class

Structural metaphors help to secure societal order. Durkheim (1983) calls this belief a "moral order" that is unassailable and ultimately the very foundation to society. As a result of adopting this worldview, chaos is adverted, according to Durkheim. A social reality is thus created which is ostensibly objective and stable. Luhmann (1982) refers to such position as a "centered" view of the social order.

Two important points are evident when conceptualizing society in this fashion. First, society has exact boundaries. Second, a system is established that defines status, normalcy, and mobility. This conceptualization of society is thought to enhance the social order of various societies. In terms of this description, the idea of structuration appears to be essential to democracy (Giddens, 1984). Sennett (1991) suggests this structural analogy conveys the impression that each component of a social system has intrinsic value. What occurs is that certain positions, rules, and classes are presumed to be more respectable than others. Most notably, this is the case when structure is combined with a hierarchical rendition of social life, as is true in most modern democracies (Murphy, Pardeck, and Chung, 1992).

Under these conditions, views from the middle or upper classes are more highly valued than those of other social positions. In essence, ideas are not assessed on their own merit but are judged first and foremost by their source. However, democracy requires a competition of ideas to work successfully. A social imagery must be created that accepts all ideas as equal, regardless of their source. Discourse is central to achieving this social imagery (Murphy, 1989). Through discourse, the cause of democracy is enhanced (Murphy, Pardeck, and Chung, 1992).

Once social class is recognized as a matter of social convention, democracy can flourish. Rationality, for example, is not indigenous to certain segments of the population and not found in others. Through the equalizing of social classes, all groups, including racial and ethnic minorities, are included in the political process. In sum, no citizen feels disenfranchised.

CONCEPTIONS OF DEMOCRACY

In philosophical terms, the notion of democracy has numerous connotations and ultimately is a complex idea (Chambers, 1987). So as not to become enmeshed in the debate over what exactly is meant by democracy, the authors will view democracy as a political system that invites all citizens to participate on an equal basis. Through this participation the most just society will emerge (Cnaan, 1988; Maas, 1984). For democracy to thrive, three basic themes must be present within a society that stress social justice (Pardeck, 1994). These are as follows:

1. Social justice exists when there is fairness in how resources within a given society are distributed to individuals and groups. There are few economic systems that achieve this noble goal; however, it should be the goal of those who are committed to a democratic society.

2. Social justice means empowerment, that is, it enables deprived citizens to seek their own personal justice on equal terms with other citizens. Through this act they are no longer passive objects that wait for the powerful to act on their behalf, but instead, are active participants in the democratic process.

3. Social justice means a commitment to the democratization of a society. Democratization, as a process, is a strategy that allows all citizens to participant on an equal basis in the political process. No society has achieved this level of development within the political social institution. The goal of democratization is often precluded by powerful vested interests that have a stake in preventing meaningful political input by citizens because the results might be a shift in economic and political power.

Fairness, participation, and empowerment should be central goals to democracy. These goals can be best achieved through discourse among citizens acting within the democratic process.

DISCOURSE AND RATIONALITY

Discourse is critical to the creation of a democratic society. Rational decision-making, an approach highly valued by technocrats, is contrary to the notion of discourse and democracy. Proponents of rational decision-making insist that when reality and interpretation are allowed to mingle, order is placed in jeopardy. Wittgenstein (1953) reminds us, however, personal or private languages do not exist. Therefore, the skeptics are wrong when they suggest that interaction cannot be sustained by language.

Wittgenstein (1953) recognizes that language use can be idiosyncratic. His claim that reality constitutes a language game testifies to this possibility. If knowledge and order are linguistically manufactured, nothing but speech acts can prevent interpretations from proliferating. Consequently, any number of esoteric versions of social reality are likely to be created.

What Wittgenstein (1953) is claiming is that language must be based in ''reflexivity.'' What this means is that citizens are able to talk about their use of language. They can challenge the rules of speech and illustrate the parameters of any particular interpretation of social reality. Especially critical is that language does not entrap its users. In fact, citizens are free to pursue any language game, in addition to moving from one interpretation of reality to another.

Wittgenstein (1953) concluded that a great deal of ''stage-setting'' is necessary before a sign has any meaning. He notes that ''non-sense'' is not an obvious trait of an event, but rather this label must be associated with a phenomenon. Information is not devoid of meaning; something must be assigned the status of nothing. The implication is thus obvious; facts are polyvalent. Accordingly, Murphy (1989) has concluded that insanity in one language is indicative of reason in another.

Hence the boundaries of rationality are impermeable. Because speech is transparent, citizens are constantly confronted by a host of interpretations. Polyvalence is never purged from language. Sartre (1963) noted that each time a person talks, more and less is expressed than intended. Language is always overflowing with numerous meanings, thereby revealing the need for clarification. Obviously, if interpretations were self-contained, interpenetration of language would never become an issue.

Interpersonal corroboration of interpretation is facilitated through the reflexivity of language (Murphy and Pardeck, 1988; Murphy and Pardeck, 1990). Above all, citizens can escape from their own region of speech, so that other modalities of reality can be entered. Accordingly, structural imperatives are not required to unite citizens; instead, the rules of decision-making can be disseminated through discourse. Through acts of iteration, information can be assessed until a common understanding among citizens is achieved; thus, sound decisions can be made that enhance the democratic process.

There is little doubt that this strategy for securing interpersonal harmony is volatile when compared to a traditional rational approach to decision-making.

As a result of exposing the limits of rationality, all other schemes for assessing judgments do not have to be dismissed as non-rational. Various styles of reason can co-exist, with each one having its own legitimacy. This portrayal of order is not hierarchical, and ultimately enhances democracy.

This new approach to the production of knowledge might be called a unified field theory of understanding (Lewin, 1958). It is noted that a reality *sui generis* does not exist; such a reality separates absolute rationality from non-rationality, interpretations are juxtaposed. In other words, an array of meanings can be associated with any event and human action is necessary to give meaning to particular events. Decision-making is grounded in discourse among citizens and has a clear existential thrust.

Decision-making is not based solely on a logic that should be uncritically accepted. Once the interpenetration of meanings has been resolved, decision-making can begin. Decision-making grounded in rationality is viewed as the ultimate source of knowledge for defining reality. Giving prominence to certain assumptions about reality is a social activity; facticity is a product of interpretation. As Weber (1958) concluded in another context, the beginning of deliberation cannot be dictated by logic. This means decision-making is neither right nor wrong but, hopefully, relevant. Such a process can only be achieved through discourse among citizens.

CONCLUSION

Crucial to democracy is the notion that no group is disenfranchised. Often those who extol the virtues of rationality are likely to promote a worldview that excludes those citizens seen as less than rational (Hisker, 1986). Because rationality is indigenous to certain segments of the population and absent in others, the source of a given proposal determines its worth. Such a view inhibits the growth of democracy.

As suggested in this chapter, democracy will fail if piecemeal planning is not avoided. Attention should focus not simply on formalities and other superficial aspects of government (Murphy, Pardeck, and Chung, 1992). Instead, a proper conceptual base should be created for the polity. In the case of democracy, conditions must be met that permit the widespread solicitation of ideas and competition among proposals from citizens.

Jacques Ellul (1964) concluded that a "technological civilization" has emerged. What this means is that whenever possible, technical remedies are employed to solve problems. Science is highly regarded in modern society and is believed to be extremely effective. Technical interventions are paramount, whereas personal insight and initiative are seen as secondary sources of information (Christensen, 1986). However, democracy is a human enterprise that is grounded in collective action of citizens. Citizens' views are the basis for decision-making in the political arena of a democracy.

In an era of complex technologies, such a view of democracy may be seen as dysfunctional. Pressures are exerted in modern societies to disregard ingredients that are not empirically based (Murphy and Pardeck, 1991; Pardeck and Murphy, 1992; and Pardeck, Murphy, and Callaghan, 1994). However, both policy makers and citizens must insist otherwise. They must demand that government assign a high priority to all views coming from citizens; if not, democracy will likely be organized around technical prescriptions. What could possibly be more undemocratic than having democracy reduced to a process that relies on technology and science as the basis for decision-making?

REFERENCES

Barthes, R. (1985) *The Grain of the Voice*. New York: Hill and Wang.

Berger, P. L., and T. Luckmann. (1966) *The Social Construction of Reality*. Garden City, NY: Doubleday.

Boden, M. (1977) *Artificial Intelligence and Natural Man*. New York: Basic Books.

Chambers, R. (1987) *Rural Development: Putting the Last First*. London: Longman.

Christensen, K. (1986) "Ethic of Information Technology." In *The Human Edge: Human Technology and Helping People*, edited by G. Geiss and N. Viswanathan. New York: The Haworth Press, pp. 72–91.

Citizens and Politics: A View From Main Street America. (1991) Dayton, OH: The Kettering Foundation.

Cnaan, R. A. (1988) "Post Industrial Technologies: Their Impact on Society and the Role of the Welfare State." *Eurosocial Newsletter* 40, no. 1: 11–12.

Durkheim, E. (1983) *Pragmatism and Sociology*. Cambridge: Cambridge University Press.

Ellul, J. (1964) *The Technological Society*. New York: Random House.

Feyerabend, P. K. (1978) *Science in a Free Society*. London: NLB.

Fitzsimmons, J. A., A. J. Schwab, and R. S. Sullivan. (1979) "Goal Programming for Holistic Budget Analysis." *Administration in Social Work* 31, no. 1: 33–43.

Freedman, J. L. (1973) *Social Psychology*. Englewood Cliffs, NJ: Prentice-Hall.

Freud, S. (1948) *An Outline of Psychoanalysis*. New York: Norton.

Gebser, J. (1985) *The Ever-Present Origin*. Athens: Ohio University Press.

Giddens, A. (1984) *The Structuration of Society*. Berkeley: University of California Press.

Guba, E. G., and Y. S. Lincoln. (1982) *Effective Evaluation*. San Francisco: Jossey-Bass.

Hisker, W. J. (1986) "The Promise of Technology: An Organizational Caveat." In *Technology and Human Productivity*, edited by John W. Murphy and John T. Pardeck. Westport, CT: Quorum Books, pp. 129–189.

Kanter, R. M. (1984) *The Change Masters*. New York: Simon and Schuster.

Kuhn, T. S. (1970) *The Structure of Scientific Revolutions*. Chicago: University of Chicago Press.

Lewin, K. (1958) "Group Decision and Social Change." In *Readings in Social Psychology*, edited by E. E. Maccoby, T. M. Newcomb, and E. L. Hartley. New York: Holt, Rinehart and Winston, pp. 197–211.

Luhman, N. (1982) *The Differentiation of Society*. New York: Columbia University Press.

Maas, H. (1984) *People and Contexts: Social Development from Birth to Old Age*. Englewood Cliffs, NJ: Prentice-Hall.

Macauley, W. A., and E. J. Heubel. (1986) "The Impact of Technology on Complex

Organizations: A Research Note.'' In *Technology and Human Productivity*, edited by J. W. Murphy and J. T. Pardeck. Westport, CT: Greenwood Press, pp. 191–201.

Mannheim, K. (1971) ''The Democratization of Culture.'' In *From Karl Mannheim*, edited by Kurt H. Wolff. New York: Oxford University Press, pp. 271–346.

Marlett, N. (1988) ''Empowerment Through Computer Telecommunications.'' In *Information Technology and the Human Services*, edited by B. Glastonburg, W. La Mendola, and S. Toole. Chichester, England: John Wiley and Sons, pp. 244–264.

Morris, M. B. (1977) *An Excursion into Creative Sociology*. New York: Columbia University Press.

Murphy, J. W. (1989) *Postmodern Social Analysis and Criticism*. Westport, CT: Greenwood Press.

Murphy, J. W., and J. T. Pardeck. (1988) ''Technology in Clinical Practice and the Technological Ethic.'' *Journal of Sociology and Social Welfare* 15, no. 1: 119–128.

———. (1990) ''Expert Systems as an Adjunct to Clinical Practice: A Critique.'' In *Computers in Human Services*, edited by J. T. Pardeck and J. W. Murphy. London: Harwood Academic Publishers, pp. 75–86.

———. (1991) *The Computerization of Human Service Agencies*. Westport, CT: Auburn House.

Murphy, J. W., J. T. Pardeck, and W. S. Chung. (1992) ''Democratization of Social Development.'' *Social Development Issues* 14, no. 1: 1–12.

Nam, D. (1986) ''The Case of the Changing Technology: Impact of Micro Computer Technology in a Fortune 500 Corporation.'' In *Technology and Human Productivity*, edited by J. W. Murphy and J. T. Pardeck. Westport, CT: Greenwood Press, pp. 191–201.

Pardeck, J. T. (1994) ''Computer Technology and Social Development.'' *Social Development Issues* 16, no. 1: 112–121.

Pardeck, J. T, and J. W. Murphy. (1992) ''Postmodernism and Clinical Practice: A Critical Analysis of the Disease Model.'' *Psychological Reports* 72: 1187–1194.

Pardeck, J. T., J. W. Murphy, and K. Callaghan. (1994) ''Computerization of Social Service: A Critical Appraisal.'' *Scandinavian Journal of Social Welfare* 3, no. 1: 2–6.

Sartre, J. P. (1963) *Search for a Method*. New York: Random House.

Sennett, R. (1991) ''Fragments Against the Ruin.'' *The Times Literary Supplement*, February 8, p. 6.

Weber, M. (1958) *The Protestant Ethic and the Spirit of Capitalism*. New York: Charles Scriber's Sons.

Williams, R. (1989) *Culture*. London: Fontana Press.

Wittgenstein, L. (1953) *Philosophical Reason*. New York: Macmillan.

8

Racist Ontology, Inferiorization, and Assimilation

Jung Min Choi

INTRODUCTION

Western thought has been overwhelmingly realistic. Consequently, writings and discussions about race/ethnic relations in the United States have been dominated by realism. While calling for equality and respect for differences, realists have continually supported an abstract set of norms that foster assimilation.

In point of fact, conservative writers throughout American history have viewed minorities consistently as inferiors who must assimilate to succeed in the mainstream of society. For example, starting with Edward Ross and Gunnar Myrdal in the early to mid-1900s, and moving to Milton Gordon and Arthur Jensen in the 1960s and 1970s to Charles Murray and Richard Herrnstein at present, race/ethnic relations in the United States have been regulated by a racist ontology that culminates in assimilation. A unique portrayal of knowledge and order, in other words, establish the conditions necessary to justify assimilation.

Assimilation hinges on a schism that demarcates two distinct ontological planes. Assimilationists adhere to tenets that support an asymmetrical relationship between the individual and society. In a Durkheimian manner, society is equated with the "sacred," while the individual occupies a more mundane, "profane" position.

This type of asymmetry has had dire consequences for minorities. To be specific, the lofty position given to society has been controlled regularly by a particular individual or group. The implication is that certain individuals or groups exemplify the pinnacle of human achievement. These specific individuals or groups have been attributed positive traits and characteristics, and are considered to be most important in maintaining society. And since these people reflect the ideals of society, they have been regarded as superior to the rest in terms of intelligence, rationality, morality, and beauty. Through a unique set of representations, white Europeans have enjoyed this seignorial position (hooks, 1992: 9–20). As Paul Gilroy states, "European particularism [has been] dressed up as universal" (Gilroy,1993a: 190).

Because whites have been linked to the ideals of social life, discussions regarding ethnic/race relations in the United States have taken a particular shape. Specifically, a policy of assimilation has been encouraged. Many immigrants throughout American history have made a concerted effort to eradicate their ethnic heritage in order to resemble their American counterparts.

Assimilation requires abandoning one identity and accepting another. What this suggests is a gradual eradication of ethnicity. The implication is that by ridding themselves of their former traits and accepting an Anglo identity, minorities will be significantly improved (Gordon, 1964: 71–72). Due to the emphasis placed on assimilation, minorities are blindly pursuing their loss of identity. In fact, some minorities support the idea that eliminating their ethnic traits is a positive move toward becoming fully American (Sowell, 1981; D'Souza, 1991). Many Asian Americans, like other minorities, at times have gone so far as to mutilate parts of their bodies in order to look European.

Nevertheless, the idea of assimilation continues to play a key role for many minorities who are striving to be included in the mainstream of social life. They are bound by the belief that true assimilation can occur if they try hard enough, because without assimilating, minorities know that the avenues of success are very limited. Thus, minorities are faced with one option: Assimilate or fail. Whether or not this has to be the case, this seems to be the prevailing option. But once this racist social ontology is challenged, social existence can be expanded. Specifically, non-dualistic and less hierarchical relationships can be envisioned.

THE INFERIOR RACE THESIS

According to Arthur Schlesinger, allowing differences to mix freely will culminate in the "disuniting of America" (Schlesinger, 1992). Balkanization is another term that has become quite popular in this regard. Clearly, the idea is that minorities should strive to emulate the American ideal, although complete assimilation is not likely to occur due to "natural inequalities" (Herrnstein and Murray, 1994: 369–388). In any case, a social organization will result that prevents society from collapsing. The resulting differentiations along class and racial lines are encouraged and reinforced, thereby preserving order.

According to Herrnstein and Murray (1994), social order should reflect a natural hierarchy based on individual abilities. Individuals or groups should be content to occupy their appointed places. As Andrew Hacker notes, Herrnstein and Murray believe that society should be ordered according to genetic capacities (Hacker, 1995: 49). And blacks, according to Herrnstein and Murray, "should accept their limitations and settle for less demanding callings. Instead of aiming for Ivy League colleges, they should hone their talents for the kinds of occupations their forbearers followed" (Hacker, 1995: 49). A strange sort of assimilation, almost predestination, is operating in this claim.

Following this type of logic, conservative writers have declared that affirmative action, along with other government assistant programs, causes more harm than good in trying to construct an egalitarian society. Much like the arguments proposed by Arthur Jensen and William Shockley in the 1970s, contemporary conservatives are suggesting that once artificial barriers, such as affirmative action programs, are removed, society will be ordered according to a natural hierarchy. Those who are superior will inhabit the top positions, while those who are inferior will occupy the less prominent levels of society. This outcome, conservative writers contend, reflects democratic ideals: society based on sheer ability, talent, and effort.

With this kind of sentiment sweeping the nation, there should be no surprise that ethnic/race relations in the United States have reached an impasse. While cheering and focusing on the latest exploits of black athletes and entertainers, the "power elites" have continuously either ignored or rejected the necessary social correctives that were once considered to be vital to combat racism (Moynihan, 1969: 9). Contrary to the policies attendant to the "Great Society," the individual is the focus of attention. And allowing nature to unveil a proper social hierarchy, in an almost social-Darwinian fashion, has become *de rigueur*.

Minorities are expected to forget the past history of slavery, segregation, mental and physical violence, and other suffering that they have endured in the name of assimilation. Past history is deemed almost irrelevant. Instead, minorities must conform to the "common culture," so that they can function as a true American. Reflecting on this sentiment, John O'Neill (1976) argues that forgetting past history is a threat to an open society. Ignoring history limits the very possibility of having a future that embodies alternate social orders. Nevertheless, historically, in one way or another, assimilationists illustrate that those who have discarded their former traits, beliefs, customs, and history have found inclusion in American society. In contrast, those who are least assimilable have remained at the bottom of the social ladder. This has been the popular explanation given for the differences between white European immigrants and blacks in the United States. While many white European immigrants were able to assimilate, blacks and other colored minorities have been hindered by their genetic or cultural factors (Herrnstein and Murray, 1994: 389–552). This is how whites have explained the hierarchical character of American society, where the underclass is dominated disproportionately by minority members.

The logic is simple. Minorities are inferior, which accounts for the disproportionately high numbers filling the lowest-paying jobs. At the same time, their limited ability is not suited to executive positions where high intelligence is necessary for important decision-making.[1] Therefore, the reason why minorities occupy consistently the lower position in the socioeconomic ladder is personal.

Their restricted capacity—mental, cultural, and to a certain extent physical—limits them from assimilating fully to the core of America (Sowell, 1981).

Faced with this kind of social imagery, true pluralism has not yet flourished. Although attempts have been made continuously to institute pluralism by celebrating differences, not much progress can be made in this regard when the "other" is dominated, subjugated, or consumed in the name of universalization and totalization. The types of pluralism that have been visible are those that stress individualism, particularism, and nationalism.[2] In each case, attention is directed to difference, but, in the end, the identity of a person or group is specified by clinging to a synoptic principle.

A person is known as black, for instance, by virtue of having a trait considered to exist *sui generis*. Due to the inability to go beyond the idea of essence, pluralism is subsumed under a variant of assimilation. What needs to be recognized, according to Cornel West, is that minorities are "neither additions to nor defections from American life, but rather *constitutive elements of that life*."[3] In other words, pluralism exists when persons are able to define and maintain themselves, rather than gaining their identities from factors they do not control, for example, economic, cultural, or metaphysical. But as long as such asymmetry is tolerated, identity can always be threatened by a so-called higher principle. When this occurs, pluralism is finished.

BEYOND RACIAL REASONING

As long as Americans understand race to be a reflection of a fixed, immutable, and permanent trait of an individual or group, any significant changes to bring about equality are unlikely. And even if a structural change does occur to include more minorities at all levels of social institutions, they will likely be compared to "monads" who pursue only self-interest. Indeed, within this scheme, "racial" groups are seen as purely "interest groups" that make "cultural, economic, or political claims on the society, on the basis of that group identity" (Bell, 1975: 160). As should be noted, according to Daniel Bell, a distinct group identity is assumed to sustain and motivate different races. Identity still exists *a priori* and is linked to a wider social system that is not questioned.

If there is any hope of fostering an egalitarian society, where race is no longer seen as an objective entity bound by some immutable genetic or biological similarities, persons must venture beyond racial reasoning when explaining the unequal distribution of wealth, power, and status. Race must not be grounded in persons' culture or genes. Instead, race must be understood to reflect the unequal relationship that exists between members of society in terms of wealth, power, knowledge, prestige, and status within the social, political, and economic arena (Marable, 1995: 363–365). Accordingly, race is a transparent concept that only becomes "real as a social force when individuals or groups behave toward each other in ways which either reflect or perpetuate the hegemonic ideology of subordination and the patterns of inequality in daily life. These are, in turn,

justified and explained by assumed differences in physical and biological characteristics, or in theories of cultural deprivation or intellectual inferiority'' (Marable, 1995: 364). As Manning Marable illustrates, race is a concept that reflects
a mode of social interaction, not an essence.

Because most Americans have been led to believe that these differences are
objective and real, no significant policy has been introduced to address the ontology of racism. Instead, the focus has been on introducing and enacting piecemeal solutions, such as affirmative action and other social programs. This is not
to suggest that social programs, such as affirmative action, are not important for
minority members.[4] The point, however, is to look beyond these social programs
and question the very foundation of American society that seems to support
massive inequality on the basis of race, gender, and cultural differences. In other
words, the reality *sui generis* that rationalizes the subordination of select persons
supported by dualism must be attacked.

POSTMODERNISM AND THE ANTI-ESSENTIALIST
TURN

According to Lawrence Grossberg, displacing or even challenging the ''already constituted moral authority'' is very difficult (Grossberg, 1992: 381). This
is because the status quo must be shown to be illegitimate. And trying to point
out the flaws to the majority, who have been taught to believe in the system, is
an arduous task. However, this is the challenge that must be met if any hope of
achieving democracy is to be kept alive.

What is to be done? Simply put, the foundationalist and dualist philosophical
enterprise that undergirds the American social system must be abandoned, so
that alternative ideas can be entertained. In this regard, West admits that he has
''a very strong anti-metaphysical bent'' (West, 1993b: 51). He claims that ''truth
is a species of the good'' (West 1993b: 123), where ''the good is defined in
relation to temporal consequences'' (West, 1993c: 40). The point is that knowledge does not exist *sui generis*, but is found among the debris left behind by
the passage of time. Truth is thus contingent and tied intimately to human desires
and aims. Truth, as West writes, is the product of ''warranted assertions
[that] are themselves value-laden and exemplary of human beings working in
solidarity for the common good'' (West, 1989: 100). In this way, West is anti-
metaphysical. Consequently, persons must be made aware that an all-
encompassing common culture is not a requirement for securing vibrant and
harmonious race relations.

Consistent with West's argument that neither assimilation nor liberal pluralism provides remedies for the injury inflicted by the beliefs of white supremacist
and images permeating U.S. society and culture, a host of writers have recognized postmodernism as furnishing alternative social imagery that is based on
''openness'' to the other. As Roland Barthes is fond of saying, postmodernists
regard persons to be open signifiers (Barthes, 1977). Indeed, writers such as bell

hooks, Paul Gilroy, Henry Louis Gates, Jr., Cornel West, and Manning Mara-ble—prominent writers in the field of race relations—agree that the critique of essentialism offered by postmodernists is paramount to establishing an egalitar-ian society.

This does not mean, however, that all the writers mentioned above consider themselves to be postmodernists. In fact, at certain times, each one criticizes postmodernism for a variety of reasons. But what is clear is that their funda-mental arguments are consistent with Lyotard's understanding of the main thrust of postmodernism: "incredulity toward metanarratives" (Lyotard, 1984: xxiv).

The result of this attack on absolutes is that the racial ontology proffered by assimilationists is no longer viable. Indeed, the asymmetrical social relationships endured by minorities based on differences in biological, cultural, or genetic factors, which have contributed to elevating particular cultures over others, can no longer be justified. Subsequent to the postmodern move—the understanding that any social relationship is a result of human *praxis* and volition—a rationale for any sort of domination and subjugation becomes vacuous. Specifically im-portant, the concept of "natural inequality" loses credibility. Any designation such as this must be referred back to its origin in social and interpretive pro-cesses.

Once the veil of objectivity is lifted from the assimilation perspective; there is nothing to justify assimilation other than a supremacist ideology. In fact, assimilation obscures the social, political, cultural, and economic factors that contribute to transforming a particular outlook into a universal reality. Accord-ingly, through the metaphysics of assimilation, a dominant culture is resurrected: a culture that reflects only one mode of reality. All others are, at the same time, inferiorized. Viewed in this light, the assimilation perspective does violence to democracy where social relationships are supposed to reflect a whole range of human interests.

Once all social relationships are understood to reflect a "discursive forma-tion," the usual justification for imperialism, the disenfranchisement of ethnic communities, and the restriction of personal expression, under the guise of se-curing a common moral order, is undermined. The usual absolutes are displaced into a melange of signifiers, none of which has the status to discredit automat-ically cultural alternatives. Accordingly, the integrity of each difference is pre-served. As a result, race relations can develop where persons practice "mature black self-love" (West, 1993d: 25). Stated clearly, West is calling for a type of love not based on "skin pigmentation or racial phenotype," but one that in-cludes "egalitarian relations within and outside black communities" (West, 1993d: 25). He is opting for ethical instead of racial reasoning, where blacks neither deify nor demonize others. This ethical reasoning, however, is not based on any *a priori* set of values. Instead, this thinking reflects what Paul Gilroy calls "grounded ethics," since human values are understood to be maintaining social relationships, rather than a reality *sui generis* (Gilroy, 1993a: 38).

The type of race relations called for by these writers is consistent with the kind of social order envisioned by postmodernists. For example, hooks contends that minorities must go beyond ''racial bonding'' if real pluralism is to arrive (hooks, 1990: 6). Similarly, Henry Louis Gates, Jr., argues that while blacks must resist viewing European particularism as the dominant mode of discourse, they must also resist ''dark essentialism'' (Gates, 1992: 100). Clearly, these writers agree with postmodernists who reject ''grand narratives'' as the source of personal or collective identity. Instead of relying on abstract principles, social order should be mediated by ''face-to-face'' meeting (Levinas, 1961: 64–70). Consistent with the social imagery advanced by Levinas, West contends that race relations should exemplify ''visceral forms of human connectedness,'' where social order embodies *praxis* (West, 1993c: 173).

Seen in this light, domination based on racial differences loses all justification. One group no longer has the high moral ground from which to judge all others. Subsequent to postmodernism and the anti-essentialist turn, the assimilation perspective must mingle with all other forms of discourse. In this regard, postmodernism provides a means for undermining supremacist ideology, while establishing a non-repressive mode of order.

A POSTMODERN IDENTITY

Given the claim that persons do not embody a certain racial essence, do postmodernists strip persons of their identity? Absolutely not. What postmodernists argue is that there is no fundamental core to a person's identity. There is no id, *psyche*, or a ''real-self,'' as symbolic interactionists are fond of saying, to sustain a person's self-concept. Instead, a person's identity reflects the relationships in which she/he is engaged. Therefore, evaluating individuals on the basis of their race lacks legitimacy, since the concept of race is a myth (Foucault, 1979: 141–160). Similar to Foucault's ''author,'' race is dissolved into the interstices of language use and *praxis*.

This anti-foundationalist maneuver made by postmodernists is praised by hooks when she states that the demise of essentialism is beneficial to blacks and other minorities (hooks, 1990: 28–29). Like West and Gates, hooks recognizes that arguments based on essentialism have been detrimental to minorities for centuries. Invoking racial and other essentialistic reasoning, minorities, especially blacks, have been systematically inferiorized. Therefore, persons must recognize the transparency of any ''self,'' so that the justification for domination is subverted. To borrow from Sartre, a self is an ongoing project that precedes the determination of any essence; identity is nothing more than a social construct.

Indeed, according to Stuart Hall, ''identity is a narrative of the self; it's the story we tell about the self in order to know who we are'' (Hall, 1991: 16). Yet, in many instances, as Lyotard suggests, the narratives of many people are dwarfed by a ''grand narrative.'' For example, under the rubric of science, a particular narrative comes to be viewed as relaying a natural story of human existence. Scientific knowledge, consequently, subsumes all other forms of narratives into a single mode of discourse. Once this happens, persons are severed effectively from telling their own meaningful story.

Therefore, Henry Louis Gates, Jr., claims that while recognizing black heritage promotes a positive step for self-pride, searching for a core to black identity must be avoided. Striving to achieve dark essentialism truncates the range of black experience (Gates, 1992: 100). As a consequence of abandoning this style of essentialism, there is no core that unites all black experience into a single mode of discourse. Furthermore, there is no "blackness" that serves to gauge true black experience, or, for that matter, inherently superior experiences of any kind.

According to postmodernists, there is no absolutely real identity. Because identities are created and sustained by linguistic practice, they are invented and destroyed many times over throughout a person's life because of her/his involvement in various linguistic communities. Thus, persons should not fear the possibility that they might be left without an identity. Persons will always have an identity. But more importantly, their identity is not sustained by some type of essence. Rather, their identities reflect certain linguistic commitments.

In this sense, Paul Gilroy is correct to note that "blackness is a necessarily multi-accentual sign," capable of sustaining a multivalent identity (Gilroy, 1993a: 112). No one, not even blacks, can claim a monopoly on "black authenticity" (Gilroy, 1993a: 113). Gilroy is certain that due to the unverifiable, yet widespread belief that blacks have a particular authentic identity—one that resembles a beast—whites have been able to systematically inferiorize blacks, and rather easily (Gilroy, 1993a: 97–113).

But how is repression possible when there is no justification for domination? Accordingly, once race is recognized to be an open "text" and not an essence, the metaphysics of oppression can be attacked. Once human interpretation is recognized to be at the heart of existence, sustaining an identity becomes a matter of exercising *praxis*. Therefore, a black identity is possible, without having an essence that unduly restricts a wide range of black experiences. Indeed, black experience can be identified without essentializing it. At the same time, an identity built on language is predictable enough to be considered stable. Surely, seen in this light, the assimilationist ideas such as "natural inequality" or "genetic inferiority" are silly. Indeed, subsequent to postmodernism, dominating others on the basis of metaphysics is no longer acceptable. To those who benefit from unequal social hierarchy, postmodernism must be scary. However, those who believe that there is "meaning for struggle," and hope for the future, might want to assess closely the tenets of postmodern identity.

POSTMODERNISM AND RADICAL ORDER

Western societies have had a penchant for a centered version of order (Luhmann, 1982: 353–355). To institute a stable society, universal and ahistorical norms have been sought by many social theorists. The belief is that without an objective standard to gauge personal actions, chaos is immanent. Thus, emphasis has been placed on the need to conform to common values as a means to secure moral order. Celebrating differences, in short, has been regarded as anathema to harmonious social relationships.

Accordingly, minorities have become suspicious of the idea of integration. Why should they attempt to assimilate when the result is a loss of ethnic heritage, without gaining any appreciable social advantage? However, because the prevailing social structure is supported by the dominant culture of assimilation, minorities are left to choose between partial integration or outright exclusion. Given this scenario, those who rebel against the idea of assimilation by celebrating difference are viewed as renegades and disrupting social harmony.

Writing against this backdrop, postmodernists believe that this type of monolithic image of society must be overcome. To be sure, postmodernists argue that a pluralistic society is possible where differences are recognized and protected without culminating in *anomie*. Such a view of order, by the way, seems to be the hallmark of democracy. According to Lyotard, social order can thrive without having a centralized and hierarchical structure. In arguing this point further, Deleuze and Guattari (1983) introduced the rhizome as an appropriate social image. A rhizome has no appropriate beginning or an end. This plant does not have a centralized root to sustain its growth. In fact, the dispersion of these plants is orderly, yet decentered (Deleuze and Guattari, 1983: 1–58). This social imagery, according to Lyotard, "refines our sensitivity to differences and reinforces our ability to tolerate the incommensurable" (Lyotard, 1984: xxv).

Consistent with the ideas presented by Lyotard and other postmodernists, Paul Gilroy, working within the field of race relations, believes that "unity within diversity . . . is an explicit feature" of postmodernism that "betrays [the] political concern" of assimilationists (Gilroy, 1993a: 116). Gilroy asserts that without exposing the assumptions that support essentialism, alternative social images that are consistent with radical pluralism will be likely overlooked and misinterpreted (Gilroy, 1993a: 1–40). Therefore, persons should not look away from social reality, but rather look beyond its facade. Withdrawal, therefore, should be replaced by alternative proposals for reality. More effort must be devoted to making real social images based on decentralization and equality. Such an image must no longer be dismissed out of hand as utopian.

Although conservative critics charge that any assault on assimilation will result in the demise of moral order, postmodernists counter that a society based on the recognition of difference will foster a vibrant moral order. According to Gilroy, a type of montage can be created where the "metaphysics of intimacy" reflects the reconciliation of differences (Gilroy, 1993b: 39). To clarify, producing homogeneity is not the only *modus operandi* for insuring social order. Instead, through interaction and interpretation, "open signifiers" can become coordinated. To borrow from phenomenologists, temporal synchronization, not an ultimate reality, can produce order. This type of order, where one anticipates the actions of the other and is open for (re)adjustment, is truly radical. In the words of Gilroy, this "syncretic" order embodies true pluralism where *change* is not repressed (Gilroy, 1993b: 101).

Developing further the idea that a society based on differences is not only possible, but required if democratic ideals are to be entertained, Gilroy introduces jazz as a model for radical pluralism. Jazz, according to Gilroy, represents the excitement of the unknown and the unanticipated, all the while carrying out a harmonious tune. Indeed, jazz reflects "a tradition in ceaseless motion—a *changing* same that strives continually towards a state of self-realization that continually retreats beyond its grasp" (Gilroy, 1993b: 122). This image provided by Gilroy is consistent with Lyotard's recommendation that persons live at the nexus of interpretive boundaries. At this juncture is where difference is shared and juxtaposed at the same time. Just as in Buber's theme of *dazwischen*, no grand arbiter is necessary to insure intimacy. As Levinas states, a robust order can arise without an intermediary.

Cornel West, like Gilroy, also cites jazz as an example that undermines a monolithic culture. Jazz, West remarks, "is [an] energy in search of political funnels that will expand American democracy" (West, 1993a: 65). Indeed, both Gilroy and West believe that social relationships can reflect the energy, improvisation, imagination, contrast, originality, and the unexpected maneuvers found in jazz. Stated clearly, a jazz ensemble opposes formalization without erupting into chaos. To Gilroy, jazz embodies a "politics of transfiguration" that defies the moral genealogy present in a "centered" society (Gilroy, 1993b: 37–38).

Through alternative images, like jazz, various authors, who write within the postmodern tradition, are calling for a new type of community based on human discourse. This new type of community should embody "at once a vision and a construction—that takes you 'beyond' yourself in order to return, in a spirit of revision and reconstruction" (Bhabha, 1994: 3). According to Homi Bhabha, radical pluralism will thrive in this kind of setting, where difference is not cast aside in the name of unity. Instead, a truly democratic society "always keep[s] open a supplementary space for the articulation of cultural knowledges that are adjacent and adjunct but not necessarily accumulative, teleological or dialectical" (Bhabha, 1994: 163). Indeed, order can be founded on people expressing and articulating different experiences of social life. A vertical hierarchy is not necessary to insure social stability. On the contrary, a lateral coexistence of language games is sufficient for sustaining society. In this sense, a human relationship is nothing more than a social bond tied together through language. Clearly, interpretation is more than adequate for securing social order amid the heteronomy of signs. According to West, this kind of social relationship represents a "healthy communitarianism," because individuals are free to pursue their destiny without sacrificing their identity (West, 1993b: 224).

CONCLUSION

Living in a society where equality is a constitutional right should be empowering to its citizens. However, as Gunnar Myrdal (1944) questions, what happens when certain groups of people are stripped of this right without just cause? According to West, ''a pervasive spiritual impoverishment grows'' within the oppressed, resulting in ''the collapse of *meaning* in life—the eclipse of hope and absence of love of self and other, the breakdown of family and neighborhood bonds'' (West, 1993d: 5). Nihilism, in other words, becomes pervasive.

Although West says that this impoverishment is widely spread among American citizens, due to the ''silent depression ravaging the country,'' minorities and blacks are hit especially hard due to their marginal status in society.[5] And given the common understanding that pervades race relations—based on assimilation and integration—no real progress will be made to support a pluralistic society. As long as persons are willing to work within the prevailing social structure and the dominant assimilationist discourse, human growth will continuously be stifled and diversity repressed. Anger and frustration, therefore, can be expected to grow. All that is left for the dominant (white) majority to do is to invest in additional social control, as a subterranean war wages. But this future is not one most persons find very appealing.

Therefore, in order to garner healthy race relations, a complete rupture with the past is necessary. Persons should not fear the onset of chaos following the demise of absolutes. While no objective base can be used to justify cultural domination and marginalization, a postmodern framework ''encourages moral assessment of the variety of perspectives held by people and selects those views based on dignity and decency that eschew putting any group of people or culture on a pedestal or in the gutter'' (West, 1993d: 28). This framework, indeed, embodies a ''new politics of difference'' that ushers in radical pluralism. Order is not abandoned, but merely precepts that reflect outmoded biases. The choice is no longer between assimilation and security or pluralism and Balkanization. As has been shown, differences can co-exist in such a way that a non-repressive order is formed.

NOTES

1. Whether it is in corporations or in entertainment, this has been the case. For example, in basketball, a sport dominated by black athletes, head coaches are predominantly white. The same scenario exists in professional football and professional baseball. In all of these sports, black general managers are just about impossible to find.

2. The popular understanding of pluralism is offered by Glazer and Moynihan, where they see ethnic groups as interest groups. The other popular view is offered by Van den Berghe. His argument is that people within the same race bond together in a natural manner because of biological similarities. The significance of understanding pluralism as outlined by these writers is that although they attempt to break away from assimilation

perspective, their rendition of pluralism does not assist in any way to liberate minorities from oppression. Furthermore, because they do not question dualism, their view of society still reflects an asymmetrical relationship.

3. See West (1993d), p. 3. Clearly, West is talking about assimilationists who are willing to let minorities "fit in" as additions to the common culture, and liberal pluralists who see minorities as separate entities who are fighting solely for group interest.

4. Although affirmative action programs are vital for minority progress, Cornel West contends that persons should view affirmative action neither as a major solution to poverty nor as a sufficient means to achieving equality. Nevertheless, it is important to support affirmative action programs since they serve to limit discriminatory practices against women and other minorities.

5. See West (1993d), p. 5. According to West, "real weekly wages of all American workers since 1973 have declined nearly 20 percent, while at the same time wealth has been upwardly distributed."

REFERENCES

Barthes, R. (1977) *Image, Music, Text*. New York: The Noonday Press.

Bell, D. (1975) "Ethnicity and Social Change." In *Ethnicity: Theory and Experience*, edited by N. Glazer and Daniel P. Moynihan. Cambridge, MA: Harvard University Press, pp. 141–174.

Bhabha, H. (1994) *The Location of Culture*. New York: Routledge.

Deleuze, G., and F. Guattari. (1983) *On the Line*. New York: Semiotext(e).

D'Souza, D. (1991) *Illiberal Education*. New York: The Free Press.

Foucault, M. (1979) "What Is an Author?" In *Textual Strategies*, edited by J. Harari. Ithaca, NY: Cornell University Press, pp. 141–160.

Gates, H. L., Jr. (1992) *Loose Canons: Notes on the Culture Wars*. New York: Oxford University Press.

Gilroy, P. (1993a) *The Black Atlantic: Modernity and Double Consciousness*. Cambridge, MA: Harvard University Press.

———. (1993b) *Small Acts*. London: Serpent's Tail.

Goldberg, D. T. (1993) *Racist Culture: Philosophy and the Politics of Meaning*. Cambridge: Blackwell Publishers.

Gordon, M. (1964) *Assimilation in American Life*. New York: Oxford University Press.

Grossberg, L. (1992) *We Gotta Get Out of This Place*. New York: Routledge.

Hacker, A. (1995) "The Crackdown on African-Americans." *The Nation*, July 10, pp. 45–49.

Hall, S. (1991) "Ethnicity: Identity and Difference." *Radical America* 23, no. 4: 9–20.

———. (1992) "What Is This 'Black' in Black Popular Culture." In *Black Popular Culture*, edited by Gina Dent. Seattle: Bay Press, pp. 21–33.

Hansen, M. L. (1952) "The Third Generation in America." *Commentary* 14 (November): 492–500.

Herrnstein, R., and C. Murray. (1994) *The Bell Curve: Intelligence and Class Structure in American Life*. New York: The Free Press.

hooks, b. (1990) *Yearning*. Boston: South End Press.

———. (1992) *Black Looks: Race and Representation*. Boston: South End Press.

Kingston, M. H. (1977) *The Woman Warrior*. New York: Vintage.

Kronenwetter, M. (1993) *Prejudice in America*. New York: Macmillan Publishing Co.

Levinas, E. (1961) *Totality and Infinity*. Pittsburgh: Duquesne University Press.

Luhmann, N. (1982) *The Differentiation of Society*. New York: Columbia University Press.

Lyotard, J. F. (1984) *The Postmodern Condition: A Report on Knowledge*. Minneapolis: University of Minnesota Press.

Marable, M. (1995) "Beyond Racial Identity Politics: Towards a Liberation Theory for Multicultural Democracy." In *Race, Class, and Gender*, edited by M. L. Andersen and R. H. Collins. Belmont: Wadsworth Publishing Company, pp. 363–366.

Moynihan, D. P. (1969) "The Professor and the Poor." In *On Understanding Poverty*, edited by Daniel P. Moynihan. New York: Basic Books, pp. 3–35.

Myrdal, G. (1944) *An American Dilemma: The Negro Problem and Modern Democracy*. New York: Harper & Brothers.

O'Neill, J. (1976) "Critique and Remembrance." In *On Critical Theory*, edited by John O'Neill. New York: Seabury Press, pp. 1–11.

Parsons, T. (1965) "Full Citizenship for the Negro American? A Sociological Problem." In *The Negro American*, edited by T. Parsons and K. B. Clark. Boston: Houghton Mifflin, pp. 709–754.

Schlesinger, A. (1992) *The Disuniting of America*. New York: W. W. Norton.

Sowell, T. (1981) *Ethnic America*. New York: Basic Books.

West, C. (1989) *The American Evasion of Philosophy*. Madison: University of Wisconsin Press.

———. (1993a) *Keeping Faith: Philosophy and Race in America*. New York: Routledge.

———. (1993b) *Prophetic Reflections*. Monroe, ME: Common Courage Press.

———. (1993c) *Prophetic Thought in Postmodern Times*. Monroe, ME: Common Courage Press.

———. (1993d) *Race Matters*. Boston: Beacon Press.

Wilkins, R. (1995) "Racism Has Its Privileges." *The Nation*, March 27, pp. 409–416.

9

Analyzing Racial Ideology: Post-1980 America

George Wilson and Jomills Braddock

INTRODUCTION

After a period of relative quiescence, issues of race in American society have undergone a dramatic transformation in the last fifteen or so years. In particular, during this period there appears to have been a conservative "backlash" to the economic and political gains made by racial minorities in the post-1965 civil rights era. In stark, material terms, the backlash has left its mark in numerous ways, such as the widening gap between the African-American and white populations in range of "life chance" outcomes, including income (Farley and Allen, 1987), wealth accumulation (Oliver and Shapiro, 1995), educational attainment (Jaynes and Williams, 1989), as well as proportional representation among this country's impoverished population (Jencks, 1991).

This backlash has manifested itself in a relatively sophisticated and appealing ideological form: specifically (couched in values that seemingly reaffirm "fair play" and "equal opportunity"), there have been growing calls for a color-blind society where no special significance, rights, or privileges attach to one's race. Evidence of growing support for a race-neutral public policy can be found in several quarters. For example, survey data indicates that during the 1980s, an increasingly large segment of the American public (at all levels of the class structure) expressed disapproval of a wide range of race-targeted government programs that are designed to address socioeconomic inequality (Kluegel and Bobo, 1991; Kluegel and Smith, 1986). In recent years, a wide variety of influential newspapers and popular periodicals including the *New York Times*, the *Washington Post*, *Newsweek*, *Time*, and the *New Republic* have changed long-standing editorial policies and expressed greater support for the principle that public policy prescriptions designed to address issues of social inequality should be race-neutral in nature.

However, even a cursory glance at American history reveals that far from being color-blind, the United States has always been an extremely color-conscious society. Indeed, this notion was perhaps no more deeply entrenched than in the two decades preceding the 1980s. During this period, government policy was rooted in the notion that race is a profound determinant to a broad array of economic opportunities. This sentiment was the basis for government policies that made possible much of the gains made by African Americans during the civil rights era. For example, the notion of persisting racial discrimination was the justification for the enactment of federal legislation such as the Civil Rights Act of 1964, the Federal Fair Housing Act of 1968, and a broad range of additional government-based initiatives (including the establishment of the Office of Federal Contract Compliance) that were designed to create a meaningful African-American middle class (see Edsall and Edsall, 1991; Collins, 1993; McAdam, 1982).

In this chapter we analyze the underpinning of the backlash—the ideological about-face in which the vision of a "color-blind" society has increasingly come to be seen as the very essence of our democratic way of life. Our overriding concern is with sketching a theoretical framework for linking the analysis of racial ideology and racial inequality in the post-1980 period. We view the search for sources of integration between racial ideology and racial inequality as a topic worthy of serious sociological investigation. Racial ideology and racial inequality are linked in ways that have not been recognized by sociologists because these two topics have tended to constitute separate provinces of sociological research. As such, we believe their separation has occurred at a serious cost: the lack of development of a more broad-based, integrated theory of racial inequality.

In undertaking this exercise, we utilize Omi and Winant's (1994) theory of "racial formation," principally because we believe it provides a way of establishing the link between racial ideology and patterns of racial inequality. We make use of their notion of "racial projects," which are conceptualized as historically contingent ideological tenets that structure "racial meaning" in everyday affairs. According to racial formation theory, "racial projects" are sufficiently broad to encompass tenets that structure patterns of social inequality in society. Race is employed as an ideological construct that plays an important role in defining individual access to the entire range of rewards and opportunities in society.

Finally, we attempt to demonstrate the utility of racial formation theory in two broad steps. First, we outline how it contributes toward understanding processes of racial inequality in general terms. Second, we apply it to the post-1980 period. Here, we are concerned with two aspects of racial theory: how it links racial ideology and racial inequality as well as how it accounts for the rise of a particular form of racial ideology in this period.

THE RACIAL FORMATION PERSPECTIVE

Approximately three decades ago, sociologists came to the full realization that race was not waning as a salient social category in America (see Stone, 1985; Glazer and Moynihan, 1975). The failure of sociologists to appreciate the fundamental role of race, until the end of the 1960s, can be attributed in large part to their having been wedded to conceptions of society that derive from the immediate preoccupations of the founding fathers of sociology, such as class conflicts engendered by nascent capitalist industry and political conflicts emanating from upheavals following the French Revolution. As such, orientations that were dominant through the 1960s (such as functionalist analysis and modernization theory) had assumed that the logical imperatives associated with industrialization would lead to the progressive erosion of distinctions based on an ascribed characteristic such as race (see Parsons, 1966; Apter, 1965; Bell, 1960).

The perception that race would not soon abate spurred sociologists to undertake a broad-based agenda of research devoted to identifying how the persistence of race is related to the structuring of socioeconomic inequality in the United States. The ensuing volume of work produced by sociologists has been enormous and has moved the analysis of race to the disciplinary center of sociology. However, this research has not been without its shortcomings. An important point of departure for this chapter is one such shortcoming: the tendency to analyze racial dynamics in terms of a series of reductionist structural properties. In particular, we believe that much of this research has failed to grasp the uniqueness of race and its immediacy in everyday experience; in these studies race and racial conflict have too often been posited not as independent dynamic forces, but as ultimately reducible to other causal, supposedly more fundamental, determinants.

To illustrate this tendency, we focus on several sociological perspectives that have come to represent predominant approaches to analyzing race relations in the United States. In particular, these labor market perspectives have tended to be rooted in principles from economics. For example, one line of sociological studies that is based on neoclassical economic thought has viewed racial discrimination as an anomaly in an equilibrium-oriented system (Williams, 1982; Thurow, 1969). This perspective views racial inequality as a product of three possibly disruptive forces that upset market equilibrium: an irrational prejudice or "taste for discrimination," monopolistic practices (which create incentive for strategically placed groups to maintain racial inequality), and disruptive state practices which interfere with the supposed equilibrating tendencies of the labor market.

Similarly, a second body of sociological research has used theories of class conflict to analyze race relations. This general perspective has tended to focus on two different sets of dynamics. The first is a "divide and rule" conception which rests on the notion of labor market "segmentation" as the key determinant of race-based inequalities (Parcel and Mueller, 1983; Rosenfeld, 1980).

According to this conception, the historic evolution of labor control and labor market processes has served to make race a fundamental criterion for allocating individuals into delineated market sectors which yield varying economic rewards. The second is an "exclusionism" perspective which maintains that a "split labor market" is the source of racial inequalities (Boswell, 1984; Bonacich and Model, 1980; Bonacich, 1972). According to this conception, racial conflict takes place between dominant and subordinate workers as the former seek to prevent the latter from bidding down the price of their labor. These exclusionary movements are not racially motivated, but are rather the product of historical accident which produced a correlation between race and the price of labor.

It is not our intention to minimize the substantial contributions that these sociological perspectives have made toward furthering our understanding of the dynamics of racial inequality. However, we maintain that their reductionist tendencies have precluded serious inquiry into important underlying sources of racial dynamics. Specifically, the focus of racial antagonism (as a manifestation of underlying economic relations) ignores the fact that ideology plays an important role in defining economic interests. As such, the sociological perspectives have tended to neglect an important prerequisite for the practices that generate racial inequality to operate—a coherent ideological formulation that sanctions and legitimates race-based differences in labor market placement, that, ultimately, result in differential economic rewards based on race.

For example, the equilibrium-based model confines itself narrowly to market relationships, while ignoring the ideological and cultural dynamics that help to define the "rightful" place of different racial groups in the labor market. Similarly, the focus of the "divide and rule" variant of class conflict theory on segmentation as the source of racial inequality places ideological forces—such as the black protest movements—that have periodically challenged the legitimacy of the segmentation system as exogenous to the model. Finally, the split labor market variant of class theory fares no better in engaging ideologies of race; instead, it imputes ideological meanings to the economically defined class and racial actors it depicts. In sum, we maintain that these sociological perspectives have not addressed the ideological context within which labor market practices (that generate racial inequality) operate. Consequently, they have missed vital aspects concerning how the supposed determinative economic practices arose and are perpetuated.

Several sociologists have advocated that studies of racial inequality would be significantly enhanced if they were infused with considerations of ideology (see Sigelman and Welsh, 1991; Omi, 1987; See, 1986). One such statement was recently made by Omi and Winant (1994: 3).

Instead of exploring how groups become racially identified, how racial identities and meanings change over time, . . . "mainstream" approaches consider race as a problem of policy, of social engineering, of state management. . . . "Radical" theories embrace class or nationalist perspectives which, while critical of the existing racial order, are often no more appreciative of the uniqueness and irreducibility of their subject than were the "established" analyses. Thus radicals too often submerge race in other social relations—most frequently class or nation-based conflicts—thought to operate as the "motor force" of history.... How one is categorized is far from a merely academic or even personal matter. Such matters as access to employment, housing or other politically or privately valued goods; social program design and the disbursement of local, state and federal funds; or the organization of elections are directly affected by ... the recognition of "legitimate" groups.

We believe that Omi and Winant's theory of racial formation begins to correct for deficiencies contained in the predominant sociological perspectives used to analyze racial dynamics in the United States. The racial formation perspective emphasizes the irreducible aspect and historical flexibility of racial ideology. As such, it stands in marked contrast to the views of race that underlie the predominant sociological perspectives used to analyze race relations—specifically, the utopian notion which views it as an illusion to somehow "get beyond," as well as the essentialist and primordial formulations which view race as something objective and fixed.

The central idea of Omi and Winant's racial formation perspective is "racial projects," which are sets of ideological tenets that structure the meaning of race in everyday life. According to Omi and Winant, racial projects racialize social structure; they shape commonsense experiences of race and condition its meaning. Thus, the most minute phenomena of everyday life, ranging from temperament, intelligence, athletic ability, aesthetic preferences, and so on, are interpreted racially. Further, such diverse issues as confidence and trust in others, ways of talking, walking, eating, and tastes in music, dance, and film become racially coded. Thus, the concept of race plays a fundamental role in representing the social world.

For the purposes of this chapter, it is especially significant to note that the ideological tenets that comprise a "racial project" extend to defining the access and relationship that racial groups have to institutions and organizations in society. As such, racial projects assign a meaning to race in structuring socioeconomic inequality. According to Omi and Winant (1994: 56), "a racial project is simultaneously an interpretation, representation or explanation of racial dynamics, and an effort to reorganize and redistribute resources along particular racial lines."

In this vein, we interpret Omi and Winant as intending that the scope of racial projects include all representations of the normative or ideal role of race in determining access to the societal reward structure. Racial projects encompass society's most valued material and symbolic outcomes: In advanced industrialized societies, such as the United States, the societal reward structure has routinely come to be interpreted broadly as including long-term trajectories to elements as diverse as the right to vote, earn income, acquire property, receive a range of government benefits, and gain meaningful employment (Oliver and Shapiro, 1995; Wilson and Royster, 1995). Consequently, a wide range of representations of the meaning of race fall within the purview of racial projects: For example, they include stereotypes held by whites that Latins are suited only for migrant work, that non-whites they encounter are servants, that non-white colleagues are less qualified persons (hired to fulfill affirmative action guidelines), and that African Americans, moving into their neighborhoods, will drive down their property values.

Two other points regarding racial formation bear mentioning. First Omi and Winant say that it is "historically contingent." By this, the authors maintain that the contents of racial projects change over time. So, for example, the processes of racial formation in the post-1980 period in the United States are present-day outcomes of a complex historical evolution. Second, racial formation is "always ascertainable." Specifically, Omi and Winant posit that at any point in time racial projects can be explained with reference to concrete and identifiable sociohistoric forces.

RACIAL IDEOLOGY IN THE POST-1980 PERIOD

We now move from the general to the specific. In particular, we focus on applying racial formation theory to a specific sociohistoric context—the post-1980 period in the United States. Toward this end, in this section we first identify the tenets of racial ideology that comprise the underpinning of the political "backlash" in the post-1980 period; all-told, the tenets of this racial ideology constitute a coherent rationale for denying any special significance to race in addressing issues of social inequality in society. Subsequent to this, we establish how this racial ideology is related to a specific, dominant "racial project." As we will show, the essence of the new mood of "social meanness" that has pervaded the United States since the 1980s is reflected in both the racial ideology and the dominant racial project that follows from it.

For several decades, sociologists have used techniques of survey research to tap the racial ideology of the American public. However, it was in the decade of the 1980s that this ideology was most extensively examined. Overall, findings from the range of studies conducted indicate that some variation in racial ideology exists among Americans, depending upon such factors as racial affect, the amount of perceived direct economic competition with other racial minorities, and the extent of adherence to the dominant American individualistic values of stratification (see Kluegel and Smith, 1986; Kluegel and Bobo, 1991). Nevertheless, despite these sources of variation in ideology, the overall trend has been for Americans to view the economic plight of racial minorities in an increasingly unsympathetic manner.

In this rendering of racial ideology, we restrict our focus to the attitudes of whites. The decision to do this is based on several factors: their numerical preponderance in the American population, the more extensive examination that has been given to tapping their racial ideology than other groups, and the more volatile nature of their racial ideology than other racial groups (see Sigelman and Welsh, 1991; Schuman, Steeh, and Bobo, 1985). From the sizable number of survey-based studies conducted on whites, it is possible to distill the following general trends in racial ideology that are relevant to formulating the dominant "racial project."

RACIAL DISCRIMINATION DOES NOT EXIST

Unlike studies conducted in the decades prior to the 1980s, white Americans surveyed since the 1980s consistently report that racial discrimination has largely been eradicated as a determinant of economic opportunities for African Americans. For example, Kluegel and Smith (1986) found this using a variety of items that measure perceptions of racial discrimination directly (e.g., "do African Americans confront additional obstacles to achieve economic success?") and indirectly (e.g., "are economic opportunities equally available for all Americans?").

AFRICAN AMERICANS ARE NOW RECEIVING PREFERENTIAL TREATMENT

Far from being the victims of discrimination, studies have consistently found that whites believe that racial minorities are receiving preferential treatment with respect to a range of economic opportunities. This perception has manifested itself in a variety of ways. For example, whites have expressed substantial support for survey items that African Americans can "get ahead" in the areas of jobs and educational opportunities without "working as hard as other groups" (see Schuman, Steeh, and Bobo, 1985). In addition, whites for the first time have expressed widespread support for the proposition that they have become the primary victims of discrimination that exists in the economic arena (see Schuman, Steeh, and Bobo, 1985).

SUPPORT FOR RACE-BASED POLICIES DESIGNED TO ALLEVIATE SOCIOECONOMIC INEQUALITY HAS DECLINED

In contrast to prior decades, overall levels of support among whites for a range of government intervention programs has declined. In particular, in the decades of the 1960s and 1970s, Americans expressed a moderate-to-strong level of support for programs that were designed to create racial equality in both economic opportunity (e.g., job training, enforcement of statutes designed to foster discrimination in the sale and rental of housing and apartments, as well as equality in educational opportunity) and economic outcome (e.g., affirmative action programs, guaranteed wage programs). However, studies conducted in the 1980s consistently found that while support for equality of opportunity programs has remained consistent, support for programs that are intended to guarantee equality of economic outcome between the races has declined drastically (see Kluegel and Smith, 1986; Schuman, Steeh, and Bobo, 1985). Rather, it appears that programs designed to ensure equality in economic outcome received similar levels of support as in prior decades only if they were implemented on the basis of social class rather than race (see Bobo and Kluegel, 1991; Kluegel and Bobo, 1991; Kluegel, 1990).

AFRICAN AMERICANS ARE PERSONALLY RESPONSIBLE FOR THEIR DISADVANTAGED STATUS

Findings from survey research indicate that in the 1980s whites took an increasingly "hard line" with respect to individualistic stratification ideology vis-à-vis the economic plight of African Americans. In particular, while levels of support for survey items that explain socioeconomic inequality between the races in terms of individualistic factors (e.g., work ethic, values, etc.) have risen dramatically, explanations that emphasize structural factors (e.g., blocked opportunities, discrimination, etc.) have declined (see Kluegel and Smith, 1986; Sigelman and Welsh, 1991).

A related development has been the crystallization of "color coding" beliefs, a phenomenon that links particular racial/ethnic groups with particular forms of extreme socioeconomic marginality (see Wilson, 1996; Quadagno, 1994). Specifically, it appears that the American public has developed stereotypical notions that African Americans disproportionately constitute the welfare-dependent population, and that this stereotypical notion is related to the predominantly individualistic explanations that Americans employ when explaining the causes of welfare dependency.

Finally, survey evidence indicates that if Americans see a culprit that has acted hand-in-hand with African Americans to explain their relative disadvantaged status, it is the state. In fact, the state appears to be the linchpin that ties many of the above tenets into a coherent ideology of race. In particular, in the 1980s, we saw a substantial increase among whites for the notion that the state has "gone too far" in advancing the rights of African Americans: the state has "legitimated groups rights," "established affirmative action programs," and "spent too much money on social programs," debilitating rather than uplifting its targeted population. In this scenario, it appears that the perceived victims of racial discrimination have dramatically shifted from African Americans to whites (see Kluegel and Smith, 1986; Schuman, Steeh, and Bobo, 1985).

Together, the above tenets constitute the heart of an ideology of race; this ideology links race with a causal framework for explaining racial inequality in society. In fact, this ideology of race has been the basis for the ascendancy of a predominant kind of racial project that attacks the legacy and logic of achievements attained by African Americans in previous decades. In the 1980s, race was rearticulated to constitute a particular kind of meaning vis-à-vis the structuring of racial inequality.

We now offer two examples of the link between this racial ideology and the dominant racial project. Both derive from the ideological tenets highlighted above. The first, a quote from Charles Murray on welfare reform, is cited by Omi and Winant (1994: 58):

My proposal for dealing with the racial issue in social welfare is to repeal every bit of legislation and reverse every court decision that in any way requires, recommends, or awards differential treatment according to race, and thereby put us back onto the track that we left in 1965. We may argue about the appropriate limits of government intervention in trying to enforce the ideal, but at least it should be possible to identify the ideal: Race is not a morally admissible reason for treating one person differently from another. Period.

Murray's statement is an example of the dominant racial project that has become ascendant in the post-1980 period in the United States. It is an analysis of the meaning of race: it is not a morally valid basis upon which to treat people differently from one another. We may notice someone's race but we cannot act upon that awareness. We must act in a "color-blind" fashion. Furthermore, this analysis of the meaning of race is linked to a conception of the role of race in the social structure: it can play no part in government action, save in "the enforcement of the ideal." Finally, Murray's statement also links the meaning of race with the structuring of racial inequality. In particular, the specific legislation and court decisions Murray mentions are legal means of defining access to economic resources on the explicit grounds of race.

We have now identified how racial ideology in the post-1980 period is linked to a dominant racial project. However, we have yet to account for the widespread adoption of this racial ideology and its concomitant racial project that advocates the ideal of a "color-blind" society. As discussed earlier, for Omi and Winant, racial projects are "historically contingent," even though they may present themselves as absolute (for all time) master narratives. These sociohistoric contingencies can be identified. In the next section, we attempt to identify the sociohistoric forces that have led to the rise of a particular kind of racial ideology.

THE SOCIOHISTORIC SOURCES OF POST-1980 RACIAL IDEOLOGY

We believe the emergence of a new form of racial ideology, which is characterized by the ideal it placed on a "color-blind" society in the 1980s, is directly related to the profound social and economic dislocations that swept across America during this period. In particular, we believe blame for a series of domestic and international economic setbacks suffered in this country led to the widespread adoption of a neoconservative ideology, which purports to "analyze" American social and economic ills. This ideology however, has a strong racial subtext. The economic factors that we identify here have been discussed in many other contexts. However, sociologists have hardly examined their implications for understanding racial ideology. In this section we attempt to accomplish this task.

Domestic

Beginning in the mid- to late 1970s, the effects of profound economic changes in this country, routinely characterized as constituting the dynamics of "industrial restructuring," began to be felt (see Cross, 1992; Wilson, 1987). Specifically, the overall opportunity structure was undergoing a transformation as traditional middle- and upper-middle-class jobs were rapidly being replaced with entry-level service slots. This transformation created levels of unemployment, underemployment, and general economic uncertainty that had been unprecedented among American workers since the Great Depression. Migration of jobs was the catalyst for this uncertainty, as a traditional range of white and blue-collar jobs and industries (such as rubber, steel, and auto production) left the "frostbelt" en masse for the sunbelt. Furthermore, the industries that replaced the departed ones—the burgeoning service and so-called "high-tech" industries—exacerbated the adverse economic conditions because of significant job and skill "mismatches."

There were other frightening signs that the economy was in a "free fall." During the same period, inflation surged to unprecedented levels, eroding consumer purchasing power, curtailing investment, and slowing economic growth. The problem of stagflation (which Keynesian policies were helpless to overcome), came to be perceived as a growing and intransigent problem. Many of the overt signs of the domestic economic malaise were well publicized: There was the near bankruptcy of major cities, property tax revolts, and the soaring federal deficit. Amid all of this domestic turmoil, in 1980 the United States elected a president whose chief commitment was to stem the tide of deterioration these events reflected.

International

In the international arena, a range of developments have also helped to shape the context for the widespread adoption of a neoconservative political ideology. In particular, the early 1980s was a period in which the formerly uncontested hegemony of the United States was seriously eroded: For the first time in memory, people in the United States were forced to contemplate the idea that we were no longer "No. 1." First, we lost in foreign wars in Vietnam, Nicaragua, and Iran in the late 1970s; international trade advantages previously enjoyed went down the tubes. Once the world's creditor, by the early 1980s the United

States had become its chief debtor. Once the chief exporter of manufactured goods, by the beginning of the 1980s the United States was their chief importer; the United States was bullied by OPEC nations who controlled our vital energy resources, and America was held "hostage" by politico-religious forces in Iran. Finally, once the model for democracy for the underdeveloped world, the United States was filled with doubt about the proper level of support for authoritarian regimes.

Significantly, the general decline of the United States in both the domestic and international spheres created an unprecedented economic insecurity and led to widespread perceptions that the American Dream was becoming increasingly unattainable. In fact, it is the ways in which the American populace experienced the severe dislocations of the late 1970s and early 1980s that created a ripe climate for a rise of right-wing politics based on the reassertion of lost traditional cultural and social values. By the 1980s a neoconservative ideology based on venerable American values such as respect for authority, mistrust of "big" government, and a defense of traditional morality had captured the popular political imagination. In sum, this neoconservative ideology represented a way of coping with the massive changes taking place in American society. Accompanying the growing economic instability was a new political fragmentation; new racial, regional, sexual, and religious groups became visible, so that there was no longer a clear notion of the "common good." The neoconservative philosophy became a vehicle by which to consolidate a new majority that could dismantle the welfare state, legislate a return to traditional morality, and stem the tide of political and cultural dislocation, which the 1970s represented.

The issue of race, of course, constituted an important aspect of the neoconservative philosophy. However, the egalitarian ideals established in the previous two decades precluded reliance on the overt kind of racism of previous generations. Racial equality had to be acknowledged as a desirable goal; no longer could Americans express open support for segregation and biological theories of racial inequality. As such, earlier themes of racial equality had to be "repackaged," infusing them with new political meaning, linking them to key elements of the neoconservative ideology.

The neoconservative philosophy touched substantially on issues relating to the role of race in the democratic process. In particular, it contained a logic that challenged the underpinnings of the 1960s ideals for social justice: It sketched out a vision of an egalitarian society where racial considerations were no longer the concern of state policy. The liberal state had become the perpetrator of a racially unjust society; this new injustice conferred groups, rights on racial minority groups, thus granting a new form of privilege—"preferential" treatment. Thus, in attempting to eliminate racial discrimination, the state went too far; It legitimated groups' rights, established affirmative action mandates, and spent money on a range of social programs which were seen as debilitating rather than uplifting of their targeted populations. In this scenario, the victims of racial discrimination had dramatically shifted from racial minorities to whites. It was time to stop "throwing good money after bad." In attempting to remedy problems of poverty and inequality, the state made them worse and instilled a parasitic dependency in its clients. A range of policy programs ranging from welfare to school busing and affirmative action now fell into widespread disfavor.

The neoconservative dogma has been particularly critical of state policies that engaged in "race-thinking" (and thus produced "reverse discrimination" and "reverse racism"). Perhaps the epitome of this logic, and the most articulate rationale for the adoption of a "color-blind" society as a resolution to excessive statism, comes from Nathan Glazer's (1976: 202) book *Affirmative Discrimination*. Affirmative action, he wrote:

has meant that we abandon the first principle of a liberal society, that the individual's interests and good and welfare are the test of a good society, for we now attach benefits and penalties to individuals simply on the basis of their race, color and national origins. The implications of this new course are increasing consciousness of the significance of group membership, an increasing divisiveness on the basis of race, color, and national origin, and a spreading resentment among the disfavored groups against the favored ones. If the individual is the measure, however, our public concern is with the individual's capacity to work out an individual fate by means of education, work, and self-realization in the various spheres of life. Then how the figures add up on the basis of whatever measure of group we use may be interesting, but should be of no concern to public policy.

Glazer's objections to affirmative action policies centered on their ineffectiveness and their challenge to the fundamental civil ideals which had made the traditional Horatio Alger "ethnic success story" possible: individualism, market-based opportunity, and the curtailment of excessive state interventionism. These civil ideals, which were the basis for the rise of American hegemony in the world, could only be recaptured if the state adopted policies that permitted only individual rights to exist.

CONCLUSION

In the past ten years, sociologists have emphasized the importance of integrating racial ideology into the analysis of racial inequality. However, they have also expressed great dissatisfaction with the efforts undertaken to integrate these two topics (see See, 1986; Omi, 1987). This chapter represents a response to this frustration: We have argued that Omi and Winant's racial formation theory can be used as a first step toward linking the sociological literatures that examine racial ideology with labor market inequality by race. As such, racial formation theory can be used as the basis for developing a broader, more inclusive theory of racial inequality.

In particular, we posited that the key to a more inclusive theory of racial inequality is the notion of "racial projects," which are historically contingent ideologies that structure the meaning of race in everyday life. Specifically, racial projects bridge the limitations of two broad sociological literatures: perspectives that focus on market dynamics (which have tended to neglect the ideological undercurrents that help to determine how different racial groups are positioned in the labor market), and studies of racial ideology (which have tended to ignore the broader structural implications of the racial ideology that they have tapped).

In addition, we have seen that the ideological tenets that comprise "racial projects" can be gleaned from empirical studies of racial attitudes and the sociohistoric sources that have been identified. As such, we maintain that the foundation for building a more inclusive theory of racial inequality is not inscrutable or elusive: The critical connections between racial ideology and racial inequality can, in fact, be made.

Applied in a specific sociohistoric context, we can now say that racial formation theory helps to shed light on the sociological significance of the post-1980 ideology, which promotes as ideal a "color-blind" society. Specifically, in the face of an ever-widening gap in levels of inequality between the races, this post-1980 ideology appears to rationalize the failure to address the historic legacy of discrimination and injustice that continues to hamper racial minorities. As such, the call for a "color-blind" society is a way of maintaining advantage for those who have not been victimized by this legacy—namely, whites.

Finally, while we have presented post-1980 racial ideology in a monolithic manner, we are mindful of the fact that it is constantly in flux. As the range of societal and economic factors that constitute the underpinning of its changes, so undoubtedly will the racial ideology. We cannot predict the form that racial ideology will take in the future. However, it is hoped that we have shown that whatever form it takes, it will be intimately related to the structuring of racial inequality.

REFERENCES

Apter, D. (1965) *The Politics of Modernization*. Chicago: University of Chicago Press.

Bell, D. (1960) *The End of Ideology*. Glencoe, IL: Free Press.

Bobo, L. and J. Kluegel. (1991) "Economic Versus Race-Targeted Policy: Public Opinion on the New Liberal Welfare Agenda." Paper presented at the Conference of the American Association for Public Opinion Research, Phoenix, Arizona, May 1991.

Bonacich, E. (1972) "A Theory of Ethnic Antagonism: The Split Labor Market." *American Sociological Review* 38 (August): 547–559.

Bonacich, E., and J. Modell. (1980) *The Economic Basis of Ethnic Solidarity*. Berkeley: University of California Press.

Boswell, T. (1984) *The Cuban-American Experience: Culture, Images, and Perspectives*. Totowa, NJ: Rowman & Allanheld.

Collins, S. (1993) "Blacks on the Bubble: The Vulnerability of Black Executives in White Corporations." *The Sociological Quarterly* 34 (August): 429–447.

Cross, M. (Ed.). (1992) *Ethnic Minorities and Industrial Change in Europe and North America*. Cambridge: Cambridge University Press.

Edsall, T., and M. Edsall. (1991) *Chain Reaction: The Impact of Race, Rights, and Taxes on American Politics*. New York: W. W. Norton.

Farley, R., and W. Allen. (1987) *The Color Line and the Quality of Life in America*. New York: Russell Sage Foundation.

Glazer, N. (1976) *Affirmative Discrimination*. New York: Basic Books.

Glazer, N., and D. Moynihan (Eds.). (1975) *Ethnicity: Theory and Experience*. Cambridge, MA: Harvard University Press.

Jaynes, G., and R. Williams. (1989) *A Common Destiny*. Washington, DC: National Academy Press.

Jencks, C. (1991) "Is the American Underclass Growing?" In *The Urban Underclass*, edited by Christopher Jencks and Paul Peterson. Washington, DC: The Brookings Institution, pp. 28–102.

Kluegel, J. (1990) "Trends in Whites' Explanations of the Black-White Gap in Socioeconomic Status, 1977–1989." *American Sociological Review* 55, no. 4: 512–525.

Kluegel, J., and L. Bobo. (1991) "Dimensions of Whites' Beliefs About the Black-White Socioeconomic Gap." In *Race and Politics in American Society*, edited by Paul Sniderman. Stanford, CA: Stanford University Press, pp. 11–41.

Kluegel, J., and E. Smith. (1982) "Whites' Beliefs About Blacks' Opportunity." *American Sociological Review* 47, no. 4: 518–532.

———. (1986) *Beliefs About Inequality: What Is and What Ought to Be*. New York: Aldine De Gruyter.

McAdam, D. (1982) *Political Process and the Development of Black Insurgency*. Chicago: University of Chicago Press.

Oliver, M., and T. Shapiro. (1995) *Black Wealth/ White Wealth: A New Perspective on Racial Inequality*. Routledge: New York.

Omi, M. (1987) "Shifting the Blame: Racial Ideology and Politics in the Post–Civil Rights Era." *Critical Sociology* 18, no. 3: 77–98.

Omi, M., and H. Winant. (1994) *Racial Formation in the United States*. New York: Routledge.

Parcel, T. and, C. Mueller. (1983) *Ascription and Labor Markets*. New York: Academic Press.

Parsons, T. (1966) *Societies: Evolutionary and Contemporary Perspectives*. Englewood Cliffs, NJ: Prentice-Hall.

Quadagno, J. (1994) *The Color of Welfare: How Racism Undermined the War on Poverty*. New York: Oxford University Press.

Rosenfeld, R. (1980) "Race and Sex Differences in Career Dynamics." *American Sociological Review* 45, no. 4: 583–609.

Schuman, H., C. Steeh, and L. Bobo. (1985) *Racial Attitudes in America: Trends and Interpretations*. Cambridge, MA: Harvard University Press.

See, K. (1986) "Ideology and Racial Stratification: A Theoretical Juxtaposition." *International Journal of Sociology and Social Policy* 6, no. 1: 75–89.

Sigelman, L., and S. Welsh. (1991) *Black Americans' Views of Racial Inequality*. Cambridge: Cambridge University Press.

Stone, J. (1985) *Racial Conflict in Contemporary Society*. Cambridge, MA: Harvard University Press.

Thurow, L. (1969) *Poverty and Discrimination*. Washington, DC: The Brookings Institute.

Williams, W. (1982) *The State Against Blacks*. New York: McGraw-Hill.

Wilson, G. (1996) ''Towards a Revised Framework for Examining Beliefs About the Causes of Poverty.'' Forthcoming in *The Sociological Quarterly*.

Wilson, G., and D. Royster. (1995) ''Critiquing Wilson's Critics: The Black Middle Class and the Declining Significance of Race Thesis.'' *Research in Race and Ethnic Relations* 8, no. 3: 63–75.

Wilson, W. (1987) *The Truly Disadvantaged*. Chicago: University of Chicago Press.

10

Neoconservatism and Freedom in Postmodern North American Culture

Norman N. Morra

INTRODUCTION

This chapter explores three issues pertinent to North American society. First, the revival of conservatism and the threat that it poses for postmodern culture is analyzed. Next, the issue of whether or not freedom has been central to democratic political, economic, and social structures is examined. Third, the continuing economic crisis is illustrated to have modified the way in which most North Americans experience their lifeworld.

The *lebenswelt*, or lifeworld, serves a dual purpose: (1) it provides the common stock of knowledge vital to forming individual and national identities; (2) it affects how persons view the world (Berger and Luckmann, 1967; Schutz, 1970). Coinciding with Mills's (1961) "social milieu," the lifeworld underpins Habermas's (1984, 1990) theory of communicative action and its corollary of communicative competence.

According to Habermas (1970: 145; 1984: 131), the blend of intersubjectivity, mutual understanding, and discourse promotes consensus in the public sphere. Ideally, rational discourse induces responsible action, which returns authority to its legitimate and primary source: the people. This chapter argues that Weberian concepts such as rationality, authority, and legitimation—once integral to the analysis of modernity—have run their course. On the other hand, Weber's often neglected theoretical concepts of irrationality and sensuality are more suitable to understanding the present postmodern era.

In the final passage of *The Protestant Ethic and the Spirit of Capitalism*, Weber predicted that rationality and utilitarianism would engulf future societies and serve as the *sine qua non* for all interpersonal relations. The Calvinist notion of a calling, or *beruf*—specialization at the expense of joy—led to the indisputable division of labor which confirmed what both Marx and Weber feared: the entrapment of the human spirit.[1] Despite its inevitability, Weber pointed to an opposing set of criteria to offset the scourge of rationalism. According to Weber (1978: 6), "The more we ourselves are susceptible to such emotional reactions as anxiety, anger, ambition, envy, jealousy, love, enthusiasm, pride, vengefulness, loyalty, devotion, and appetites of all sorts, and to the 'irrational' conduct which grows out of them, the more readily can we empathize with them."

The irrational, incoherent, obscene, and erratic aspects of technological society are at the heart of postmodernity. These themes underpin the writings of Beckett, Baudrillard, Bataille, Bakhtin, Benjamin, and Lyotard among others. Lyotard (1984), for instance, argues that consensus is illusory because it rarely guarantees harmony or progress in intellectual activity. Indeed, the contractual agreement, which underlies most of today's social and sexual relations, serves as little more than a "skin of currency" (Lyotard, 1993: 85). For Lyotard, consensus is prohibitive because it tends to stultify bold, innovative, anarchic thought, which challenges "the power center whose behavior is governed by a principle of homeostasis" (Lyotard, 1984: 63). Furthermore, computerization sets new standards of performativity requiring speedy and insightful arguments—mini-narratives—to free up the weighty abundance of traditional knowledge. According to Baudrillard (1983: 138), technology outstrips the social and produces "Raw industrial violence, aiming to induce behaviors of terror and of animal obeisance. All of that no longer has any meaning."

Lyotard and Baudrillard share the conviction that two major technological forces—computers and television—supplant the existential subject. Both forces have restructured the economic base and will transform work, ideology, and culture in the next century (Rifkin, 1995). Therefore, does this technological shift forward signal a rescindment of the democratic spirit and a possible return to conformity?

THE DEMOCRATIC SPIRIT VERSUS NEOCONSERVATISM

Mannheim's (1992) notions of "de-distantiation" and "de-hierarchization" form the basis of the democratic spirit—in work and culture. He advanced these notions in the early 1930s, prior to the Nazi dominance of Europe. "A democratizing trend is our predestined fate, not only in politics, but also in intellectual and cultural life as a whole" (Mannheim, 1992: 171). In 1934, Bertrand Russell, sensing the rise of fascism, wrote an essay that paid tribute to Thomas Paine as an exemplar of freedom and democracy.[2] According to Russell, "It was his [Paine's] fate to be always honoured by Opposition and hated by Governments." The point they are making is that equality, free speech, and action have always sustained democracy and have been the antidote for totalitarian thinking.

In the midst of war, suffering, genocide, and AIDS, freedom gives meaning to human existence. Existentialists such as Sartre (1960) and Camus (1957) defined freedom in terms of authentic action and rebellion, divorced from any systematic *a priori* values. In Sartre's words, "I alone have to realize the meaning of the world and my own existence; values are not transcendental givens, independent of human subjectivity" (Sartre, 1960: 115–116). Accordingly, for postmodernism to defy the present conservative onslaught it must revitalize the notion of self as a person—a thinking agent with social awareness (Taylor, 1991). This is an ethical stance, but ethics are required to combat the religious right who undermine equally pleasure and scientific truth. For example, several school boards are being pressured to admit creationism into the curriculum as a valid alternative to Darwin's Theory of Evolution.

North America is experiencing a conservativivism similar to the conformity of the 1950s. This so-called new conservatism heralds the rebirth of a decade that discouraged independent thought and promoted respect for legitimate authority, bureaucracy, the state, and religion—for orthodoxy in general. This respect for hierarchical institutions such as the family, church, and government has serious implications for postmodernism, which espouses an egalitarian, heterogeneous, hedonistic, and carnivalesque culture (Bakhtin, 1968; Bataille, 1985; Featherstone, 1991; Stallybrass and White, 1986). Conservatism threatens on two fronts: by imposing draconian economic restraints and by chipping away the cornerstone of North American society—democracy. Specifically, recent cuts in jobs and social programs, along with massive technological change, have diminished society's broad consumer base of lower- and middle-class citizens. This raises a critical question: Does the current malaise, along with the neoconservatism, jeopardize the welfare of millions, as well as the democratic spirit at the heart of postmodernism?

For the last fifteen years, many persons have endured a demoralizing recession that threatens democratic principles. One principle is the right of citizens to participate openly in the decision-making process that affects their everyday lives. The following illustrates this point from a Canadian perspective. Throughout this century, Ontario has been a thriving industrial and financial region of North America. Between the 1950s and 1960s, Ontario helped to sustain a strong Canadian dollar that equalled and surpassed—albeit briefly—the American dollar as a leading world currency. Additionally, in light of its steadily deteriorating economy, Canadian elites now distance themselves from the expanding underclass whose function is to serve the rich and powerful (Galbraith, 1979).

This dismal situation affects other Western democracies, including the United States and Britain. For instance, California has suffered economically as much as any region in Britain or Canada. The economic decline in California is attributable less to the influx of illegal immigrants from Mexico—as conservatives argue—than from federal policy enacted over the last decade, specifically the North American Free Trade Agreement (NAFTA).

The most obvious reasons for this economic morass is the shutting down of industries in Canada and the United States, as well as the coalescence of government and corporate interests in Canada, Mexico, and the United States, manifested as NAFTA. Theoretically, NAFTA aimed to bind North America into a single political and economic union in order to combat the growing European and Asian economic communities. The accord's real goal, however, was to increase profits for corporate owners by reducing tariffs and opening up domestic markets.

Preceding NAFTA was the U.S-Canada Free Trade Agreement (FTA), which the two countries drafted *in camera*, away from the scrutiny of the public and the media. Chief negotiators Peter Murphy and Canadian Simon Reisman (1988) carefully guarded the details of the pact and excluded the input of citizens. As representatives of the Mulroney and Reagan administrations, Murphy and Reisman intentionally squelched public debate on both sides of the border. Simply, Canadians and Americans were prevented from deciding their own economic futures. Consumer advocate Ralph Nader put it this way: "This difficulty in obtaining and understanding the actual agreements is not an accident; it reflects a purposeful effort by government negotiators to conceal the terms and effect of the agreements from the public, the news media, and even Congress" (Nader, 1993: 5).

Reisman (1988) openly despised the media and doubted the average Canadian's ability to understand NAFTA or determine its import to their lives. Between 1986 and 1988, he assured Canadians that free trade would stimulate job growth and raise the standard of living in both Canada and America. He termed the media "dummies" and proclaimed that the public would learn, in due course, the true meaning of the agreement. In one sense Reisman was correct. Canadians and Americans, economists and laypersons alike, failed to grasp the true meaning of free trade. This was due mainly to the agreement's convoluted language, but also to the general lack of will on the part of North Americans to confront the state. The political mandarins refused to clarify the accord or listen to a public debate concerning its merits or faults. Emphatically, the powerful never discussed the foreboding effects in store for workers and others at the bottom of the socioeconomic order, including the young, old, disabled, and those on society's margins.

Instead of creating more jobs and higher wages, NAFTA gave companies that were hunting cheap labor and lax environmental laws the opportunity to relocate in Mexico. Today, there is talk of bringing Chile into the accord—but for what reason? By closing factories and setting up business in Mexico, corporate structures abandoned both Canadian and American workers. Some pro-NAFTA advocates, such as New Jersey senator Bill Bradley (1993), argued that "NAFTA will provide less incentive to move production to Mexico and not more." But the job growth and higher wages never materialized. Instead, companies capitalized on their newfound and unrestricted right to set up shop outside of Canada and the United States. This is what followed. Similar to the Great Depression, workers now scramble for the few decent paying jobs that corporations make available. Recently, more than 50,000 turned out at a General Motors plant in

Ontario to apply for a handful of unskilled jobs. Another closure of a GM plant in Flint, Michigan entailed the loss of 35,000 jobs.[3] Closing factories and cutting jobs has contributed to a pessimism that seriously alters the way in which most North Americans view their lifeworld and its democratic ideals.

This state of affairs has taken place gradually and took root in advance of free trade, but has certainly been facilitated by recent developments. This brings forward another significant issue related to Habermas's concept of communicative competence: the alternative solution of worker ownership of plants. As an attempt to forestall plant closings in the early 1980s, worker ownership only temporarily resolved the issue of corporate abandonment of the workplace. Aside from the effects of free trade, two reasons account for this: (1) technological progress threatens the traditional idea of work and the worker, and (2) corporate mergers reestablish patterns of hierarchical dominance that threaten open discourse throughout all sectors of society.

Workers' participation in corporate decisions and the liberalization of the workplace appear to be a short-term answer to the problem of plant closures. Canadian workers own and operate Algoma Steel in Sault St. Marie, Ontario, but the upper-level decisions rest in the hands of board directors and not with the workers. In effect, the right to strike has been removed because the next strike will be the last strike.

The current economic situation forces critics to reexamine the once viable and optimistic notion of worker ownership as an alternative to unemployment cause by plant closings. This challenges the idea of solidarity/consensus basic to Habermas's concept of communicative competence and his grand theory of communicative action. The power of language as fundamental to discourse and action—critical in resolving ethical and pragmatic problems—is paramount for several theorists (Chomsky, 1972; 1975; 1989; Murphy, 1984; Habermas, 1970; 1984; Taylor, 1991). Yet, despite the ability of workers to contribute to the decision-making process, they have never transcended the structure of ''organizational hegemony'' (Murphy, 1984: 294). The reason is communicative competence has a basic flaw: the assumption that reflective thought is sufficient to undermine structurally entrenched power. The one element that bonds workers is the reality of the physical or sensuous aspects of life. In other words, they are facing cultural mandates, including economic and political imperatives, that are enforced through various forms of violence. Unemployment and physical and political attack are real fears. And as Stanley Fish (1989: 342–355) points out, critical reflexivity may constitute a start, but is insufficient to undermine these threats.

COMMUNICATIVE COMPETENCE: LANGUAGE, DEMOCRACY, AND ACTION

Integral to Habermas's theory of communicative competence is the work of linguist Noam Chomsky. Habermas (1970: 131) based his theory on Chomsky's notion that language is an innate "monological capability" of humans bound by an "abstract system of rules." Avoiding the analysis of semantics—integral to Chomsky's thesis—Habermas adds another dimension to the argument of linguistic competence. By stressing the importance of language along with a knowledge of grammatical rules, Habermas attempts to show that discourse and empathy are key to resolving conflict. Simply put, both Chomsky and Habermas assume that because people communicate through language, they can easily theorize and develop the ability to critique various aspects of society. True competence, however, rests on the ability to conceptualize, form a perspective, and modify one's position accordingly. This is beyond the scope of most people, due to the fact that the social conditions necessary for them to engage in critical reflection have not been established. They are pitted against a version of reality that constantly inferiorizes the value of critique.

Chomsky (1989) argues that because people can analyze issues in the realm of sport, they also have a capacity to discuss important political issues. By overemphasizing rationality and logic as the guiding principle of everyday life, Chomsky and Habermas misconstrue what genuinely solidifies the masses—the element of the body and enjoyment—already mentioned in respect to Weber. Moreover, workers deal with the economy rationally, trying to analyze and predict what is going to happen, and thereby fail to recognize and overcome the rationale for their alienation and exploitation. Philosophy, sociology, and education have downplayed enjoyment, leisure, and the body as the centrifugal force in the expression of democracy. For example, contrast Habermas's description of the "ideal speech situation," which stresses three related types of action (success, instrumental, and strategic) with the concrete notion of carnival put forward by Bakhtin, and the excremental culture of Baudrillard and Bataille. In the latter case, the body defiles claims about absolute logic and reveals the limits of any system of rationality, including economic rationality. Accordingly, the world is rendered open for change, which is now possible with the proper motivation.

Excremental Culture and Authoritarianism

The masses perpetrate a discourse that leads to a kind of consensus that Baudrillard (1990: 31) terms "obscenity." This obscenity permeates an entire culture where oversignification, a superfluidity of images and babble—has destroyed any sense of the real. "When everything is oversignified, meaning itself becomes impossible to grasp" (p. 60). One example of this is the forum of talk radio and TV— places where the lowest form of argument passes as definitive and meaningful discourse. Geraldo Rivera, Jenny Jones, Jerry Springer, Phil Donahue, Oprah Winfrey, and Larry King compete with one another for the truth of a particular social issue, including abortion, incest, adultery, or guilt and innocence in the O. J. Simpson trial. For sure, discourse abounds but not as rational, purposeful and reflective language. This form of talk is nonsensical, passionate, reactive, and at times barbaric, but gives full value to freedom of speech. In short, the current financial and political situation affects the way that many express their deepest sentiments on personal and world affairs. Fragmented and frenetic speech, in other words, has become the norm. If this is the legitimate forum for free speech, perhaps Baudrillard is correct in depicting television as God. This may signal the decline of postmodernity, and a return to authoritarian thinking and one-dimensional society governed by ''the logic of domination'' (Marcuse, 1966: 142).

Authoritarianism Revisited

The early 1950s was a period of economic boom with low unemployment and a burgeoning middle class in North America. Despite this prosperity, the memory of the Great Depression and the Second World War prevented many Americans from embracing the cultural diversity that accompanied the wave of postwar immigration. Besides wealth, the 1950s represented the apex of fear, insecurity, and intolerance for others. The threat of a final nuclear holocaust—''The Cold War''—and the spread of communism—''The Red Scare''—induced a sense of panic among Americans fearful of losing their new security. McCarthyism, racism, and ethnocentrism ushered in the repression of free discourse in both academic and public forums. Besides racism, there was discrimination against intellectuals in the culture industry (actors, directors, screenwriters, and producers) who espoused so-called un-American points of view. Terms such as ''un-American'' and ''liberal'' suggested paranoia and hysteria on both sides: among the xenophobes themselves and among those they chose to target. Writings critical of American society, Steinbeck's *The Grapes of Wrath* and Arthur Miller's *Death of a Salesman*, were considered by conservatives as indicative of inflammatory leftist ideology. This tension culminated in the social revolution of the Beat and Hippie generations during the 1950s and the late 1960s. Both rejected middle-class values of industriousness and propriety, which were considered to be remnants of the Protestant ethic. The dominant bourgeois society spawned a counterculture that defied the industrial military technocracy and pursued freedom of expression and the right to criticize the establishment.

The Cold War gave rise to Beat writers such as Kerouac and Ginsberg, who, through their novels and poetry, brought the notion of democratization to the growing masses of American youth. Seminal to the Beat Generation was the poetry of Walt Whitman (1991), whose *Leaves of Grass* was the first authentic declaration of freedom from oppressive labor and bourgeois beliefs. Moreover, Whitman's poetry celebrated the pleasures of the body, a theme common to postmodern writings (Bakhtin, 1968; Stallybrass and White, 1986). From the mid-1950s to the early 1970s, the trend in music, art, and literature was toward self-expression or ''doing your own thing.'' Both public protests and rock concerts shared the same mood of celebration and solidarity. Further, liberalization in literature, art, academia, and work occurred throughout the 1970s and early 1980s. The electronic age of television, followed by computers, provided information to millions almost instantly. People would now know and act on the basis of what they learned through TV and computers. In this context, the reinstatement of conservatism in Britain, France, and North America signals the end of diversity, dedistantiation, and freedom from hierarchical dominance in society. More critically, conservativism threatens to stamp out play, symbol, and festivity—the roots of creativity and common culture (Gadamer, 1982).

From the 1950s until the present, industry has devised efficient technological methods to achieve greater productivity for the "maximation of profits" (Galbraith, 1979: xiii). Presently, fewer workers create more products for the marketplace. Braverman (1975: 206) pointed to the automobile industry assembly line as one industrial method that inhibits worker creativity for the sake of mass production. Since the 1970s, automobile manufacturers—domestic and foreign— have supplanted workers with robots. This switch has eliminated jobs and taken away the livelihood of many workers in smaller centers throughout North America. Automobile companies distort reality by using television commercials that depict workers expressing satisfaction with their work and the quality of their products. Still, fewer workers now produce more vehicles to ensure larger profits for the automobile industry. And the division of labor that Durkheim, Marx, and Weber envisaged as central to society has become a moot sociological point. The reasons for this outcome are twofold. First, as corporations merge there is less and less labor to divide; and second, as Baudrillard (1975: 74–75) has argued, the great theorists, Marx particularly, grounded their analysis largely in the material aspect of work or the production of material commodities.

Despite the fact that leisure, fragmentation, and irrationality have now transposed labor, solidarity, and rationalization, this hardly diminishes the theses of Marx, Durkheim, and Weber. To refute these early concepts on the grounds that they failed to predict the current state of affairs suggests that the early major theorists understood the future trajectory of technology and mass culture. This reasoning falters, because applying contemporary perspectives to the past is little more than a presentist kind of analysis.

For instance, Marx's interpretation of capitalism is understandable in the context of his time, as is Weber's study of rationalization. The explosion of the symbolic disorder, as well as the death of the social that Baudrillard (1983; 1987; 1990; 1994) convincingly describes, coincided with the advent of television in the 1950s. What Baudrillard (1994: 26) encounters now differs from Marx's reality, and to relegate Marxist philosophy to the "dustbins of history" and to await the "sacred excrement of the dialectic" to surface is unfair.

Durkheim (1966: 41) wrote that "whatever opinion one has about the division of labor, everyone knows that it exists, and is more and more becoming one of the fundamental bases of the social order." Durkheim argued correctly that specialization was unavoidable and essential to the function of the workplace and society in general. The economic and political reality of the twentieth century has shown that technological progress depended on specialization and efficiency. Alienation and routinization of labor, along with the loss of creative expression in bourgeois capitalism, anchored the bulk of Marx and Weber's humanist argument (Lowith, 1993). For Durkheim (1973), however, individual creativity was secondary to solidarity and progress based on social morality. Indeed, as both Durkheim (1973) and Weber (1958) had professed, specialization and efficiency were the keystones of economic progress. None of the three envisaged the dawn of a postmarket era when work would cease (Rifkin, 1995).

To maximize profits, industry continues to streamline its operations by downsizing, restructuring, and centralizing knowledge. Lyotard (1984: 66) envisioned that computerization and designing information for the widest public use would give rise to new and creative mini-narratives, and thereby emphasize "the heteromorphous nature of language games." The dissemination of knowledge would help to instate fresh narratives essential to the flourishing of postmodern culture. But the opposite occurred! Instead of expanding markets, computerization centralized power in the workplace, decreased the labor force, and set an example for the public sector. By following private industry, different levels of government in Canada and the United States have implemented drastic fiscal cuts. The Canadian government, for example, intends to abolish 45,000 civil service jobs, many directly related to health and welfare. This exemplifies the way in which a bureaucratic answer to a problem can override both the consensus of the majority and the attempt to find creative solutions to problems. The rationale for this austerity is simple: Governments need to curb spending and lower their massive public debt for the public good.

Inevitably, corporate structures and governmental agencies aim their cuts at those who most need assistance—students, the elderly, and the unskilled. For instance, federal governments push to end billion dollar subsidies, such as student loans and home fuel assistance for older and poorer Americans. Politicians, regardless of orientation, draw up social contracts that benefit the powerful at the expense of the majority. Contractual agreements between the state (democrat, fascist, or communist) and its citizens are not feasible for this reason. Good faith solidifies contractual agreements, and neither corporations nor the state hold a genuine regard for workers as persons. Social contracts exist as unilateral dictums meant to further the agenda of the powerful. According to Ellul (1981), the state is without a moral sense and shows scant interest in the welfare or empowerment of its citizens. Thus, the state's main concern is economic, political, and institutional dominance or power (Chomsky, 1993; Ellul, 1973; 1981; Foucault, 1977; Galbraith, 1972). The rebirth of conservatism—moral and cultural—underpins the current austerity that broadens the gap between the affluent and others (Galbraith, 1992).

DEMOCRATIZATION OF CULTURE: MYTH AND REALITY

In 1956, Mannheim (1992: 175) asked a pertinent question: "But what if it could be shown that political democracy is merely one manifestation of a per-

vasive cultural principle?'' This question represents Mannheim's thesis on culture and democratization, and has set the stage for Habermas's theory of
communicative action via the lifeworld and linguistic competence. The theories
of communicative action and democratization have been presented as a possible
way for workers to achieve consensus and control their destinies (Murphy,
1984). But is controlling one's economic reality, through worker ownership and
solidarity, also a way to create a strong cultural base? When society rests on
the broadest and lowest-level cultural base—what Kroker (1986) terms "excremental culture"—is it possible to achieve a widespread, rational, and articulate
consensus? Mannheim's and Habermas's notions are questionable, when one
takes a good look at the lifeworld that infuses the reality or hyperreality of late
capitalism. How can democracy be forthcoming from persons who are alienated,
terrified, and view one another as adversaries? Moreover, democratization can
be manipulated according to one's ideological perspective. In this regard, Mannheim (1992: 173) argues that liberty can slip from the grasp of liberals when
"conservative or reactionary forces get the upper hand as the result of the free
play of political forces."

The legitimation crisis that Habermas (1975) outlined two decades ago continues unresolved. The inveterate moral majority leaders, such as Jerry Falwell
and Pat Buchanan as well as conservative writers and talk-show hosts Rush
Limbaugh and G. Gordon Liddy, fail to understand that the discrepancy between
the dismal economic reality and the means with which to survive it is insur-
mountable. Democratization in postmodern culture is epitomized in the form of
social contracts that governments propose for the benefit of their citizens. Social
contracts such as the Republicans' "Contract With America" are simply codes
for legalized indenture where the lower and middle classes take massive cuts in
Medicare and Medicaid.

Terms such as restructuring and downsizing translate into lower wages, part-
time jobs, early retirement, and outright dismissals for workers, regardless of
skill or senority. The cyclical crisis that Marx cited as endemic to capitalism
have become less intermittent and more sustained. Cutbacks are common in
practically all areas of society and affect jobs in factories, offices, universities,
and the arts. In the United States, the Republican-dominated Congress has threatened to withdraw funding for public television while the Canadian government
plans to cut 45,000 jobs in the public sector. In desperation, many now embrace
conservativism as a way to save their jobs and to salvage the remnants of a
traditional workplace with an easily discernible hierarchy of power.

With their emphasis on deficit reduction, return to religion, and overall conformism, conservatives threaten the liberty of workers and others in North America. The concepts of work and liberty are long-standing social and philosophical
issues that remain unresolved in contemporary consumer culture. Will the return
to traditional structures and values in both organizations and culture destroy the
lifeworld of North America? This last section of the chapter will outline a possible answer to this dilemma.

Liberty, however, has a different meaning for Marxists, neoconservatives, and postmodern theorists. For Marx, freedom had a threefold significance: (a) escape from life's exigencies, (b) open criticism of authority, and (c) the ability to realize one's creative potential. Regardless of political orientation, most theorists agree on the first and third points. However, to readopt the Protestant ethic, as many conservative politicians, writers, and talk-show hosts urge, is to refurbish the iron cage (Weber, 1958). Although theorists such as Baudrillard (1983; 1994) discern society and culture to be on the verge of oblivion, the realities of work, livelihood, and freedom persist. Despite what he believes, different forms of common culture—media, sport, religion, and politics—all constitute the basis for social reality. And from within these dimensions is where freedom and democracy will be realized. Conservatives, nonetheless, ignore this prospect because of their commitment to *laissez-faire*, authority-based tradition, and cultural conformity and assimilation.

The Right to Enjoyment: The Bakhtinian Answer

Directly opposed to conservatism is the liberational philosophy of Mikhail Bakhtin (1968). Bakhtin's starting point is the temporality of life and the demise of the body. Mortality and suffering underlie all philosophies and religions, as well as the social sciences. For Bakhtin, suffering unites the writings of disparate but similar authors such as Dostoevski and Rabelais. Enjoyment, pleasure, and sensuality are what liberate persons from the grim absurdity of the human condition. Pleasure, in fact, is the basis for seduction in literature as well as life (Barthes, 1975).

Conservative authoritarianism seeks to control the masses' right to pleasure and desire for diversity, with a return to the homogenous conformity of the 1950s. The phrase ''common wealth'' has no meaning to those who see the term as a way to centralize and monopolize the resources of a nation. This is Bakhtin's interpretation of the phrase. The material bodily principle is contained not in the biological individual, not in the bourgeois ego, but in the people who are continually growing and renewed. This is why, in Bakhtin's work, all that is bodily becomes grandiose, exaggerated, immeasurable (Bakhtin, 1968:19).

Metaphorically, the body represents the single most common example used in art, literature, and sociology. The body has been the unifying principle in discussions related to social organization. Comte and Durkheim used the organic analogy to explain how society could function and grow with the changing times, so long as there was a moral authority guiding this development (Collins and Makowsky, 1972). But the combination of morality and functionalism underpinned the largely conservative approach to the social sciences in post–World War II America. This new imagery appeared to be more scientific and rational.

The body was used in another sense, and sensuality took on different meanings. As a metaphor for democracy (the body politic for example), the body was used by Petronius (1959). Rabelais (1967), Bataille, Bakhtin, Walt Whitman, and Kurt Vonnegut, to both disrupt and to unify. As individuals, persons constitute a heterogeneous whole, and the social bond (before language and abstraction) is the sense of pleasure. This notion dates back to the Ancient Greek philosophers Democritus and Epicurus. This search for sensual fulfillment is what unites conservatives and liberals and is the phenomenological basis of social existence. As Marcuse reminds his readers, "the memory of gratification is at the origin of all thinking" (Marcuse, 1962: 29).

Dehierarchization hinges on the dismantling of power, and ribald laughter is the natural, dialogical response to the "tendency toward the stability and completion of being, toward one single meaning, one single tone of seriousness" (Bakhtin, 1968: 101). Classical Roman satirist Petronius (1959) showed how laughter combined with disrespect could remove social barriers, and shorten the gap between the Roman citizens and their slaves. Within the context of the feast is where the slave could entertain his masters, with limericks, puns, and farce, and gain his freedom. Duty went by the board. A slave's ability to generate laughter gained him his freedom. Once freed, however, former slaves were bound to the larger society by civil obligations.

In the poetry of Walt Whitman (1981), an amalgam of the body and soul becomes the true embodiment of American democracy. With Whitman there is a disregard for work unless this labor brings pleasure and self-expression, and unites persons to the cosmic realm. Although Marx (1818–1883) and Whitman (1819–1892) were separated geographically and had different educational backgrounds, both were kindred spirits in the sense that they had witnessed human suffering firsthand and despised what they saw. Marx, as editor of the *Rheinische Zeitung*, watched the Mosel peasants die from the cold and lack of food during the winter of 1842, forbidden by law to pick up the dead wood in the Rhine forest under penalty of death. This incident prompted Marx to abandon Hegelian idealism and to battle "the material forces of production in society" (Marx, 1959: 42–46).

Whitman opposed racism and sexism in America. While Marx focused on liberation from the division of labor and the oppression associated with social inequality, Whitman served as a medic during the Civil War and understood the meaning of suffering and death. The reaction to the insane wasting of human potential in both Europe and America—in the name of capitalism and racism—was what bonded Whitman and Marx. Liberation from tradition and hierarchical authority was what substantiated that bond.

In defense of Charles Dickens, against one American critic who attacked Dickens's portrayal of the misery under British capitalism in the nineteenth century, Whitman said this:

A "democratic writer," I take it, is one the tendency whose pages is to destroy the old land-marks which pride and fashion have set up, making impassable *distinctions* [italics mine] between the brethren of the Great Family . . . the familiarity with low life wherein Mr. Dickens places his readers is a wholesome familiarity. (Quoted in Dutton, 1961: 8)

Common culture and the masses, the vast majority of people who inhabit the lifeworld, form the basis for postmodern culture. But how does this culture thrive in a world where the basic necessities are threatened to be withdrawn? Outside of violence the only means left is laughter. If persons are caught in a quagmire of terror, obscenity, illusion, and death—where is the way out? Vonnegut (1973) decries the same condition as Baudrillard but his answer is laughter, and in this sense writers of any age who use this device can be referred to as postmodern. America was founded on gunpowder and greed, and this claim is the main theme of *Breakfast of Champions*. The superiority of the white race, and the institution of laws to favor the culturally content at the expense of a much larger majority, should be contested on all levels. Moore's attempt to deal with General Motors, with a mix of confrontation and laughter, was the only alternative to deadening the horrific imposition of power by corporate America.

Bakhtin and Race Relations

At this time, social democracy is rarely tied to economic democracy. As C. W. Mills says, social problems are presumed to be the result of personal faults (Mills, 1961: 5). Consistent with the emphasis that has been placed lately on *laissez-faire*, individuals are blamed for the recent increases in poverty and unemployment. Witness the rise in prominence, for example, of Charles Murray, Glen Lowry, and Thomas Sowell. To these writers, social justice is the product of personal responsibility and private morality.

In race relations, this conservative strategy has become very visible in recent days. Although some radical and progressive elements were present, the Million Man March was dominated by spokespersons who seemed to be most interested in propitiating the prevailing social and economic system. Theses such as atonement, self-help, and personal responsibility were prevalent. Of course, these ideas are a central part of the conservatives' credo. In the end, the message is that the victims of discrimination, economic dislocation, and the globalization of the economy are blamed for their current predicament.

Although, at times, there were calls for more jobs, many of the March's leaders seemed to be paying tribute to the "culture of poverty" thesis, particularly in terms of how this position has been outlined by Edward Banfield (Banfield, 1968). That is, those at the bottom of the well, to borrow the imagery provided by Derrick Bell (1992), are in this position because of personal and cultural traits.

As August Meier notes, however, "in periods of discouragement Negroes have adopted doctrines of self-help, racial solidarity, and economic development," instead of more radical proposals (Meier, 1968: 24). Regardless of whether the race relations has been taken over by conservatives or inundated by despair, the issue of change has been deflected away from racist institutions and social policies. The point is that little attention is devoted to developing more embodied institutions, ones that are not autonomous and likely to remain the privileged domain of the powerful.

Postmodernists, as mentioned in the previous section, can assist in this endeavor. As recognized by Stanford Lyman, in his most recent discussion of postmodern culture, there is no equivocation about dualism in postmodernism (Lyman, 1994). Suggested by talk about the flesh, sexual climax, laughter, and the carnivalesque is that the formation of social reality is a bodily process. Work and the workplace are the culmination of this activity. Human *praxis*, in other words, is at the root of any institutions.

Looking inward, accordingly, is simultaneously looking outward. This insight should not be lost on critics of race relations. The traditional separation of inward and outward should be viewed as a ploy to have minorities internalize the guilt for racism and economic discrimination. After all, subsequent to the collapse of dualism, this differentiation does not make sense. The so-called internal domain, accordingly, is simply a dimension of existing in the world as a thoroughly embodied being.

Personal salvation, accordingly, requires that the worldly conditions be present to foster this sort of renewal. This sublation of inward and outward, as Merleau-Ponty writes, means that individuals are always being-in-the-world (Merleau-Ponty, 1968: 130–155). The general upshot of this collapse of dualism is that personal freedom, for example, requires economic democracy. These issues no longer occupy parallel planes. In terms of constructing a world, if these facets of social life are intertwinted, they must be linked at the level of policy. To do otherwise would make no sense.

This is where laughter becomes relevant. For Bakhtin, laughter is not vacuous, similar to that encouraged by situational-comedy television programs. Instead, laughter shatters the facade of those who promote the reification of reality. Laughter rips away the legitimacy from those who try to convince persons that the present condition represents the best of all possible worlds. Laughter exposes the futility of the political intrigues supported by those in power to delude the masses. In this sense, laughter is a weapon to be used against those who take too seriously the urgency of the present reality.

Also illustrated by laughter is the intimate connection between motives and reality. As persons laugh at the populist claims made by corporate America, for example, the real interests of capitalists are exposed. Accordingly, the connecction can be made between the ability to shape reality and what is accepted as real. This awareness has the potential to promote social change. New motives, in other words, can gain acceptance and alter the present social configurations.

CONCLUSION

The point of this chapter is to argue that democracy does not exist in a vacuum. Significant segments of the civil rights movement nowadays, at least that which is receiving public attention, seem to be falling into this trap. The victims of discrimination are either being asked to atone for their sins or to become a more productive force in their communities. But working individually or with communities is usually futile, when this effort is usurped by a stifling economic system.

In capitalism, social reality has been constituted in several layers. This arrangement is neither natural nor inevitable, but the result of decisions made by powerful interests about what is most important in this kind of society. What is about to be said, therefore, is not an attempt to resurrect the standard base-superstructure argument. Nonetheless, within capitalism, primacy is given to the economic dimension of social life. The ability to be creative culturally, for example, depends on whether persons have at their disposal certain economic resources.

Accordingly, social democracy is incumbent on democratizing economy, unless democratic activity is going to be restricted to particular enclaves. This would be a utopian vision, as Marx notes, that is practically worthless. Before democracy can be truly exercized, the economic barriers that stifle this progress must be subverted. They must no longer be viewed as representing an inviolable reality. Clearly, this is the message conveyed by postmodernists.

Both Marxists and postmodernists critique the autonomy of economic reality within capitalism. However, their respective strategies are very different. Postmodernists illustrate that this task can be accomplished without invoking grand schemes such as history and naturalistic laws. Instead, claims about economic necessity can be revealed to be bombastic, as a result of demonstrating the fleshy or carnivalesque character of this reality. This maneuver, claim postmodernists, can be made without metaphysical props. And subsequent to this critique of economics, democracy is made possible; political motivation can move the polity in this direction.

NOTES

1. This represents the gist of Bryan S. Turner's insightful introduction to Lowith (1993).

2. See ''The Fate of Thomas Paine'' in Bertrand Russell, *Why I Am Not a Christian* (London: Unwin, 1975).

3. Mike Moore's sardonic documentary film *Roger and Me* gives a bittersweet account of Moore's attempt to meet with General Motors president Roger Smith to discuss saving the automobile plant in Flint, Michigan.

REFERENCES

Bakhtin, M. (1968) *Rabelais and His World*. Cambridge, MA: MIT Press.

Banfield, E. (1968) *Unheavenly City*. Boston: Little, Brown.

Barthes, R. (1975) *The Pleasure of the Text*. New York: Hill and Wang.

Bataille, G. (1985) *Visions of Excess: Selected Writings, 1927–1939*. Minneapolis: University of Minnesota Press.

Baudrillard, J. (1975) *The Mirror of Production*. St. Louis: Telos Press.

———. (1983) *Simulations*. New York: Semiotext(e).

———. (1987) *The Ecstasy of Communication*. New York: Semiotext(e).

———. (1990) *Fatal Strategies*. New York: Semiotext(e).

———. (1994) *The Illusion of the End*. Stanford, CA: Stanford University Press.

Bell, D. (1992) *Faces at the Bottom of the Well: The Permanence of Racism*. New York: Basic Books.

Berger, P., and T. Luckmann. (1967) *The Social Construction of Reality: A Treatise in the Sociology of Knowledge*. Harmondsworth, UK: Penguin.

Bradley, B. (1993) "NAFTA Is about Opportunity." *USA Today*, November 8, p. 13A.

Braverman, H. (1975) *Labor and Monopoly Capital*. New York: Monthly Review Press.

Camus, A. (1957) *The Rebel: An Essay on Man in Revolt*. New York: Random House.

Chomsky, N. (1972) *Language and Mind*. New York: Harcourt Brace Jovanovich, Inc.

———. (1975) *Reflections on Language*. New York: Random House.

———. (1989) *Necessary Illusions: Thought Control in Democratic Societies*. Toronto, ON: CBC Enterprises.

———. (1993) *Rethinking Camelot: JFK, The Vietnam War, and U.S. Political Culture*. Montreal, QC: Black Rose Books.

Collins, R., and M. Makowsky. (1972) *The Discovery of Society*. New York: Random House.

Derber, C. (1979) *The Pursuit of Attention: Power and Individualism in Everyday Life*. New York: Oxford University Press.

Durkheim, E. (1966) *The Division of Labor in Society*. New York: Free Press.

———. (1973) *Moral Education*. New York: Free Press.

Dutton, G. (1961) *Whitman*. London: Oliver & Boyd Ltd.

Ellul, J. (1973) *Propaganda: The Formation of Men's Attitudes*. New York: Random House.

———. (1981) "The Ethics of Propaganda: Propaganda, Innocence and Amorality." *Communications* 6, no. 2: 159–175.

Featherstone, M. (1991) *Consumer Culture and Postmodernism*. London: Sage Publications.

Fish, S. (1989) *Doing What Comes Naturally*. Durham, NC: Duke University Press.

Foucault, M. (1972) *Discipline and Punishment*. Harmondsworth, UK: Penguin Books.

Gadamer, H. G. (1982) *Truth and Method*. New York: Crossroad Publishing Company.

Galbraith, J. K. (1979) *The New Industrial State*. New York: The New American Library.

Habermas, J. (1970) "Toward a Theory of Communicative Competence." In *Recent Sociology: Patterns of Communicative Behavior*, no. 2, edited by Hans Dreitzel. New York: Macmillan, pp. 115–148.

———. (1975) *Legitimation Crisis*. Boston: Beacon Press.

———. (1984) *The Theory of Communicative Action, Vol. 2: Lifeworld and System: A Critique of Functionalist Reason*. Boston: Beacon Press.

———. (1989) *The New Conservatism: Cultural Criticism and the Historians' Debate*. Cambridge, MA: MIT Press.

———. (1990) *Moral Consciousness and Communicative Action*. Cambridge, MA: The MIT Press.

Kroker, A. (1986) *The Postmodern Scene: Excremented Culture and Hyperaesthetics*. New York: St. Martin's Press.

Lowith, K. (1993) *Max Weber and Karl Marx*. London: Routledge.

Lyman, Stanford, M. (1994) *Color, Culture, Civilization: Race and Minority Issues in American Society*. Champaign, Urbana: University of Illinois Press.

Lyotard, J. F. (1984) *The Postmodern Condition*. Minneapolis: University of Minnesota Press.

———. (1993) *Libidinal Economy*. Bloomington: Indiana University Press.

Mannheim, K. (1992) *Essays on the Sociology of Culture*. London: Routledge.

Marcuse, H. (1966) *One Dimensional Man*. Boston: Beacon Press.

———. (1962) *Eros and Civilization*. Boston: Beacon Press.

Marx, K. (1959) *Contribution to the Critique of Political Economy*. In *Marx and Engels: Basic Writings on Politics and Philosophy*, edited by L. Feuer. New York: Doubleday, pp. 42–46.

Meier, A. (1968) *Negro Thoughts in America, 1880–1915*. Ann Arbor: University of Michigan Press.

Merleau-Ponty, M. (1968) *The Visible and the Invisible*. Evanston, IL: Northwestern University Press.

Mills, C. W. (1961) *The Sociological Imagination*. New York: Grove Press.

Murphy, J. (1984) ''Organizational Issues in Worker Ownership.'' *American Journal of Economics and Sociology* 43, no. 3: 287–299.

Nader, R. (1993) ''Free Trade and the Decline of Democracy.'' In *The Case Against Free Trade: GATT, NAFTA, and the Globalization of Corporate Power*. San Francisco: Earth Island Press, pp. 1–12.

Petronius, A. (1959) *The Satyricon*. New York: New American Library.

Rabelais, F. (1967) *Gargantua and Pantagruel*. New York: AMS Press.

Reisman, D. (1988) ''Retiring Trade Negotiator Reisman Blasts 'Offensive' Questions.'' *Toronto Star* 5 (August): A3.

Rifkin, J. (1995) *The End of Work*. New York: G. P. Putnam's Sons.

Sartre, J. P. (1960) *To Freedom Condemned*, translated by Wade Baskin. New York: Philosophical Library.

Schutz, A. (1970) *Reflections on the Problem of Relevance*. New Haven, CT: Yale University Press.

Stallybrass, P., and A. White. (1986) *The Politics and Poetics of Transgression*. Ithaca, NY: Cornell University Press.

Taylor, C. (1991) ''The Person.'' In *The Category of the Person*, edited by M. Carrithers, S. Collins, and S. Lukes. New York: Cambridge University Press, pp. 257–281.

Vonnegut, K. (1973) *Breakfast of Champions*. New York: Bantam Books.

Weber, M. (1958) *The Protestant Ethic and the Spirit of Capitalism*. New York: Charles Scribner's Sons.

———. (1978) *Economy and Society, Vol. 1*, edited by G. Roth and C. Wittich. Berkeley: University of California Press.

Whitman, W. (1981) *Leaves of Grass and Selected Prose*, edited by L. Buell. New York: Modern Library.

Selected Bibliography

Albee, G. (1988) "The Politics of Nature and Nurture." *American Journal of Community Psychology* 10, no. 3: 4–28.

Alderfer, C. P. (1994) "A White Man's Perspective on the Unconscious Processes Within Black-White Relations in the United States." In *Human Diversity: Perspectives on People in Context*, edited by E. J. Trickett, R. J. Watts, and D. Birman. San Francisco: Jossey-Bass Publishers.

Alexander, J. C. (Ed.) (1987) *The Micro-Macro Link*. Berkeley: University of California Press.

Aomori, T. (1994) "Chusei" [The Middle Ages]. In *Buraku no Rekishi*, edited by B. K. Kenkyujo. Osaka: Kaiho.

Apter, D. (1965) *The Politics of Modernization*. Chicago: University of Chicago Press.

Asante, M. K. (1987) *The Afrocentric Idea*. Philadelphia: Temple University Press.

Aston, W. G. (1956) *Nihongi: Chronicles of Japan from the Earliest Times to A.D. 697*. London: Allen & Unwin.

Austin, J. L. (1962) *How to Do Things with Words*. Cambridge, MA: Harvard University Press.

Bakhtin, M. (1968) *Rabelais and His World*. Cambridge, MA: MIT Press.

———. (1981) *The Dialogic Imagination*. Austin: University of Texas Press.

Banfield, E. (1968) *Unheavenly City*. Boston: Little, Brown.

Barlow, J. P. (1995) "Welcome to Cyberspace." *Time* 145, no. 12 (Spring): 4–11.

Barr, C. W. (1996) "Failed Foreign Marriages in Japan: Boom or Bust?" *The Christian Science Monitor*, March 14, pp. 1, 8.

Barthes, R. (1975) *The Pleasure of the Text*. New York: Hill and Wang.

———. (1977) *Image, Music, Text*. New York: The Noonday Press.

———. (1982) *Mythologies*. New York: Hill and Wang.

———. (1985) *The Grain of the Voice*. New York: Hill and Wang.

Baudrillard, J. (1983) *Simulations*. New York: Semiotext(e).

———. (1987) *The Ecstasy of Communication*. New York: Semiotext(e).

————. (1990) *Fatal Strategies*. New York: Semiotext(e).

————. (1993) *Symbolic Exchange and Death*. Thousand Oaks, CA: Sage.

————. (1994) *The Illusion of the End*. Stanford, CA: Stanford University Press.

Bell, D. (1960) *The End of Ideology*. Glencoe, IL: Free Press.

————. (1975) "Ethnicity and Social Change." In *Ethnicity: Theory and Experience*, edited by N. Glazer and D. P. Moynihan. Cambridge, MA: Harvard University Press, pp. 141–174.

————. (1992) *Faces at the Bottom of the Well: The Permanence of Racism*. New York: Basic Books.

Benjamin, W. (1978) *Reflections*. New York: Harcourt Brace Jovanovich.

Berger, P., and T. Luckmann. (1967) *The Social Construction of Reality: A Treatise in the Sociology of Knowledge*. Harmondsworth, UK: Penguin.

Bhabha, H. K. (1994) *The Location of Culture*. London: Routledge and Kegan Paul.

Binet, A. (1896) *On Double Consciousness: Experimental Psychological Studies*. Chicago: The Open Court Publishing Company.

————. (1897) *The Psychic Life of Micro-Organisms*. Chicago: The Open Court Publishing Company.

————. (1899) *The Psychology of Reasoning: Based on Experimental Researches in Hypnotism*. Chicago: The Open Court Publishing Company.

————. (1913) *A Method of Measuring the Intelligence of Young Children*. Lincoln, IL: The Courier Company.

Binet, A., and T. Simon. (1914) *Mentally Defective Children*. London: Edward Arnold.

Blumer, H. (1969) *Symbolic Interactionism*. Englewood Cliffs, NJ: Prentice-Hall.

Bobo, L., and K. James. (1991) "Economic Versus-Race-Targeted Policy: Public Opinion on the New Liberal Welfare Agenda." Paper presented at the Conference of the American Association for Public Opinion Research, Phoenix, Arizona, May 1991.

Boden, M. (1977) *Artificial Intelligence and Natural Man*. New York: Basic Books.

Bonacich, E. (1972) "A Theory of Ethnic Antagonism: The Split Labor Market." *American Sociological Review* 37: Vol. 38, August: 547–559.

Bonacich, E., and J. Modell. (1980) *The Economic Basis of Ethnic Solidarity*. Berkeley: University of California Press.

Bond, H. M. (1934) *The Education of the Negro in the American Social Order*. New York: Prentice-Hall.

Bornoff, N. (1991) *Pink Samurai: Love, Marriage and Sex in Contemporary Japan*. New York: Simon & Schuster.

Boswell, T. (1984) *The Cuban-American Experience: Culture, Images, and Perspectives*. Totowa, NJ: Rowman & Allanheld.

Braddock, J. H., II, and M. P. Dawkins. (1993) "Ability Grouping, Aspirations, and Attainments: Evidence from the National Educational Logitudinal Study of 1988." *Journal of Negro Education* 62, no. 3: 324–336.

Bradley, B. (1993) "NAFTA Is about Opportunity." *USA Today*, November 8, p. 13A.

Braverman, H. (1975) *Labor and Monopoly Capital*. New York: Monthly Review Press.

Buber, M. (1970) *I and Thou*. New York: Charles Scribner's Sons.

Buffon, G. L. L., Compte de. (1812) *Natural History, General and Particular: The History of Man and the Quadrapeds*. London: T. Cadell and W. Davies.

Burger, J. (1995) *Zusetsu Sekai no Senjumin* [The Gaia Atlas of First Peoples: A Future of the Indigenous World]. Tokyo: Akashi Shoten.

Buss, A. R. (1976) "Galton and the Birth of Differential Psychology and Eugenics: Social, Political, and Economic Forces." *Journal of the History of the Behavioral Sciences* 12, no. 1: 47–58.

Callaghan, K. A., and J. W. Murphy. (1983) "Changes in Technological Social Control: Theory and Implications for the Workplace." In *The Underside of High-Tech*, edited by J. W. Murphy, A. Mickunas, and J. J. Pilotta. Westport, CT: Greenwood Press, pp. 17–28.

Campbell, J., and B. Moyers. (1988) *The Power of Myth*. New York: Doubleday.

Camus, A. (1957) *The Rebel: An Essay on Man in Revolt*. New York: Random House.

Chambers, R. (1987) *Rural Development: Putting the Last First*. London: Longman.

Chomsky, N. (1969) *The Acquistion of Syntax in Children from 5 to 10*. Cambridge, MA: MIT Press.

———. (1975) *Reflections on Language*. New York: Random House.

———. (1989) *Necessary Illusions: Thought Control in Democratic Societies*. Toronto, ON: CBC Enterprises.

———. (1993) *Rethinking Camelot: JFK, The Vietnam War, and U.S. Political Culture*. Montreal, QC: Black Rose Books.

"Chosen-go Towa Donna Kotobaka" [What Kind of Language Is Korean?]. (1984) *Kikan Sanzenri* (May): 38.

Christensen, K. (1986) "Ethic of Information Technology." In *The Human Edge: Human Technology and Helping People*, edited by G. Geiss and N. Viswanathan. New York: The Haworth Press, pp. 72–91.

Chuang Tzu. (1974) *Inner Chapters*. New York: Vintage.

Churchill, W. (1992) *Fantasies of the Master Race*. Monroe, ME: Common Courage Press.

Clarke, S. H., and G. G. Koch. (1976) "The Influence of Income and Other Factors on Whether Criminal Defendants Go to Prison." *Law & Society Review* no. 1:11, 57–92.

Cnaan, R. A. (1988) "Post Industrial Technologies: Their Impact on Society and the Role of the Welfare State." *Eurosocial Newsletter* 40, no. 1:11–12.

Collins, R., and M. Makowsky. (1972) *The Discovery of Society*. New York: Random House.

Collins, S. (1993) "Blacks on the Bubble: The Vulnerability of Black Executives in White Corporations." *The Sociological Quarterly* 34 (August): 429–447.

Comte, A. (1865) *A General View of Positive Religion*. London: Trubner.

Cross, M. (Ed.) (1992) *Ethnic Minorities and Industrial Change in Europe and North America*. Cambridge: Cambridge University Press.

Darwin, C. (1911) *The Origin of Species*. London: John Murray.

Deluze, G., and F. Guattari. (1983) *On the Line*. New York: Semiotext(e).

Derber, C. (1979) *The Pursuit of Attention: Power and Individualism in Everyday Life*. New York: Oxford University Press.

Derrida, J. (1977) "Introduction." In *The Origin of Geometry*, by E. Husserl. New York: Nicolas Hays.

Dowell, P. (1995) "Immaterial Girl." In *These Times* (July 10–23): 28–29.

Dower, J. (1986) *War without Mercy*. New York: Pantheon.

D'Souza, D. (1991). *Illiberal Education*. New York: The Free Press.

Durkheim, E. (1938) *The Rules of Sociological Method*. New York: Free Press.

———. (1951) *Suicide, a Study in Sociology*. Glencoe, IL: Free Press.

————. (1965) *The Elementary Forms of the Religious Life*. New York: Free Press.

————. (1966) *The Division of Labor in Society*. New York: Free Press.

————. (1973) *Moral Education*. New York: Free Press.

————. (1983) *Pragmatism and Sociology*. Cambridge: Cambridge University Press.

————. (1993) "Individualism and the Intellectuals." In *Readings in Social Theory*, edited by J. Farganis. New York: McGraw-Hill, pp. 88–96.

Dutton, G. (1961) *Whitman*. London: Oliver & Boyd Ltd.

Edsall, T., and M. Edsall. (1991) *Chain Reaction: The Impact of Race, Rights, and Taxes on American Politics*. New York: W. W. Norton.

Egon, G. (1990) *The Paradigm Dialogue*. Thousand Oaks, CA: Sage.

Ellul, J. (1973) *Propaganda: The Formation of Men's Attitudes*. New York: Random House.

————. (1981) "The Ethics of Propaganda: Propaganda, Innocence and Amorality." *Communications* 6, no. 2: 159–175.

Fanon, F. (1963) *Black Skin, White Masks*. New York: Grove.

Farley, R., and W. Allen. (1987) *The Color Line and the Quality of Life in America*. New York: Russell Sage Foundation.

Featherstone, M. (1991) *Consumer Culture and Postmodernism*. London: Sage Publications.

Feyerabend, P. K. (1978) *Science in a Free Society*. London: NLB.

Fish, S. (1989) *Doing What Comes Naturally*. Durham, NC: Duke University Press.

Fitzsimmons, J. A., A. J. Schwab, and R. S. Sullivan. (1979) "Goal Programming for Holistic Budget Analysis." *Administration in Social Work* 31, no. 1: 33–43.

Foucault, M. (1970) *The Order of Things*. New York: Pantheon.

————. (1979a) *Discipline and Punish: The Birth of the Prison*. New York: Vintage.

————. (1979b) "What Is an Author?" *In Textual Strategies*, edited by J. Harari. Ithaca, NY: Cornell University Press, pp. 141–160.

Freedman, J. L. (1973) *Social Psychology*. Englewood Cliffs, NJ: Prentice-Hall.

Freud, S. (1948). *An Outline of Psychoanalysis*. New York: Norton.

Gadamer, H. G. (1975) *Truth and Method*. New York: Seabury Press.

————. (1981) *Reason in the Age of Science*. Boston: MIT Press.

Galbraith, J. K. (1979) *The New Industrial State*. New York: The New American Library.

Gates, H. L. (1992) *Loose Canons: Notes on the Culture Wars*. New York: Oxford University Press.

Gebser, J. (1985) *The Ever-Present Origin*. Athens: Ohio University Press.

Giddens, A. (1984) *The Structuration of Society*. Berkeley: University of California Press.

Gilroy, P. (1993a) *The Black Atlantic: Modernity and Double Consciousness*. Cambridge, MA: Harvard University Press.

————. (1993b) *Small Acts*. London: Serpent's Tail.

Glazer, N. (1976) *Affirmative Discrimination*. New York: Basic Books.

Glazer, N., and D. Moynihan (Eds.). (1975) *Ethnicity: Theory and Experience*. Cambridge, MA: Harvard University Press.

Goldberg, D. T. (1993) *Racist Culture: Philosophy and the Politics of Meaning*. Cambridge, MA: Blackwell Publishers.

Gordon, M. (1964) *Assimilation in American Life*. New York: Oxford University Press.

Gould, S. J. (1975) "Racist Arguments and IQ." In *Race and IQ*, edited by A. Montagu. New York: Oxford University Press, pp. 129–144.

————. (1981) *The Mismeasure of Man*. New York: Norton.

Grathoff, R. (1983) *Sozialitsaet und Intersubjecktivitaet*. Muneneh: Wilhelm Fink Verlag.

Grossberg, L. (1992) *We Gotta Get Out of This Place*. New York: Routledge.

Guattari, F. (1984) *Molecular Revolution*. Middlesex, England: Penguin Books.

Guba, E. G. (1990) *The Paradigm Dialog*. Newbury Park, CA: Sage.

Guba, E. G., and Y. S. Lincoln. (1982) *Effective Evaluation*. San Francisco: Jossey-Bass.

Habermas, J. (1970) "Toward a Theory of Communicative Competence." In *Recent Sociology: Patterns of Communicative Behavior*, no. 2, edited by Hans Dreitzel. New York: Macmillan, pp. 115–148.

———. (1975) *Legitimation Crisis*. Boston: Beacon Press.

———. (1984a) *Reason and the Rationalization of Society*. Boston: Beacon.

———. (1984b) *The Theory of Communicative Action, Vol. 2: Lifeworld and System: A Critique of Functionalist Reason*. Boston: Beacon Press.

———. (1989) *The New Conservatism: Cultural Criticism and the Historians' Debate*. Cambridge, MA: The MIT Press.

———. (1990) *Moral Consciousness and Communicative Action*. Cambridge, MA: The MIT Press.

"Hachiju Yonin Ga 'Shinpo Hitsuyo' " [84 Diet Members Agreed that "A New Law Is Necessary"]. (1995) *The Asahi Shimbun*, December 3, p. 34.

Hacker, A. (1995) "The Crackdown on African-Americans." *The Nation*, July 10, pp. 45–49.

Hall, S. (1991) "Ethnicity: Identity and Difference." *Radical America* 23, no. 4: 9–20.

———. (1992) "What Is This 'Black' in Black Popular Culture." In *Black Popular Culture*, edited by Gina Dent. Seattle: Bay Press, pp. 21–33.

Hansen, M. L. (1952) "The Third Generation in America." *Commentary* 14 (November): 492–500.

Harris, M. (1968) *The Rise of Anthropological Theory: A History of Theories of Culture*. New York: Thomas Y. Crowell Company.

Harry, B., and M. G. Anderson. (1994) "The Disproportionate Placement of African American Males in Special Education Programs: A Critique of the Process." *Journal of Negro Education* 63, no. 4: 602–619.

Hayashida, C. T. (1976) *Identity, Race, and the Blood Ideology of Japan*. Dissertation for the University of Washington, AAC 7625413.

Hazel, C. V. (1992) "Multicultural Wars." In *Black Popular Culture, a Project by Michele Wallace*, edited by G. Dent. Seattle: Bay Press, pp. 189–197.

Heidegger, M. (1962) *Being and Time*. New York: Harper & Row.

Herrnstein, R. J., and C. Murray. (1994) *The Bell Curve: Intelligence and Class Structure in American Life*. New York: Free Press.

Hinkle, R. C. (1980) *Founding Theory in American Sociology 1881–1915*. Boston: Routledge and Kegan Paul.

Hisker, W. J. (1986) "The Promise of Technology: An Organizational Caveat." In *Technology and Human Productivity*, edited by J. W. Murphy and J. T. Pardeck. Westport, CT: Quorum Books, pp. 129–189.

hooks, b. (1990) *Yearning*. Boston: South End Press.

———. (1992) *Black Looks: Race and Representation*. Boston: South End Press.

———. (1994) *Outlaw Culture, Resisting Representations*. New York: Routledge.

Hume, D. (1973) *A Treatise of Human Nature*. London: Oxford University Press.

————. (1982) "Of National Characters." In *The Philosophical Works*, edited by T. H. Green and T. H. Groce. London: Aalen, Scientia Verlag, pp. 244–257.

Husserl, E. (1962) *Ideas: General Introduction to Pure Phenomenology*. New York: Collier.

————. (1970) *The Crisis of European Sciences and Transcendental Phenomenology*. Evanston, IL: Northwestern University Press.

————. (1975) *The Paris Lectures*. The Hague: Nijhoff.

————. (1977) *The Origin of Geometry*. New York: Nicholas Hays.

Iguchi, K. (1981) "Kindai Nihon Ni Okeru Chosenkan No Kozo" [Structure of Images of Koreans in Modern Japan]. In *Zainichi chosenjin—Rekishi To Genjo*, edited by T. Yamada and C. Pak. Tokyo: Akashi Shoten, pp. 63–84.

Ikeda, R. (1992) *Ie to kazoku: A Shift in the Communication Pattern of the Japanese Family*. Master's thesis, University of Oklahoma.

Inoue, M. (1993) "Kodai" [The Ancient Period]. In *Buraku no Rekishi*, edited by Buraku Kaiho Kenkyujo. Osaka: Kaiho Shuppansha, pp. 1–24.

Jaynes, G., and R. Williams. (1989) *A Common Destiny*. Washington, DC: National Academy Press.

Jencks, C. (1991) "Is the American Underclass Growing?" In *The Urban Underclass*, edited by C. Jencks and P. Peterson. Washington, DC: The Brookings Institution, pp. 28–102.

Johnson, L., Jr. (1993) "Race and Enlightenment: Situating the Concept of Race." Paper presented at the Seventy-ninth Annual Meeting of the Speech Communication Association, Miami Beach, Florida (November).

Kallen, H. M. (1956) *Cultural Pluralism and the American Idea*. Philadelphia: University of Pennsylvania Press.

Kant, I. (1929) *Critique of Pure Reason*. New York: St. Martin's Press.

Kanter, R. M. (1984) *The Change Masters*. New York: Simon & Schuster.

Kato, E. (1990) "Wa-ism no Teisho" [Proposal of *Wa*-ism]. *Chuo Koron* (November): 80–85.

Kayano, S. (1994) "The Current Situation of the Ainu in Japan." In *Gathering in Ainumoshir, the Land of the Ainu: Messages from Indigenous Peoples in the World*, edited by Nibutani Forum Organizing Committee. Tokyo: Eikoh Educational and Cultural Institute, pp. 15–35.

Kierkegaard, S. (1941) *Concluding Unscientific Postscript*. Princeton, NJ: Princeton University Press.

Kingston, M. H. (1977) *The Woman Warrior*. New York: Vintage.

Klineberg, O. (1935) *Negro Intelligence and Selective Migration*. New York: Columbia University Press.

Kluegel, J. (1990) "Trends in Whites' Explanations of the Black-White Gap in Socioeconomic Status, 1977–1989." *American Sociological Review* 55, no. 4: 512–525.

Kluegel, J., and L. Bobo. (1991) "Dimensions of Whites' Beliefs About the Black-White Socioeconomic Gap." In *Race and Politics in American Society*, edited by Paul Sniderman. Stanford, CA: Stanford University Press, pp. 11–41.

Kluegel, J., and E. Smith. (1982) "Whites' Beliefs About Blacks Opportunity." *American Sociological Review* 47, no. 4: 518–532.

————. (1986) *Beliefs About Inequality: What Is and What Ought to Be*. New York: Aldine De Gruyter.

Kramer, E. (1988) *Television Criticism and the Problem of Ground, 2 Vols.* Ann Arbor, MI: University Microfilms International, no. 8816770.

———. (1992a) "Consciousness and Culture." In *Consciousness and Culture: An Introduction to the Thought of Jean Gebser,* edited by E. Kramer. Westport, CT: Greenwood Press, pp. 1–60.

———. (1992b) "Terrorizing Discourses and Dissident Courage." *Communication Theory* 1, no. 4: 336–346.

———. (1993a) "Investigative Journalism in Bulgaria: A Postponed Renaissance." In *Creating a Free Press in Eastern Europe,* edited by A. Hester and K. White. Athens: University of Georgia, The James M. Cox, Jr., Center for International Mass Communication Training & Research, The Henry W. Grady College of Journalism and Mass Communication, the University of Georgia, pp. 111–159.

———. (1993b) "Mass Media and Democracy." In *Open Institutions: The Hope for Democracy,* edited by J. W. Murphy and D. Peck. Westport, CT: Praeger, pp. 77–98.

———. (1993c) "The Origin of Television as Civilizational Expression." In *Semiotics 1990: Sources in Semiotics, Vol. XI,* edited by J. Deely et al. Lanham, MD: University Press of America, pp. 28–37.

———. (1994) "Making Love Alone: Videocentrism and the Case of Modern Pornography." In *Ideals of Feminine Beauty,* edited by K. Callaghan. Westport, CT: Greenwood Press, pp. 79–98.

Kramer, E. M., and R. Ikeda. (1996) "Japanese Clocks: Semiotic Evidence of the Perspectival Mutation." Forthcoming.

Kristeva, J. (1986a) "Revolution and Poetic Language." In *The Kristeva Reader,* edited by T. Moi. New York: Columbia University Press, pp. 89–136.

———. (1986b) "Word, Dialogue, and Novel." In *The Kristeva Reader,* edited by T. Moi. New York: Columbia University Press, pp. 34–61.

Kristof, N. D. (1995) "Japanese Outcasts Better Off Than in Past But Still Outcast." *New York Times,* November 30, pp. A1, A8.

Kronenwetter, M. (1993) *Prejudice in America.* New York: Macmillan Publishing Co.

Kuboi, N. (1993) *Kindai no Sabetsu to Nihon Minshu no Rekishi* [Discrimination and Japanese People's History in the Modern Era]. Tokyo: Akashi Shoten.

Kuhn, T. (1962) *The Structure of Scientific Revolutions.* Chicago: University of Chicago Press.

Langan, P. A. (1991) *Race and Prisoners Admitted to State and Federal Institutions, 1926–1986.* Washington, DC: U.S. Government Printing Office.

Lemelle, A. L. (1993) "Review of Ralph C. Gomes and Linda Faye Williams, from Exclusion to Inclusion: The Long Struggle for African-American Political Power." *Contemporary Sociology* 22, no. 1 (January): 60–78.

Levi-Strauss, C. (1969) *The Raw and the Cooked.* Chicago: University of Chicago Press.

———. (1978) *Myth and Meaning.* New York: Schocken Books.

Levinas, E. (1961) *Totality and Infinity.* Pittsburgh: Duquesne University Press.

Lewin, K. (1958) "Group Decision and Social Change." In *Readings in Social Psychology,* edited by E. E. Maccoby, T. M. Newcomb, and E. L. Hartley. New York: Holt.

Lewis, O. (1959) *Five Families: Mexican Case Studies in the Culture of Poverty.* New York: Random House.

———. (1961) *The Children of Sanchez.* New York: Random House.

———. (1966) *La Vida: A Puerto Rican Family in the Culture of Poverty.* New York: Random House.

Linnaeus, K. (1806) *A General System of Nature Through the Three Grand Kingdoms of Animals, Vegetable, and Minerals.* London: Lackington, Allen, and Company.

Lowith, K. (1993) *Max Weber and Karl Marx.* London: Routledge.

Luhmann, N. (1982) *The Differentiation of Society.* New York: Columbia University Press.

Lyman, S. M. (1994) *Color, Culture, Civilization.* Urbana: University of Illinois.

Lyotard, J. F. (1984) *The Postmodern Condition: A Report on Knowledge.* Minneapolis: University of Minnesota Press.

———. (1993a) *Libidinal Economy.* Bloomington: Indiana University Press.

———. (1993b) *The Postmodern Explained.* Minneapolis: University of Minnesota Press.

Maas, H. (1984) *People and Contexts: Social Development from Birth to Old Age.* Englewood Cliffs, NJ: Prentice-Hall.

Macauley, W. A., and E. J. Heubel. (1986) "The Impact of Technology on Complex Organizations: A Research Note." In *Technology and Human Productivity*, edited by J. W. Murphy and J. T. Pardeck. Westport, CT: Greenwood Press, pp. 191–201.

Mann, C. R. (1993) *Unequal Justice: A Question of Color.* Indianapolis: Indiana University Press.

Mannheim, K. (1971) "The Democratization of Culture." In *From Karl Mannheim*, edited by Kurt H. Wolff. New York: Oxford University Press, pp. 271–346.

———. (1992) *Essays on the Sociology of Culture.* London: Routledge.

Marable, M. (1995) "Beyond Racial Identity Politics: Towards a Liberation Theory for Multicultural Democracy." In *Race, Class, and Gender*, edited by M. L. Andersen and R. H. Collins. Belmont, CA: Wadsworth Publishing Company, pp. 363–366.

Marcuse, H. (1962) *Eros and Civilization.* Boston: Beacon Press.

———. (1966) *One Dimensional Man.* Boston: Beacon Press.

Marger, M. N. (1991) *Race and Ethnic Relations.* Belmont, CA: Wadsworth.

Marlett, N. (1988) "Empowerment Through Computer Telecommunications." In *Information Technology and the Human Services*, edited by B. Glastonburg, W. La Mendola, and S. Toole. Chichester, England: John Wiley and Sons, pp. 244–264.

Marx, K. (1959) "Contribution to the Critique of Political Economy." In *Marx and Engels: Basic Writings on Politics and Philosophy*, edited by L. Feuer. New York: Doubleday, pp. 42–46.

———. (1967) *Capital Vol. 1.* New York: International Publishers.

Matsushita, S. (1985) *Kyushu Hisabetsu-burakushi Kenkyu* [Research on the Oppressed Buraku People in Kyushu]. Tokyo: Akashi Shoten.

Mattelart, A. (1994) *Mapping World Communication: War, Progress, Culture.* Minneapolis: University of Minnesota Press.

Mauer, M. (1990) *Young Black Men and the Criminal Justice System: A Growing National Problem.* Washington, DC: The Sentencing Project.

McAdam, D. (1982) *Political Process and the Development of Black Insurgency.* Chicago: University of Chicago Press.

McLuhan, M. (1962) *The Gutenburg Galaxy.* Toronto: University of Toronto Press.

———. (1969) "A Candid Conversation with the High Priest of Popcult and Metaphysician of Media." *Playboy* (November): 63–81.

McLuhan, M., and Q. Fiore. (1967) *The Medium Is the Message: An Inventory of Effects.* New York: Bantam.

Meier, A. (1968) *Negro Thoughts in America, 1880–1915.* Ann Arbor: University of Michigan Press.

"Menkyo Nakutemo Kyodan De Kirari" [Without Licence, Brilliant in Classroom]. (1995) *The Asahi Shimbun,* November 31.

Mensh, E., and H. Mensh. (1991) *The IQ Mythology: Class, Race, Gender, and Inequality.* Carbondale: Southern Illinois University Press.

Merleau-Ponty, M. (1968) *The Visible and the Invisible.* Evanston, IL: Northwestern University Press.

———. (1973) *The Prose of the World.* Evanston, IL: Northwestern University Press.

Metzger, P. L. (1971) "American Sociology and Black Assimilation: Conflicting Perspectives." *American Journal of Sociology* 76, no. 4: 627–647.

Michell, H. R. (1981) *Zainichi Chosenjin no Rekishi* [The Korean Minority in Japan]. Tokyo: Sairyusha.

Mickunas, A. (1995) "Consciousness Critique of Universal Culturalism." Paper delivered at the XIV Annual Gebser Conference, November 4, Governors State University, Matteson, Illinois.

Milgram, S. (1974) *Obedience to Authority.* New York: Harper & Row.

Mills, C. W. (1961) *The Sociological Imagination.* New York: Grove Press.

Miyata, N. (1990) "Tashinkyo Bunka no Jidai" [The Era of Polytheistic Culture]. *Shokun* (December).

Montagu, A. (1945) "Intelligence of Northern Negroes and Southern Whites in the First World War." *American Journal of Psychology* 58 (April): 161–188.

Montagu, A. (Ed.) (1975) *Race and IQ.* New York: Oxford University Press.

Moore, R. B. (1992) "Racist Stereotyping in the English Language." In *Race, Class and Gender in the United States, An Integrated Study*, edited by P. S. Rothenberg. New York: St. Martin's Press, pp. 331–341.

Morris, M. B. (1977) *An Excursion into Creative Sociology.* New York: Columbia University Press.

Moynihan, D. P. (1967) "The Negro Family: The Case for National Action." In *The Moynihan Report and the Politics of Controversy*, edited by L. Rainwater and W. L. Yancy. Cambridge, MA: MIT Press, pp. 39–132.

———. (1969) "The Professor and the Poor." In *On Understanding Poverty*, edited by D. P. Moynihan. New York: Basic Books, pp. 3–35.

———. (1986) *Family and Nation.* San Diego: Harcourt, Brace, Jovanovich.

Murphy, J. W. (1984) "Organizational Issues in Worker Ownership." *American Journal of Economics and Sociology* 43, no. 3: 287–299.

———. (1989) *Postmodern Social Analysis and Criticism.* Westport, CT: Greenwood Press.

———. (1994) "Symbolic Violence and the Disembodiment of Identity." In *Ideals of Feminine Beauty*, edited by K. A. Callaghan. Westport, CT: Greenwood Press, pp. 69–78.

Murphy, J. W., and J. T. Pardeck. (1988) "Technology in Clinical Practice and the Technological Ethic." *Journal of Sociology and Social Welfare* 15, no. 1: 119–128.

———. (1990) "Expert Systems as an Adjunct to Clinical Practice: A Critique." In

Computers in Human Services, edited by J. T. Pardeck and J. W. Murphy. London: Harwood Academic Publishers, pp. 75–86.

———. (1991) *The Computerization of Human Service Agencies*. New York: Auburn House.

Murphy, J. W., J. T. Pardeck, and W. S. Chung. (1992) "Democratization of Social Development." *Social Development Issues* 14, no. 1: 1–12.

Murray, C., and R. J. Herrnstein. (1994) "Race, Genes and I.Q.—An Apologia." *The New Republic*, October 31, pp. 27–37.

Murray, D. J. (1988) *A History of Western Psychology*. Englewood Cliffs, NJ: Prentice-Hall.

Nadamoto, M. (1991) "Sabetsugo To Ikani Mukiauka [How One Should Face Discriminated Terms]. In *Buraku no Kako Genzai Soshite*, edited by K. Henshubu. Kyoto: Kyoto Burakushi Kenkyujo, pp. 100–137.

Nader, R. (1993) "Free Trade and the Decline of Democracy." In *The Case Against Free Trade: GATT, NAFTA, and the Globalization of Corporate Power*. San Francisco: Earth Island Press, pp. 1–12.

Nakatsuka, A. (1991) "Zainichi Chosenjin no Rekishiteki Keisei" [Koreans in Japan Created in History]. In *Zainichi chosenjin—Rekishi To Genjo*, edited by T. Yamada and C. Pak. Tokyo: Akashi Shoten, pp. 85–115.

Nam, D. (1986) "The Case of the Changing Technology: Impact of Micro Computer Technology in a Fortune 500 Corporation." In *Technology and Human Productivity*, edited by J. W. Murphy and J. T. Pardeck. Westport, CT: Greenwood Press, pp. 191–201.

Neary, I. (1989) *Political Protest and Social Control in Pre-war Japan: The Origins of Buraku Liberation*. Atlantic Highlands, NJ: Humanities Press International.

Niebuhr, R. (1976) *Love and Justice*. Glouster, MA: P. Smith.

Nietzsche, F. (1974) *The Gay Science*. New York: Vintage.

Nitobe, I. (1905) *Bushido: The Soul of Japan*. New York: G. P. Putnam's Sons.

O'Neill, J. (1976) "Critique and Remembrance." In *On Critical Theory*, edited by J. O'Neill. New York: Seabury Press, pp. 1–11.

Oakes, J. (1988) *Keeping Track: How Schools Structure Inequality*. New Haven, CT: Yale University Press.

Oblas, P. B. (1995) *Perspectives on Race and Culture in Japanese Society: The Mass Media and Ethnicity*. Lewiston, NY: The Edwin Mellen Press.

Oliver, M., and T. Shapiro. (1995) *Black Wealth/White Wealth: A New Perspective on Racial Inequality*. New York: Routledge.

Omi, M. (1987) "Shifting the Blame: Racial Ideology and Politics in the Post-Civil Rights Era." *Critical Sociology* 18, no. 3: 77–98.

Omi, M., and H. Winant. (1986) *Racial Formation in the United States: from the 1960s to the 1980s*. New York: Routledge and Kegan Paul.

Pak, C. (1991) "Zainichi Chosenjen no Shakai Keizai Seikatsu." [The Social and Economic Life of Koreans in Japan]. Edited by T. Yamada and C. Pak. Tokyo: Akashi Shoten, pp. 209–243.

Pak, K. S. (1957) "Nihon Teikokushugi Ka ni okeru Zainichi Chosenjin Undo" [The Korean People's Movement in Japan Under the Rule of Japanese Imperialism], part 1. *Chosen Geppo* 2, no. 4: 6–36.

Parcel, T., and C. Mueller. (1983) *Ascription and Labor Markets*. New York: Academic Press.

Pardeck, J. T. (1994) "Computer Technology and Social Development." *Social Development Issues* 16, no. 1: 112–121.

Pardeck, J. T, and J. W. Murphy. (1992) "Postmodernism and Clinical Practice: A Critical Analysis of the Disease Model." *Psychological Reports* 72: 1187–1194.

Pardeck, J. T., J. W. Murphy and K. Callaghan. (1994) "Computerization of Social Service: A Critical Appraisal." *Scandinavian Journal of Social Welfare* 3, no. 1: 2–6.

Park, R. E., and E. W. Burgess. (1969) *Introduction to the Science of Sociology.* Chicago: University of Chicago Press.

Parsons, T. (1965) *Societies: Evolutionary and Contemporary Perspectives.* Englewood Cliffs, NJ: Prentice-Hall.

———. (1966a) "Full Citizenship for the Negro American? A Sociological Problem." In *The Negro American*, edited by T. Parsons and K. B. Clark. Boston: Houghton Mifflin, pp. 709–754.

———. (1966b) *Societies.* Englewood Cliffs, NJ: Prentice-Hall.

Petronius, A. (1959) *The Satyricon.* New York: New American Library.

Pilotta, J., and A. Mickunas. (1990) *Science of Communication: Its Phenomenological Foundation.* New York: Lawrence Earlbaum.

Popkin, R. H. (1973) "The Philosophical Basis of Eighteenth Century Racism: Racism in the Eighteenth Century." *Studies in Eighteenth Century Culture* 3, no. 2: 245–262.

———. (1974) "The Philosophical Basis of Modern Racism." In *Philosophy and the Civilizing Arts*, edited by C. Walton and J. P. Anton. Athens: Ohio University Press, pp. 126–163.

Postman, N. (1984) *Amusing Ourselves to Death.* New York: Penguin.

Quadagno, J. (1994) *The Color of Welfare: How Racism Undermined the War on Poverty.* New York: Oxford University Press.

Rabelais, F. (1967) *Gargantua and Pantagruel.* New York: AMS Press.

Rauch, J. (1992) *The Outnation: A Search for the Soul of Japan.* New York: Little, Brown and Company.

Rifkin, J. (1995) *The End of Work.* New York: G. P. Putnam's Sons.

Rose, N. (1979) "The Psychological Complex: Mental Measurement and Social Administration." *Ideology and Consciousness* 5: 5–68.

Rose, P. I. (1968) *They and We.* New York: Random House.

Rosenfeld, R. (1980) "Race and Sex Differences in Career Dynamics." *American Sociological Review* 45, no. 4: 583–609.

Saeki, S., S. Hirakawa, and N. Miyata. (1990) "Tashinkyo Bunka no Jidai" [The Time of Polytheism]. *The Shokun* (February): 54–65.

Sarashina, G. (1970) *Ainu To Nihonjin* [Ainu and Japanese]. Tokyo: Nippon Hoso Shuppan Kyokai.

Sartre, J. P. (1960) *To Freedom Condemned.* New York: Philosophical Library.

———. (1963) *Search for a Method.* New York: Random House.

———. (1969) *Anti-Semite and Jew.* New York: Schocken.

Sennett, R. (1991) "Fragments Against the Ruin." *The Times Literary Supplement* 8 (February): 6.

Schlesinger, A. (1992) *The Disuniting of America.* New York: W. W. Norton.

Schuman, H., C. Steeh, and L. Bobo. (1985) *Racial Attitudes in America: Trends and Interpretations.* Cambridge, MA: Harvard University Press.

Schutz, A. (1970a) *On Phenomenology of Social Relations.* Chicago: University of Chicago Press.

———. (1970b) *Reflections on the Problem of Relevance.* New Haven, CT: Yale University Press.

See, K. (1986) "Ideology and Racial Stratification: A Theoretical Juxtaposition." *International Journal of Sociology and Social Policy* 6, no. 1: 75–89.

Selden, S. (1977) "Conservative Ideology and Curriculum." *Educational Theory* 27, no. 3: 205–222.

Shafarivic, I. (1991) "Rosafobia." In *Jest Li U Rossii Buduscheje?* Moscow: Sovietskij Pisatel, pp. 383–406.

Sigelman, L., and S. Welsh. (1991) *Black Americans' Views of Racial Inequality.* Cambridge: Cambridge University Press.

Smith, J. D. (1993) *The Eugenic Assault on America.* Fairfax, VA: George Mason University Press.

Sorano, Y. (1995) "Hanshin Daishinsai To Zainichi Chosenjin no Jinken" [The Kobe Earthquake and Human Rights of Koreans in Japan]. In *Zainichi Chosenjin no Seikatsu To Jinken*, edited by Y. Sorano and C. Y. Ko. Tokyo: Akashi Shoten, pp. 135–139.

Sowell, T. (1981) *Ethnic America.* New York: Basic Books.

———. (1994) *Race and Culture.* New York: Basic Books.

Spohn, C. C. (1995) "Courts, Sentences, and Prisons." In *Daedaulus* 124, no. 1 (Winter): 119–143.

Sprinker, M. (1987) *Imaginary Relations.* London: Verso.

Stallybrass, P., and A. White. (1986) *The Politics and Poetics of Transgression.* Ithaca, NY: Cornell University Press.

Stark, W. (1963) *The Fundamental Forms of Social Thought.* New York: Fordham University Press.

Sternberg, R. J. (1995) "For Whom the Bell Curve Tolls: A Review of *The Bell Curve.*" *Psychological Science* 5, no. 6: 257–261.

Stone, J. (1985) *Racial Conflict in Contemporary Society.* Cambridge, MA: Harvard University Press.

Suginohara, J. (1982) *The Status Discrimination in Japan—Introduction to Buraku Problem.* Kobe: The Hyogo Institute of Buraku Problem.

Tanaka, H. (1995) *Zainichi GaikOkujin* [Foreigners in Japan]. Tokyo: Iwanami Shoten.

Taniguchi, S. (1985) "Buraku Sabetsu To Shoukyo To Jinken" [Buraku Discrimination, Religion, and Human Rights]. In *Koza Sabetsu To Jinken* (vol. 2), edited by E. Isomura, Y. Ichibangase, and T. Harada. Tokyo: Yuzankaku Shuppan, pp. 223–257.

Taylor, C. (1991) "The Person." In *The Category of the Person*, edited by M. Carrithers, S. Collins, and S. Lukes. New York: Cambridge University Press, pp. 257–281.

Taylor, J. (1983) *Shadows of the Rising Sun: A Critical View of the "Japanese Miracle."* New York: Quill.

Teraki, N. (1984) "Hisabetsu-buraku no Rekishi" [History of the Oppressed Buraku People]. In *Koza sabetsu To Jinken* (vol. 1), edited by E. Isomura, Y. Ichibangase, and T. Harada. Tokyo: Yuzankaku Shuppan, pp. 15–59.

———. (1993) "Kindai" [The Early Modern Period]. In *Buraku no Rekishi*, edited by B. K. Kenkyujo. Osaka: Kaiho Shuppansha, pp. 171–265.

Thompson, J. B. (1984) *Studies in the Theory of Ideology.* Berkeley: University of California Press.

Thurow, L. (1969) *Poverty and Discrimination.* Washington, DC: The Brookings Institute.

Todorov, T. (1993) *On Human Diversity: Nationalism, Racism, and Exoticism in French Thought.* Cambridge, MA: Harvard University Press.

Troyka, L. Q. (1993) *Simon & Schuster Handbook for Writers*, 3d ed. Englewood Cliffs, NJ: Simon & Schuster.

Tuner, J. H., R. Singleton, Jr., and D. Musick. (1984) *Oppression.* Chicago: Nelson-Hall.

U.S. Department of Commerce, Bureau of the Census. (1993) ''Poverty in the United States, 1991.'' In *National Commission on American Urban Families, Families First.* Series P-60, no. 181. Washington, DC: U.S. Government Printing Office.

U.S. Department of Health and Human Services. (1993) *Vital Statistics of the United States, Vol. 1, 1991: Natality.* DHHS Publication No. PHS 93–1100. Washington, DC: U.S. Government Printing Office.

Ueda, T. (1995) *Zainichi Kankokujin no Sokojikara* [Power of Koreans in Japan]. Tokyo: Nisshin Hodo.

Umehara, T. (1981) *Shotoku Taishi II, Kenpo 17jo* [Prince Shotoku, the Constitution of 17 Articles]. Tokyo: Shogakukan.

———. (1990) ''Isshinkyo Kara Tashinkyo e [From Monotheism to Polytheism]. *Chuo Koron* (February): 84–90.

Vonnegut, K. (1973) *Breakfast of Champions.* New York: Bantam Books.

Waldenfels, B. (1971) *Zwischenreich des Dialogs.* The Hague: Martinus Nijhoff.

Walinsky, A. (1995) ''The Crisis of Public Order.'' *The Atlantic Monthly* (July): 39–54.

Walker, S. (1993) *Taming the System: The Control of Discretion in Criminal Justice, 1950–1990.* New York: Oxford University Press.

Watzlawick, P., J. Beavin, and D. Jackson. (1967) *Pragmatics of Human Communication.* New York: Norton.

Weber, M. (1958) *The Protestant Ethic and the Spirit of Capitalism.* New York: Charles Scriber's Sons.

———. (1978) *Economy and Society, Vol. 1*, edited by G. Roth and C. Wittich. Berkeley: University of California Press.

Weiner, M. (1994) *Race and Migration in Imperial Japan.* London: Routledge.

West, C. (1989) *The American Evasion of Philosophy.* Madison: University of Wisconsin Press.

———. (1993a) *Keeping Faith: Philosophy and Race in America.* New York: Routledge.

———. (1993b) *Prophetic Reflections.* Monroe, ME: Common Courage Press.

———. (1993c) *Prophetic Thought in Postmodern Times.* Monroe, ME: Common Courage Press.

———. (1994) *Race Matters.* New York: Vintage.

Whitman, W. (1981) *Leaves of Grass and Selected Prose*, edited by L. Buell. New York: Modern Library.

Wilkins, R. (1995) ''Racism Has Its Privileges.'' *The Nation*, March 27.

Williams, R. (1989) *Culture.* London: Fontana Press.

Williams, W. (1982) *The State Against Blacks.* New York: McGraw-Hill.

Williams, W. E. (1989) ''Campus Racism.'' *National Review*, May 5, pp. 36–38.

Wilson, G. (1996) ''Towards a Revised Framework for Examining Beliefs About the Causes of Poverty.'' Forthcoming in *The Sociological Quarterly.*

Wilson, G., and D. Royster. (1995) "Critiquing Wilson's Critics: The Black Middle Class and the Declining Significance of Race Thesis." *Research in Race and Ethnic Relations* 8, no. 3: 63–75.

Wilson, W. (1987) *The Truly Disadvantaged.* Chicago: University of Chicago Press.

Wittgenstein, L. (1953) *Philosophical Reason.* New York: Macmillan.

———. (1958) *Philosophical Investigations.* Oxford, England: Basil Blackwell.

———. (1969) *On Certainty.* Oxford, England: Basil Blackwell.

———. (1971) *Prototractatus.* London: Routledge and Kegan Paul.

———. (1974) *Philosophical Grammar.* Oxford, England: Basil Blackwell.

———. (1975) *Philosophical Remarks.* Oxford, England: Basil Blackwell.

Yamaguchi, Y. (1994) "Futatsu no Gendaishi" [Two Modern Histories]. In *Senso Sekinin, Sengo Sekinin.* Tokyo: Asahi Shimbunsha, pp. 221–265.

Yuasa, S. (1993) *Nippon Wa Naze Koritsusurunoka* [Why Is Japan Isolated from the Rest of the World?]. Tokyo: Taiyo Shuppan.

Yun, K. (1987) *Ishitsu Tono Kyozon* [Co-existence with Differences]. Tokyo: Iwanami Shoten.

Name Index

Adorno, T. W., 41, 48, 163
Albee, G., 46, 48, 163
Alderfer, C. P., 46, 48, 163
Alexander, J. C., 18, 28, 163
Alger, Horatio, 140, 163
Allen, W., 129, 142, 163
Anderson, M. G, 42, 48, 163
Anderson, M. L., 127, 163
Anton, J. P., 49, 163
Aomori, T., 82, 100, 163
Apter, D., 131, 141, 163
Aston, William G., 79, 80, 100, 163
Athena, 8, 163

Bacon, Francis, 14
Bakhtin, Mikhail, 51, 64, 146, 147, 150,
    151, 155, 156, 158, 159, 163
Banfield, E., 157, 159, 163
Barlow, John Perry, 4, 14, 163
Barr, C. W., 98, 100, 163
Barthes, Roland, 22, 23, 28, 106, 112,
    119, 126, 155, 159, 163
Bataille, G., 146, 147, 150, 155, 159, 163
Baudrillard, Jean, 66, 76, 146, 150, 151,
    152, 155, 160, 163, 164
Beavin, J., 13, 15
Beckett, Samuel, 146

Bell, Derrick, 118, 126, 131, 141, 157,
    160, 164
Benjamin, Walter, 17, 28, 146, 164
Berger, P. L., 107, 112, 145, 160, 164
Berghe, Pierre van den, 21
Bhabha, Homi K., 22, 23, 25, 28, 124,
    126, 164
Binet, Alfred, 37, 38, 39, 41, 44, 45, 46,
    47
Birman, D., 48, 164
Blumer, Herbert, 17, 28, 164
Bobo, L., 129, 134, 135, 136, 141, 142,
    164, 168
Boden, M., 107, 112, 164
Bonacich, E., 132, 141, 164
Bond, Horace Mann, 44, 48, 164
Bornoff, N., 98, 100, 164
Boswell, T., 132, 141, 164
Bourdieu, Pierre, 67
Bourne, Randolph, 21
Braddock, J. H. II, 42, 48, 164
Bradley, Bill, 148, 160, 164
Braverman, Harry, 152, 160, 164
Brown, Tony, 11, 12, 14, 164
Buber, Martin, 51, 64, 124, 164
Buchanan, Pat, 154, 164
Buffon, G. L. L, 35, 36, 37, 48, 164
Burger, J., 100, 164, 173

Subject Index

About the Editor and Contributors

JOMILLS BRADDOCK received his doctorate from Florida State University. Prior to joining the University of Miami as Professor and Chair of Sociology, he served as director of the Center of Research on Effective Schooling for Disadvantaged Students at Johns Hopkins University. He has also held faculty/research appointments in the Department of Sociology at the University of Maryland and at Johns Hopkins University's Center for Social Organization of Schools/Department of Sociology. His broad research interests in issues of inequality and social justice have been supported by public and private grants and contracts addressing equality of opportunities in education, employment, and sports. His work on these topics typically involves secondary analyses of large-scale, national longitudinal data and addresses public policy issues.

KAREN A. CALLAGHAN is Associate Professor of Sociology and Department Chair at Berry University. Ms. Callaghan earned her doctorate from Ohio State University. She teaches courses on sociological theory; sociology of race, class, and gender; marriage and the family; and juvenile delinquency. She has edited a collection of essays on women and images of beauty, and co-authored a book on the cultural politics of race, violence, and democracy, in addition to publishing several articles on the contemporary family, adolescence, and social theory.

JUNG MIN CHOI is Assistant Professor of Sociology, Barry University, Florida. He has published several articles and is co-author, with John W. Murphy, of *The Politics and Philosophy of Political Corrections.*

WOO SIK CHUNG was born in Korea and received his B.A. degree at Sogang University, Seoul, and his doctorate in Social Work at St. Louis University. His research and writing are in the field of correctional social work. He is the founder of the Institute of Korean Correctional Work and is the current director in Korea. Currently, he is focusing on structural equation modeling and the validation of latent constructs in major social work concepts. His most recent work deals with Korean American prostitutes who were formerly married to American soldiers.

RICHIKO IKEDA is Assistant Professor of International Relations at The International Christian University in Tokyo, Japan. She has authored several papers and made several international presentations. Her most recent book is *Nippon o Gokaisansenai Eikaiwa* [A Discussion of Contemporary Japan], with K. Miura. Her interests are in women's issues and the cross-cultural study of time.

ERIC MARK KRAMER is Assistant Professor of Communication at the University of Oklahoma. He has published several articles and book chapters. His most recent book is *Consciousness and Culture: An Introduction to the Thought of Jean Gebser* (Greenwood Press, 1992). He is interested in intercultural, international, and mass communication.

LONNIE JOHNSON, JR., is a doctoral candidate at the University of Oklahoma. Mr. Johnson has presented several papers, and his interest is in race relations.

ALGIS MICKUNAS received his doctorate from Emory University. He has studied at the universities of Cologne, Freiburg, and Chicago. He is currently Professor of Philosophy at Ohio University. He has authored, co-authored, translated, and co-edited several works, and has published numerous articles in diverse fields including pedagogy, sociology, comparative cultures, communications, semiotics, hermeneutics, and critical phenomenology. He has lectured at academic institutions and read papers at conferences throughout Eastern and Western Europe, Japan, the Middle East, and North America.

NORMAN N. MORRA received his doctorate in Sociology from York University in Toronto, Canada. His areas of research are cultural studies, violence, and theory. He has written on sport, gender, and violence from a theoretical perspective, and has published several articles.

JOHN W. MURPHY is Professor of Sociology at the University of Miami, Florida. He received his doctorate at Ohio University, and has been working in the area of social theory. He is author and editor of fifteen books and numerous articles. His most recent book is *The Politics of Culture* (with Jung Min Choi and Karen Callaghan).

JOHN T. PARDECK is Professor of Social Work in the School of Social Work at Southwest Missouri State University. He received his doctorate in Social Work from St. Louis University. Professor Pardeck has published over 100 articles in academic and professional journals. His most recent books include *Computers in Human Services: An Overview for Clinical and Welfare Services* (with John W. Murphy) (1990), *The Computerization of Human Services Agencies: A Critical Appraisal* (with John W. Murphy) (1991), *Issues in Social Work: A Critical Analysis* (with Roland G. Meinert and William P. Sullivan) (1994), and *Social Work Practice: An Ecological Approach* (1994).

GEORGE WILSON received his doctorate in Sociology from Johns Hopkins University. He is currently an Assistant Professor of Sociology at the University of Miami, Florida. His current research interests focus on the institutional production of racial and ethnic inequality in the workplace and the social structural determinants of beliefs about the causes of racial and economic inequality.

ISBN 0-275-95367-X

90000>

EAN

9 780275 953676

HARDCOVER BAR CODE